Theory and Practice in the History of European Expansion Overseas

ESSAYS IN HONOUR OF RONALD ROBINSON

Theory and Practice in the History of European Expansion Overseas

ESSAYS IN HONOUR OF
RONALD ROBINSON

Edited by
Andrew Porter and Robert Holland

LONDON AND NEW YORK

First published in 1988 in Great Britain by
FRANK CASS AND COMPANY LIMITED

Published 2015 by Routledge
2 Park Square, Milton Park, Abingdon, Oxfordshire OX14 4RN
711 Third Avenue, New York, NY 10017

First issued in paperback 2015

*Routledge is an imprint of the Taylor and Francis Group,
an informa business*

Copyright © 1988 Frank Cass & Co. Ltd.

British Library Cataloguing in Publication Data

Theory and practice in the history of
    European expansion overseas: essays in
    honour of Ronald Robinson.
    1. European imperialism, 1815–1960
    I. Porter, Andrew II. Holland, Robert
    III. Robinson, Ronald, 1920– IV. Journal
    of imperial and commonwealth history
325′.32′094

ISBN 13: 978-1-138-86799-4 (pbk)
ISBN 13: 978-0-7146-3346-6 (hbk)

Library of Congress Cataloging in Publication Data

Theory and practice in the history of European expansion overseas:
    essays in honour of Ronald Robinson/edited by Andrew Porter and
    Robert Holland.
        p. cm.
    'Special issue . . . of the Journal of Imperial and Commonwealth
    history, vol. XVI, no. 3' – T.p. verso.
    'Published writings by R.E. Robinson': p.
    ISBN 0-7146-3346-1: £20.00 (est.)
    1. Great Britain – Colonies – History. 2. Europe – Colonies –
History. 3. Robinson, Ronald Edward, 1920– . I. Robinson,
Ronald Edward, 1920– . II. Porter, Andrew. III. Holland, Robert
JV1011.T43 1988
325′.34′09–dc19   88–2583
                                                 CIP

This group of studies first appeared in a Special Issue on 'Theory and Practice in the History of European Expansion Overseas: Essays in Honour of Ronald Robinson' of *The Journal of Imperial and Commonwealth History*, Vol. XVI, No. 3, published by Frank Cass & Co. Ltd.

All rights reserved. No part of this publication may be reproduced, stored in a retrieval system, or transmitted in any form, or by any means, electronic, mechanical, photocopying, recording or otherwise, without the prior permission of Frank Cass and Company Limited.

Contents

Editors' Note	**Andrew Porter and Robert Holland**	vii
Ronald Robinson: Scholar and Good Companion	**George Shepperson**	1
Centre and Periphery in the Making of the Second French Colonial Empire, 1815–1920	**C.M. Andrew and A.S. Kanya-Forstner**	9
Scottish Missions and Education in Nineteenth-Century India: The Changing Face of Trusteeship	**Andrew Porter**	35
The Giant that was a Dwarf, or the Strange History of Dutch Imperialism	**H.L. Wesseling**	58
Decentralized Violence and Collaboration in Early Colonial Uganda	**Michael Twaddle**	71
Spoils of War: Sub-Imperial Collaboration in South West Africa and New Guinea, 1914–20	**Colin Newbury**	86
Imperial Collaboration and Great Depression: Britain, Canada and the World Wheat Crisis, 1929–35	**Robert Holland**	107
Sir Alan Cunningham and the End of British Rule in Palestine	**Wm. Roger Louis**	128
Africa and the Labour Government, 1945–51	**Ronald Hyam**	148
Ronald Robinson and the Cambridge Development Conferences, 1963–70	**D.K. Fieldhouse**	173
Published Writings by R.E. Robinson		200
Notes on Contributors		200

Editors' Note

These essays have been written to mark the retirement of Ronald Robinson as Beit Professor of the History of the British Commonwealth at the University of Oxford. The contributors have all at various times worked closely with 'Robbie' as pupils, colleagues and friends. They offer this volume to him with their thanks and great affection, both in recognition of his immense contribution to the revival and development of imperial or commonwealth history, and in the conviction that he has still much to offer all scholars in the field.

Andrew Porter
Robert Holland

Ronald Robinson: Scholar and Good Companion

by

George Shepperson

The retirement of Ronald Robinson from the Beit Chair of the History of the British Commonwealth at Oxford University in the autumn of 1987 came almost a century after the conclusion of the West African Conference of Berlin in 1885. That gathering marked, even if it did not cause, the partition of Africa by the Powers of Europe and was a pointer to what, by 1902, was coming to be called 'Imperialism'. In that year J.A. Hobson published his seminal book on the making of new empires as Europe, America and Japan divided up among themselves ancient and modern cultures around the world in a kaleidoscope of domination.

Since Ronald Robinson published his first article in the British Colonial Office's *Journal of African Administration* in January 1949 (two years after the beginnings of the British exit from empire, symbolized by the independence of India, Pakistan, Ceylon and Burma), the Powers of Europe have relinquished political control over their African possessions and most of their other overseas territories. Ronald Robinson's career, since he was demobilized in 1945 from the Royal Air Force in which he gained the Distinguished Flying Cross as a bomber pilot, mirrors this process. Following his return to St. John's College, Cambridge, to take his undergraduate and postgraduate degrees, and after spending two years as Research Officer in the African Studies Branch of the Colonial Office, he has made distinguished contributions, in theory and practice, to the transformation and ending of overseas empires in the second half of the twentieth century and to the beginnings of their development as modern, independent states.

I

Like many young British airmen in the Second World War, Ronald Robinson carried out some of his training as a pilot in Southern Rhodesia; and it was there that his interest in Africa and Imperialism was quickened. The wheel came full circle when he went back as a member of the United Kingdom team of observers of the election in February 1980, two months after which Cecil Rhodes's creation became independent as the Republic of Zimbabwe. During these four decades, through membership of influential British committees, such as the Bridges Committee on Training in Public Administration, and through the key part which he played in eight important conferences in the 1960s and 1970s at Cambridge University on development in Africa and the Third World, Ronald Robinson's practical contributions to the transformation of Imperialism were a constant feature of his career. It seems appropriate that in 1970 he should have been made a Commander of the Order of the British Empire.

But, while these contributions must never be forgotten and were, indeed, a valuable concomitant of his specifically academic career, stimulating and shaping the range of his publications, it is surely through his historical writings on the creation and collapse of colonialism that Ronald Robinson will be most remembered by future generations of historians in his own country and in the world far beyond it. His influence on his contemporaries, especially in Britain, Europe, Africa and the United States, is already firmly established; writing as one of them and paying my respects to his achievements, I wish that I could be alive in the next century to see what future historians of the expansion and contraction of Europe will take into their permanent stock of facts and frames of reference from Ronald Robinson's contributions to the study of that history.

Much of his thought about the past has been formed in the shadow of three great British institutions, one of which, the Colonial Office, went out of existence in 1966, but the other two of which, St. John's College, Cambridge, and Balliol College, Oxford, are very much alive. If there is such a thing as 'Oxbridge', Ronald Robinson is a quintessentially Oxbridge man; and academic visits to the United States and Africa, together with marriage to a charming American, have helped to make him into an energetic ambassador of the Oxbridge diaspora.

Ronald Robinson's career has spanned four decades: 22 years as Fellow of a Cambridge college; 16 as Fellow of an Oxford college. His career as a Lecturer in History at Cambridge culminated in a final five years as Smuts Reader in the History of the British Commonwealth; and he has held the Beit Chair at Oxford for 16 years. It all seems, at first sight, very much of an Establishment career.

But anyone who is inclined to this view should note that Ronald Robinson was born in Clapham and attended Battersea Grammar School. This area of London, from the anti-slavery activities of the Clapham Sect at the beginning of the nineteenth century to the work for the British and international labour movements of men such as John Burns and Shappurji Saklatvala, socialist and communist Members of Parliament for Battersea at the start of the twentieth century, has never lacked a dissenting tradition. I have no doubt that something of this tradition has remained with Ronald Robinson at Cambridge and Oxford.

It was at Cambridge that he entered into the now famous academic partnership with the late John Gallagher of Trinity College: a partnership that made 'Robinson and Gallagher' almost as famous an expression in historical circles, for a time, as 'Marx and Engels'. Much of the work, however, of this famous Cambridge team was aimed at Marxist pretensions, particularly in their Leninist form, in the interpretation of modern history. The major product of this partnership was a celebrated article and a celebrated book: 'The Imperialism of Free Trade' in *The Economic History Review* in 1953 and *Africa and the Victorians. The Official Mind of Imperialism* in 1961. Both article and book coined phrases which have become part of the currency of historical writing today, even when their users may be unaware of their origins and may be employing them in wider contexts than their originators intended: 'the imperialism of free trade' and 'the official mind', sometimes – but not always – with 'of imperialism' attached to it. It is given to few historians in their lifetimes to have a book written about their ideas; but selections from the work of this famous partnership and commentary on their ideas appeared, under William Roger Louis's editorship, in *Imperialism. The Robinson and Gallagher Controversy* (New York and London, 1976), to which the interested reader is referred as a starting point for the study of their place in modern historiography.

In his first year as Beit Professor at Oxford, Ronald Robinson published an important article, 'Non-European Foundations of European Imperialism: Sketch for a theory of Collaboration' in Roger Owen and Bob Sutcliffe (eds.), *Studies in the Theory of Imperialism* (London, 1972). This article indicated that his thoughts were moving in an increasingly theoretical direction. Many of those who subsequently witnessed him both at work and in splendid form in stimulating discussions early in 1985 in Berlin (at the centenary conference on the West African Conference of Berlin, under the auspices of the Deutsches Historisches Institut, London) might well have taken away a similar impression.

As the formal side of Ronald Robinson's career has drawn to its close, many of his colleagues and potential writers of the inevitable theses on his work have doubtless begun to make their assessments of his place in historiography. In aid of these, I would offer an apparently paradoxical suggestion which I leave to them to interpret: look for its origins on both the right and the left wings of the traditions of historical scholarship at Cambridge University, from Sir John Seeley's occupancy of the Chair of Modern History (1869–95) to the Cambridge Left of the 1930s and 1940s. Whether envisaged as Scylla and Charybdis or as Castor and Pollux, I feel that these polarities of the modern Cambridge historical tradition, far more than any Oxford historiographical patterns, have determined much in the writings of Ronald Robinson.

Admirers have often seen Ronald Robinson putting the imperialist Sir John Seeley in his place. But the more that I look at Ronald Robinson's writings, the more Seeley's two famous statements seem as characteristic of the Beit Professor's approach to his chosen fields of historical study as they do to Seeley's: 'We [the English] seem, as it were, to have conquered and peopled half the world in a fit of absence of mind' (*The Expansion of England*, 1895) and 'History is past politics, and politics present history' (*The Growth of British Policy*, 1895).

The first of these famous statements on the often apparently reluctant nature of British imperialism poses a problem, as I see it, which much of *Africa and the Victorians* is devoted to answering. The second seems to me particularly pertinent to the comments on this celebrated book and its milieu by a representative of the old Cambridge Left, V.G. Kiernan, in an article, 'Farewells to Empire', originally published in a socialist journal of 1964 and given wider circulation when it was reprinted in its author's *Marxism and Imperialism* ten years later. 'Before the last war [1939–45],' said Victor Kiernan (p. 82), 'the "jolly old empire" was very much a part of Cambridge orthodoxy, and students who declined to take it at its face value were regarded by their seniors as very abandoned characters.' Ronald Robinson has never taken the British Empire at its face value; and, in retrospect, it seems to me that he has employed the insights of both the right and the left in the British political traditions, especially at Cambridge, to raise and often to answer important questions about Imperialism, proto-, past, present and future. Whether, however, he thereby falls into a Cambridge category of 'abandoned characters' is another question altogether.

II

Undoubtedly, there is a refreshingly reckless element in his character which thesis writers of the future should not overlook. It is part of what I would call, echoing the famous novel of another Cambridge man, the good companion side of Ronald Robinson's nature. His students and colleagues alike have experienced it; and, surely, it has been an element of strength in his approach to history, whether as a teacher or as a writer.

I had a fascinating experience of this dimension of his personality in the autumn of 1960 when we both attended the Leverhulme Inter-Collegiate History Conference at the young University College, as it was then called, of Rhodesia and Nyasaland in the city of Salisbury, which has now reverted to its original African name of Harare in Zimbabwe. For the first and only time in my life I had a research assistant, acting-unpaid but most willing: the future Beit Professor. But that is to anticipate our venture to the interior after the Salisbury Conference was over.

Under the wise leadership of the late Professor Eric Stokes and the energetic secretaryship of Dr Terence Ranger (now Rhodes Professor of Race Relations at Oxford University), the conference brought together a lively collection of young historians from Europe and, because of the restrictive nature of laws on race in Southern Rhodesia in those days, a much smaller number of scholars from Africa. Ronald Robinson's gregarious nature soon eased the awkward relationships implicit at a conference held under these kind of racial restrictions.

He and I were contemporaries as undergraduates at St. John's College, Cambridge, before and after our periods of war service; and I had been aware of Ronald Robinson's reputation as a College and a University footballer. (Today, however, he lists his recreations in *Who's Who* not as soccer but as 'room cricket', the transition to which should make a very interesting footnote in one of those theses of the future, particularly if composed by a transatlantic student not completely familiar with the ramifications and refinements of these very English sports.) It was not, however, until the Salisbury 1960 Conference that I was to experience at first hand his considerable ability to help put at their ease a very widely assorted company of scholars.

Ronald Robinson did this as much by his frankness in debate in formal Conference sessions as by his good fellowship in what may be described discreetly as extra-mural meetings. *Africa and the Victorians* was in the press at the time of this 1960 conference; but, in his paper to this gathering and in his discussion of it, he presented the thesis of this now celebrated volume. Some of the African students at the University College who heard his presentation were, at first, resentful of the apparent fact that much of their peoples' destinies in the epoch of Imperialism appeared to have originated and to have been settled in a very off-hand, almost absent-minded, manner in the Foreign Office in far-off London. Patiently, however, Ronald Robinson dealt with their difficulties in appreciating his thesis, and indicated to them the complexities of the metropolis-colonial situation and the importance in European policies towards the hitherto unpartitioned world of internal factors in overseas territories, especially in Africa, in pulling the attention of imperialist countries towards them. In such discussions, he was adumbrating ideas which he was to assemble more formally in his article of 1972 on 'Non-European foundations of European imperialism'. It is a very great pity for the study of the history of ideas of Imperialism that there is, apparently, no recording available of these discussions and of the African, particularly the young African, presence at them.

On the Conference bus trip, over three days, to the Zimbabwe Ruins, Ronald Robinson's knowledge, as an exponent of University ball games, of what have come to be called 'rugby songs' eased many a weary mile over dusty and bumpy roads. When his own throat was getting a little sore with British sporting songs, he persuaded one of the African members of the conference, Ndabaningi Sithole, treasurer of the National Democratic Party in Southern Rhodesia and author of the recently published book, *African Nationalism*, to render the great southern African national song, 'Nkosi sikeleli' i Afrika', which many of the members of the conference heard for the first time. Again, how sad it is that we do not have a tape recording of this exercise on the move in European and African popular minstrelsy.

After the Salisbury Conference was over, I had planned a visit to Nyasaland, in its pre-Malaŵi days, to renew acquaintance with African nationalists there, with whom I had been in touch while making a study of John Chilembwe and the Nyasaland Native Rising of 1915. When Ronald Robinson heard of this, he said that he would like to come along and look at Nyasaland's position and prospects in the Central African Federation *in situ*. He made an excellent companion, particularly because, at the end of our venture to the interior, I was indisposed with intestinal problems, and he arranged to have the doctor from the Seventh-day Adventist Malamulo Mission bring me back to health.

When we were comfortably settled in Ryall's Hotel in Blantyre, after a rather bumpy flight from Salisbury, I got in touch with Orton Chirwa, who was then legal adviser to the Malawi Congress Party which had emerged from the imprisonment in Southern Rhodesia of the Nyasaland African Congress leaders after the declaration of a State of Emergency in their country in March 1959. I had known Orton Chirwa since 1952, especially during his days as a student for the Bar in London; and he had been very helpful in providing me with African testimony about the Chilembwe Rising. He immediately invited Ronald Robinson and me to supper with him and his wife, Vera, at their house in Limbe. Then, over coffee, and as dusk was almost upon the Shire Highlands, he broke out in excitement with the news that he had discovered the son of John Gray Kufa Mapantha, African medical assistant at the Church of Scotland Blantyre Mission, who had been one of John Chilembwe's main supporters and who, with other protagonists of the Native Rising, had been executed in early 1915. With his family, B.W. (Willie) J. Gray Kufa Mapantha was living in a small house on the Mlinde Estate. Orton Chirwa was anxious to take us to him, in search of further evidence about the impact of the 1915 Rising upon the Africans of the Protectorate.

And so, in mid-September 1960, in the dusk which was rapidly becoming thick darkness, Ronald Robinson and I set off with Orton Chirwa, in his car to find this little house. It was not one of the easiest of journeys; but, eventually, we found it. The family was having supper, and they were anxious to tidy up before we went into their living room. We, therefore, waited outside for a while, listening to drumming and other nocturnal sounds. Eventually, however, we were all seated around a tiny table, lit by a flickering little home-made oil lamp. John Gray Kufa's son told us the sad story of his father's part in the Chilembwe Rising; of his going into hiding after its collapse; of his betrayal, for a Government reward, by the man who married John Gray Kufa's wife after his death; of his last letter to his five children (Fraser, Willie, Albert, Agnes and Daisy) who had been born between 1898 and 1910, telling them to go to the Blantyre Mission where the Scots missionary in charge, Alexander Hetherwick, would look after them ('Muli Kusala mmanja mwa Dr Hetherwick akakusungani bwino lomwe ndithu'); and, at the end, of John Gray's execution.

I was attempting, in the little time at our disposal, not only to question John Gray's son about his account of his father's last days but also to take down his answers in writing. But it was all becoming too much for me, when Ronald Robinson volunteered to take notes and, as I have said, thereby became my first – and last – research assistant. How he managed to write so neatly and comprehensively in the cramped and ill-lit conditions in which we were working, I do not know. But I still have his notes; and, one day, I may try to make them part of another study of John

Chilembwe and his milieu. Perhaps a few lines from these notes may convey something of their pathos as well as the kernel of constitutional thinking in them, looking towards the independence of Nyasaland which ensued 49 years after John Gray Kufa's execution. 'He asked permission [said John Gray's son, of his father] to see his family for the last time. We left home for Blantyre . . . and we saw him in a motor bicycle side-car going to Zomba Central Prison. On his trial in the Court, he refused to say that there was "war" but "rising". Chilembwe's followers were taught not to accept the word "war" . . . if "war" had been accepted, the Europeans would have been declared conquerors of the country'.

During our week in Nyasaland, Ronald Robinson and I went from one end of the spectrum of independence to the other: from this interview with the son of one of Chilembwe's chief followers in 1915 to a meeting with Dr Hastings K. Banda who had been released from prison in April 1960. Ronald Robinson had a second meeting with him; but I was not able to accompany him because I had been taken ill at Ryall's Hotel. However, he later gave me an account of this second interview with the leader of the Malaŵi Congress Party who was to become his country's first President. Ronald Robinson and I also went into Kanjedza Prison to see, shortly before their release, three other leaders of the Nyasaland move towards independence: the late Dunduzu and Yatuta Chisiza and Henry M. Chipembere.

Our trip to Nyasaland was not all observations of the African side of the colonial equation. We also saw something of the European way of life. One greatly appreciated manifestation of the Caledonian character of much of this in the Protectorate was when we visited the Reverend Andrew Doig and his wife at the Blantyre manse of the Church of Central Africa Presbyterian, where, in good Scottish fashion, and in spite of the blazing hot sun outside, we were entertained with morning coffee and freshly made, hot, buttered scones. And, in a hired car, with Ronald Robinson at the wheel, we made the ascent to the Kuchawe Inn for lunch. By this time, I felt very much in his debt; and, with my mind on his choral abilities on the road to Fort Victoria and the Zimbabwe Ruins, I entertained him with a number of soldiers' songs which I had learned during my service with the King's African Rifles. One, which began with 'sole' ('sorry'), took his fancy, although I like to think that it fascinated him more as evidence of the hardships suffered by Nyasaland askari and other migrants northward during and after the First World War than because of any musical talents on my behalf:

> Sole, sole! Sole, sole!
> Anyamta kutawa,
> Kutawa ku Kenya:
> Ku Kenya kuli sole!

Or, in rough translation:

> Sorry, sorry! Sorry, sorry!

> The boys are off to Kenya,
> They are running away to Kenya:
> In Kenya they'll be sorry!

But we, indeed, were also sorry when our week in Nyasaland came to an end.

Back in Salisbury, we continued our researches in the Central African Archives. I wanted to look at African Watch Tower materials and the ramifications of the Chilembwe Rising into contemporary Southern Rhodesia. Ronald Robinson took the opportunity of searching out oddments on the career of Cecil Rhodes. I well remember his castigation of the founder of Southern Rhodesia for his morosely-expressed criticisms of the fondness for females of one of his prospective employees in the new British colony in Central Africa. It is from that time that I trace my interest in the sexual patterns of the life of Cecil Rhodes.

Looking back on this fortnight with Ronald Robinson, over a quarter of a century ago, in the Federation of Rhodesia and Nyasaland when its end was clearly in sight, I feel that I was privileged to be with a scholar who was also a good companion, at a historic moment. Twenty-eight years later, as Ronald Robinson reaches retirement, I – and I am sure I may speak here also for the contributors to this volume whose scholarly articles develop areas of interest in which he pioneered – want to thank him deeply for his contributions to the history of the Commonwealth and Africa and to the emergence of a general theory of Imperialism. Above all, I am grateful to him for helping to keep the historical profession, in the face of what appears these days both from within and without to be almost insuperable difficulties, wholehearted and humane.

Centre and Periphery in the Making of the Second French Colonial Empire, 1815–1920

by

C.M. Andrew and A.S. Kanya-Forstner

French colonial expansion, a prominent colonial publicist concluded in November 1883, 'has always been the product of isolated enterprises, of individual initiatives occasionally supported by public opinion but rarely understood by governments which, in the long run, caused them all to fail through lack of foresight, blindness, unwarranted timidity or misplaced temerity'.[1] The defects which Gabriel Charmes blamed for the loss of the first French colonial empire were just as evident in the construction of the second. Nineteenth-century French governments rarely pursued any consistent imperial design. Except for occasional bursts of enthusiasm, the French public, too, seemed either indifferent or actively hostile to empire. For most of the nineteenth century, empire-building proceeded by fits and starts, more often than not through the initiative of military agents on the imperial frontiers over whom metropolitan governments exercised little or no control. Similarly, those who finally gave French expansion some sense of direction after 1890 were for the most part members of the small but powerful French 'colonial party'. The incomprehension of governments, the indifference of public opinion and the influence of small groups on the periphery or at the centre were the dominant features of French expansion after 1815, and their interaction helps to explain how the second-largest colonial empire in the world came to be built.

I

Inconstancy and incoherence bedevilled official approaches to imperial expansion throughout the nineteenth century. During the early years of the Restoration, ambitious plans were made for building a second French India in the West African interior and for developing a lucrative trade with Indochina, only to be abandoned when the Senegal proved not to be another Ganges and the Vietnamese showed no interest in resuming their former ties with France.[2] The Restoration's most important colonial undertaking, the Algiers expedition of 1830, reflected no imperial priorities at all; its sole objective was to shore up Charles X's faltering regime. But as one of the King's ministers noted, it was far too late 'for opinion to be distracted by military successes'.[3] A month after the fall of Algiers, the Bourbons themselves were overthrown.

The Orleanists did not welcome their Algerian legacy and hesitated till 1834 before deciding to occupy the Algerian coast permanently. Nor were they interested in the creation of a tropical empire. Senegal was relegated to the status of a 'simple trading factory' in 1830; the French toe-holds along the coast of Madagascar were evacuated in 1831; and appeals for protection from French missionaries in Indochina were consistently ignored. The pace of French expansion, it is true, did pick up during the 1840s. In 1841 the July Monarchy finally began the 'total conquest' of Algeria. In 1842 the Marquesas islands in the South Pacific were occupied; the West African naval squadron was reinforced and the government authorized the construction of fortified naval stations along the West African coast. In 1843 a naval division was posted to the Far East with orders 'to protect and if necessary to defend our political and commercial interests', to negotiate a commercial agreement with China, and to establish a naval base somewhere off the Chinese coast.[4] But these initiatives did not amount to a coherent imperial strategy. Louis-Philippe himself was never an imperialist; his overriding concern was to keep the peace in Europe and to stay on good terms with the other Powers. Though hopeful that an African empire would offer 'immense opportunities for our activity and future greatness', the King's Foreign Minister, François Guizot, was also convinced that France lacked the resources for empire-building on a global scale. His so-called *politique des points d'appui* was intended merely to give France independent bases 'in those parts of the world which are destined to become major centres of trade and navigation'. To avoid 'grandiose projects which are then aborted', Guizot resolutely opposed any idea of conquering Madagascar and vetoed any occupation of the Indochinese coast.[5] In the face of Spanish objections to the occupation of Basilan in the Sulu archipelago, he soon dropped his plans for a Far Eastern naval base as well. Little was done to encourage trade with China either. Although a commercial agreement was signed in 1844, a *chargé d'affaires* was not sent to Canton until 1847. By 1850 the French colony in Shanghai still numbered only ten, half of them members of the consul's family.[6]

To begin with, the Second Empire was no more interested in overseas expansion than the July Monarchy, and Napoleon III's policies were just as firmly Eurocentric as those of Louis-Philippe. '[I regret] that France has colonies,' the Emperor once told the British ambassador: 'It is so difficult to maintain them in a prosperous state, [and] they are a burden to the Mother Country.'[7] In 1854 the new governor of Senegal was warned not to regard his appointment as 'the start . . . of a warlike era', and his colony's modest budget of 1.5 million francs was described as 'a very considerable financial sacrifice'. The government was equally dubious about the prospects of empire-building in South-East Asia. As the Minister of Marine and Colonies pointed out, India gave Britain a position of strength which the French could never hope to challenge. According to a senior official in the Foreign Ministry, French interests in the Far East were minimal even in comparison to those of the Dutch and the Americans.[8]

Napoleon III did eventually embark upon a series of adventures overseas. In 1857, responding to a concerted missionary campaign, he authorized the establishment of a French protectorate over Cochinchina. He then sent French troops to participate in the Chinese campaigns of 1858–60, to protect the Christians of Lebanon during the Druze uprising of 1860 and finally to make the Archduke Maximilian Emperor of Mexico. But these adventures were not the product of a carefully considered policy of imperial expansion. The Cabinet as a whole showed little enthusiasm for a Cochinchinese protectorate and approved 'a relatively small expedition' to occupy the Vietnamese port of Tourane only because the Emperor himself was in favour of it. Tourane itself soon proved untenable and was evacuated in 1860. By 1862, 'through force of circumstances' rather than by design, the French had acquired a fully-fledged colony in Cochinchina with Saigon as its capital. Two years later they almost gave it up in return for a large Vietnamese indemnity.[9] French intervention in Syria was no better conceived. One of its purposes may have been to create a client Arab state in the Levant, but such a fanciful scheme would have entailed the break-up of the Ottoman empire, and it was never seriously pursued.[10] The objectives of the Mexican expedition, 'to regenerate a people, implant our ideas of order and progress, and open vast markets to our trade', were the most unrealistic of all, and here the result was total failure.[11]

The driving force behind all these overseas adventures was the Emperor's determination to raise French prestige. 'For the sake of national greatness,' he declared in 1861, 'we must maintain our incontestable rights everywhere in the world, defend our honour wherever it is attacked, lend our assistance wherever it is sought in support of a just cause.' The Chinese campaigns were undertaken 'to avenge our honour in the Far East', the Syrian expedition 'to defend Christians against blind fanaticism', and Mexico 'to protect our nationals and suppress attacks against humanity and the rights of man'. But a preoccupation with national honour was no substitute for settled policies, as Napoleon himself was eventually forced to admit. 'Our overseas expeditions do not represent the execution of any preconceived plan,' he told Parliament in November 1863; 'they have been driven by force of circumstance.'[12]

Public attitudes to empire occasionally reflected a similar obsession with prestige. 'As a point of honour, out of national vanity and to avoid doing less than the Restoration', Frenchmen were determined not to abandon Algeria.[13] Their determination was all the greater because Great Britain had originally opposed the expedition and continued to press for Algeria's evacuation. Anti-British sentiments grew even sharper after the Eastern Crisis of 1839–41. France's diplomatic defeat, Guizot later acknowledged, 'revived all the old feelings of distrust and hostility against England . . . and made a deep and bitter impression on the people'. When he tried to defuse a minor Anglo-French crisis in 1844 by repudiating the unauthorized annexation of Tahiti, he and his colleagues were immediately accused of 'acting out of weakness and pusillanimity towards the British . . . All the popular feeling against Britain was mobilized against us.' For a time, the Tahiti affair threatened to bring down the government.[14]

But patriotic enthusiasm was not enough to make the French public imperialist. Only in Marseilles was the conquest of Algeria ever popular. Parliament and the press frequently criticized its cost, and the notorious corruption of the Algerian administration became a standard theme in nineteenth-century French literature. 'We are still confronted with an anti-African party which includes several prominent and influential people,' Guizot told the governor-general of Algeria in 1846, 'and their views have the silent but no less real support of many others.'[15] Except in Bordeaux, Marseilles and a few other port cities with colonial trading interests, French businessmen remained quite indifferent to the commercial prospects of West Africa and Indochina. French missionaries in the Far East and their supporters at home did plead constantly for government intervention on their behalf, and the decision to occupy Cochinchina was in large part a response to their pressure.[16] But when the occupation proved more difficult than the missionaries had predicted, their influence rapidly declined. By the 1860s, indeed, overseas expansion was losing its appeal as brilliant victories on distant battlefields no longer aroused the enthusiasm of a population increasingly anxious for peace. 'The country is tired of war,' the *procureur général* for Paris noted in August 1863: 'It coldly calculates the cost in men and money of the most glorious expeditions . . . It wants peace, a lasting peace, with all the force of settled conviction.'[17] In Parliament, the budget commission repeatedly insisted on the need to control colonial expenditures and 'to avoid all expeditions which are not absolutely necessary'. Though the Cochinchinese Estimates were progressively reduced from 22.5 million francs in 1862 to 8.5 million francs in 1865, the budget commission still described them as 'very high' and called for the colony to become self-supporting as quickly as possible.[18] Mexico, Napoleon's most ambitious overseas adventure, was also the most unpopular. By the time French troops were finally withdrawn in 1867, the Mexican expedition had become 'the scapegoat on which everything is blamed', and a lasting source of grievance 'against the government which undertook it without the consent of public opinion'.[19]

The creation of the second French colonial empire was less the work of central governments than of soldiers and sailors on the periphery who generated their own expansive drives and launched France on a series of conquests far more sweeping than their masters in Paris had ever contemplated. Algeria was the classic example. Even before the expedition set sail, its commander-in-chief, Marshal Bourmont, was telling everyone that Algeria would be French forever. Having captured

Algiers, Bourmont on his own initiative occupied the towns of Bône and Oran and began to organize a permanent administration. His successor, General Clauzel, reoccupied Oran in 1831, again without instructions. During his second tour of duty in 1836, Clauzel browbeat the government into sanctioning an expedition against Constantine, the disastrous failure of which forced Paris to approve a second and successful expedition in 1837. Two years later Marshal Valée, once more without permission, led his troops through territory belonging to the Algerian leader Abd el-Kader, and thus set the stage for Algeria's 'total conquest'. Under Valée's successor, Thomas-Robert Bugeaud, military insubordination was raised to the level of an art. 'In the face of the enemy,' Bugeaud once declared, 'one must never accept any precise instructions or plans imposed from above. . . Sovereigns and ministers, far from the scene of action, are often incapable of judging a situation dispassionately . . . One should burn instructions so as to avoid the temptation of reading them.' In direct violation of his orders, the governor-general invaded Morocco in August 1844. By 1845 he was publicly feuding with the government over his plans for military colonization. In 1847 he invaded Kabylia, again in violation of his instructions. When the Minister of War ordered him to stop, he insolently replied: 'I have received your despatch. It is too late. My troops . . . have already left, and I am on my way to join them. If we succeed, France and the government will have the honour. If we fail, the responsibility will be mine alone.'[20]

On a more modest scale, the Algerian experience was repeated in West Africa. 'Having served in Algeria,' wrote Senegal's energetic governor, Louis Faidherbe, in 1858, 'I [have] to be in favour of a more serious occupation of Senegal.'[21] As in Algeria, serious occupation meant conquest. In 1859 Faidherbe sent a punitive expedition into southern Senegal, later explaining that the need for immediate action to preserve security prevented him from seeking the government's prior approval. Though ordered to halt his advance, Faidherbe was not instructed to evacuate the newly occupied territory. Six months later he led another campaign in the south, this time with the government's permission.[22]

French naval officers in the Far East demonstrated a similar inclination and ability to slip the metropolitan leash. In 1842 Admiral Dupetit-Thouars, having taken possession of the Marquesas, sailed to Tahiti and on his own initiative placed the island under a French protectorate. In 1843, again without instructions, he abrogated the protectorate, annexed Tahiti and arrested the leading English missionary there. In 1847 the commander of the Far Eastern naval division, despite orders to avoid the use of force, sank five Vietnamese ships off Tourane and then made a farcical attempt to land French missionaries on the coast of Korea. The naval governors of Cochinchina were just as difficult to control. In 1862 Admiral Bonard, on his own initiative, negotiated a treaty whereby Vietnam ceded the three eastern provinces of Cochinchina to France. In August 1863 his successor, Admiral La Grandière, signed a treaty placing Cambodia under a French protectorate one week before the government sent him instructions not to intervene in Cambodian affairs. In June 1867 La Grandière seized the three western provinces of Cochinchina, despite explicit orders 'to avoid anything which might upset the court of Hué [Vietnam's capital]'.[23]

Metropolitan governments rarely possessed the strength of will needed to control their headstrong military agents. The weak and unstable governments of the 1830s in particular were quite incapable of controlling the Algerian generals. Fifteen different ministries came and went between August 1830 and October 1840. Between July 1834 and May 1835 alone, the Ministry of War, the department responsible for Algeria, changed hands six times. The Molé government of September 1836 disapproved of Clauzel's plans for an expedition against Constantine but dared not veto them. Instead, it simply refused to send Clauzel any reinforcements, 'a truly shameful way of escaping its responsibility by placing a general's prudence at odds with his sense of honour'. None of the three 'unhappy' ministers under whom Valée served was strong enough 'to dominate such a man' either.[24]

Not all governments under the July Monarchy were short-lived. The Soult–Guizot ministry of October 1840, for example, lasted more than seven years. But even stable governments had to give the generals and admirals wide powers to deal with local crises as they arose, even when the latter were responsible for provoking them. Though Bugeaud was told to keep Paris informed of his plans, he was left free 'to make whatever dispositions you think immediately useful'.[25] Considerations of security and prestige also made it difficult for Paris to disavow the results of military insubordination. Once Valée had goaded Abd el-Kader into attacking French settlements on the outskirts of Algiers, 'the destruction of Abd el-Kader's power . . . by all the means at [our] command' had to become the government's overriding objective. Guizot too felt obliged to approve the unauthorized protectorate over Tahiti, if not the island's unauthorized annexation. Having just established a permanent presence in the South Pacific with the occupation of the Marquesas, he later admitted, the French could not afford 'to appear uncertain and timid'.[26]

In addition, military commanders had their supporters within the government itself. The July Monarchy's three leading politicians were all in favour of Algeria's conquest. As Minister of War and Prime Minister, the venerable Marshal Soult was largely responsible for the decision to keep Algiers in 1834 and to appoint Bugeaud as governor-general in 1840. An Algerian partisan almost from the start, Adolphe Thiers was firmly convinced that 'something useful and important could be done' there if one adopted 'a sweeping plan of conquest'. As Minister of the Interior in 1835, he engineered Clauzel's reappointment to the governor-generalship. As Prime Minister in 1836, he gave his blessing to the attack on Constantine, though his government fell before the expedition could be mounted. Guizot, too, soon overcame his initial doubts about the value of a North African empire. He helped Soult to arrange Bugeaud's appointment in 1840 and thereafter became the governor-general's most influential, though not uncritical, supporter in the government.[27] The governors of Cochinchina under the Second Empire had equally powerful allies. Prosper de Chasseloup-Laubat, the minister responsible for colonial affairs from March 1859 to January 1867, believed fervently in the creation of a French Indochina.[28] He approved Bonard's acquisition of Cochinchina's eastern provinces in 1862 and urged the Emperor to accept La Grandière's protectorate over Cambodia in 1863. He was also responsible for blocking the retrocession of Cochinchina in 1864. On two critical occasions, La Grandière enjoyed the Emperor's support as well. Napoleon personally ordered the ratification of the Cambodian protectorate despite the strenuous objections of the Foreign Ministry, and he accepted the seizure of western Cochinchina in 1867 despite the hesitation of Chasseloup-Laubat's successor at the Ministry of Marine.

By 1867, however, French colonial expansion was clearly running out of steam. In 1863 Chasseloup-Laubat had unceremoniously dismissed Faidherbe's grandiose plans for extending French control over the Niger and raising the *tricolore* over Timbuktu. Preoccupied by his efforts to save Cochinchina, the minister had no time for visions of a new French India in the Western Sudan. When Faidherbe left Senegal in 1865, his dreams of empire went with him and were not to be revived for another decade.[29] After La Grandière's return to France, in 1868, Cochinchina, too, lapsed into relative obscurity. Faced with the growing threat of war in Europe, the French public lost all interest in colonial affairs, and even the Mexican adventure was gradually, though by no means completely, forgotten. 'On returning to France after many years overseas,' wrote the explorer Francis Garnier in April 1869, 'one is struck by the public's profound indifference to all aspects of the colonial contribution to our national greatness . . . There seems to be no connection between the overseas interests which one has just defended and that metropolitan power which, sunk back on itself, does not even dream of seeking overseas outlets for the restless activity consuming it at home.'[30]

II

The Franco-Prussian war and the uncertain beginnings of the Third Republic ruled out any prospect of empire-building in the years immediately after 1871. All the resources of the State had now to be devoted to internal reconstruction and metropolitan defence. Colonial expenditures were slashed and governors forbidden to exceed their meagre budgets. 'We must be patient, prepare for more prosperous times, allow France to regain her strength and rebuild herself militarily, economically and politically,' the governor of Cochinchina was warned in 1873: 'We can recover from our misfortunes, but only with a great deal of prudence and the strictest possible economies.'[31] Defeat in Europe, which most Frenchmen blamed on Napoleon's reckless waste of men and money overseas, also made continued expansion politically unacceptable. '*L'Empire a dégoûté notre pays d'aventures*', Jules Ferry complained in 1882: 'The disasters of an insane war, undertaken without alliances or preparation, filled the masses with a stubborn belief in peace.'[32]

Only in Indochina was this determination to avoid new overseas commitments briefly challenged. From December 1872 onwards the governor of Cochinchina, Admiral Dupré, bombarded Paris with requests to occupy Hanoi and the mouth of the Red River in Tonkin. Such decisive action, he argued, would force the Vietnamese to accept the loss of western Cochinchina and give France access to the rich markets of South China. It was thus 'a matter of life and death for the future of our domination in the Far East'.[33] In October 1873 Dupré sent Francis Garnier with 170 men to Hanoi, ostensibly to expel a French gun-runner, Jean Dupuis, and open the Red River to French trade. The true purpose of Garnier's expedition, however, was 'to conquer the country'.[34] Two weeks after his arrival, Garnier stormed Hanoi's citadel and occupied several positions in the Red River Delta. A month after that he was killed in a skirmish with Chinese irregulars – the notorious Black Flags – outside Hanoi. The Black Flags also killed Dupré's hopes for conquering Tonkin. Hanoi was immediately evacuated, and on 15 March 1874 a new Franco-Vietnamese treaty confirmed French sovereignty over the whole of Cochinchina, opened the Red River to trade and imposed a measure of French control over Vietnam's foreign relations. Except for two small garrisons at Hanoi and Haiphong, all French troops were withdrawn from Tonkin. For the next five years, French objectives in South-East Asia were simply 'to avoid conflicts and additional sacrifices by limiting ourselves to the maintenance of our existing positions'.[35]

The prevailing distaste for empire-building after 1871, however, was not universally shared. Some Frenchmen at least saw overseas expansion not as the cause of France's downfall but as the source of its regeneration, the only way it could regain the status and power lost in Europe.[36] Their arguments gradually converted influential moderate Republicans to the imperialist cause. The two most prominent Republican leaders, Léon Gambetta and Jules Ferry, did not become imperialists overnight. Both men had condemned Napoleon III's overseas adventures and both had toyed with the idea of sacrificing some part of the French empire for the return of Alsace-Lorraine. This thought still 'obsessed' Gambetta in 1876. But Gambetta had many friends among French settlers in Cochinchina and had assured one of them in 1871 that 'colonies will play a preponderant role in the reconstitution of our national wealth'.[37] In 1874 his newspaper, *La République Française*, led a brief but strident campaign for the retention of Tonkin.[38] By 1880 Ferry too had been converted: 'We had to dispel the widely-credited myth that France, after her disasters, had resigned herself to introspective and impotent withdrawal . . . France would not easily be content to count for no more in the world than a big Belgium.'[39]

As the post-war period of *recueillement* drew to a close, support for colonial expansion revived. In 1879 the public's imagination was captured by yet another extravagant plan to carve out 'a vast colonial empire' in the

West African interior, this time by building a railway from Algeria across the Sahara desert to Senegal.[40] Partisans of Indochinese expansion also renewed their agitation, and by 1881 the *Société des Etudes Coloniales et Maritimes* was noting with evident satisfaction: 'Public opinion, normally so uninterested in colonial expansion, seems to have emerged from its customary indifference and to have become aware of what people are starting to call, inaccurately, the Tonkin question.'[41]

Official policies appeared to change decisively as well. Charles de Freycinet, the Minister of Public Works in the Waddington government of 1879, responded to the publicity surrounding the trans-Sahara railway by establishing an official commission to study the plan. When he became Prime Minister at the end of the year, he proclaimed the government's duty 'to look beyond our frontiers and investigate what peaceful conquests it can undertake . . . Africa, on our doorstep, has a special claim to our attention'. In February 1880 Admiral Jean Jauréguiberry, Freycinet's Minister of Marine and Colonies and a former governor of Senegal, submitted an ambitious programme of Senegalese railway-building to Parliament, and in September he placed the Upper Senegal under military command. Jauréguiberry had equally ambitious plans for Indochina. As Minister of Marine in the previous government he had already drawn up detailed proposals for the military occupation of Tonkin. In April 1881 the Ferry ministry sent troops into Tunisia and placed the Regency under a French protectorate. Gambetta's short-lived *grand ministère* may have been planning for decisive action in Tonkin. It was almost certainly planning for joint Anglo-French intervention in Egypt and was supposed to have prepared an expeditionary force of 6,000 men for that purpose. Jauréguiberry's return to office in the second Freycinet administration gave a fresh impetus to French expansion in West Africa and Indochina. Commandant Rivière was sent to Hanoi with 500 men in April 1882, and in October Jauréguiberry revived his plans for the occupation of Tonkin. In August 1882 he authorized the occupation of Bamako on the Upper Niger and the construction of gunboats to patrol the river as far downstream as they could sail. To complete his plans for a West African empire, he then asked the Foreign Ministry to negotiate treaties giving France unrestricted commercial access to the Lower Niger and political control along the Benué, so opening 'Lake Chad and the rich markets of Bornu and Adamawa' to French trade and influence.[42]

For the second Ferry ministry (February 1883–March 1885), empire-building became almost an obsession. In 1883 the government launched a small-scale war aimed at imposing a French protectorate over the northern half of Madagascar. At the Berlin West Africa Conference of 1884–85, it secured international recognition for French claims in the Congo and French primacy along the Upper Niger. Most significantly of all, it committed France to the conquest of Indochina. In August 1883 Hué was bludgeoned into accepting a French protectorate, together with the imposition of French military control over Tonkin. Massive reinforcements were sent out, and by January 1884 the Tonkin expeditionary force totalled 15,000 men. The occupation of Tonkin led in turn to a war with China. In March 1883 Ferry had repudiated an earlier agreement partitioning Tonkin into French and Chinese spheres of influence, and by the end of the year French troops were fighting Chinese regulars as well as the Black Flags. In July 1884 Ferry issued an ultimatum demanding Chinese acceptance of the French protectorate over Annam, the immediate withdrawal of Chinese troops from Tonkin, and the payment of a huge indemnity. In August a French squadron destroyed the Chinese arsenal at Foochow, and in October the French seized Keelung on Formosa. In February 1885 the Tonkin expeditionary force occupied Langson near the Chinese frontier, and in March a French column crossed the border into Chinese territory.[43]

The governments responsible for this impressive wave of colonial expansion, however, were by no means consistent in their purposes. Freycinet and Jauréguiberry, the architects of the West African empire, differed sharply over the blueprints for its construction. The former believed in the peaceful expansion of trade and influence; the latter was determined 'to extend our domination to the Niger' and beyond by military means. Though Britain and Germany had effectively offered Tunisia to France at the Congress of Berlin in 1878, successive governments vacillated for three years before establishing the protectorate. Gambetta was initially opposed to any action for fear of upsetting the Italians. The President of the Republic, Jules Grévy, was staunchly opposed to all foreign adventures and once dismissed Tunisia as 'not worth a five-cent cigar'. Ferry himself at first considered the operation far too risky. 'An expedition to Tunis during an election year', he told his Foreign Minister in January 1881, scarcely two months before the invasion, 'my dear [Barthélemy] Saint-Hilaire you cannot think of it.' Only when Gambetta changed his mind could the expedition proceed.[44] Egyptian policy was even more uncertain. Gambetta's plans for intervention did not survive his fall from office. Grévy was firmly opposed to any French involvement in Egypt, and Freycinet was much more under the President's influence than Gambetta.[45] In June 1882 the government pledged not to send any troops to Egypt. When Freycinet requested approval for a limited operation to protect the Suez Canal a month later, the Chamber threw him humiliatingly out of office. The conquest of Tonkin was beset by similar hesitations. The Waddington government fell before it could act on Jauréguiberry's proposals in 1879. By the time Jauréguiberry persuaded Freycinet to approve them in July 1880, that government too was on its last legs. The Ferry ministry's Tonkin policy in 1881 was 'above all to avoid the risks of a military conquest'. Though Freycinet approved Rivière's dispatch to Hanoi in March 1882, he was opposed to any form of occupation, however limited. Jauréguiberry trotted out his plans for an expedition yet again in October and obtained Prime Minister Duclerc's support. But President Grévy then persuaded the rest of the Cabinet to reject them.[46] The Tonkin expeditionary force did not set sail until the summer of 1883, almost four years after Jauréguiberry had first proposed it.

Nor were the Third Republic's imperial objectives any more realistic than those of the Second Empire. The creation of a North-West African empire was no more than a pipedream, and the trans-Sahara railway never got past the planning stage. The Senegal-Niger railway also turned into an expensive farce and was effectively abandoned in 1885. Plans for controlling the Upper Niger by means of gunboats proved equally fanciful, as did the attempt to challenge British supremacy on the Lower Niger.[47] The dominant motive behind French expansion in the 1880s, as it had been in the 1860s, was to maintain and enhance French prestige. For Gambetta and those who persuaded him to support the invasion, Tunis was above all proof that 'France is becoming a great power again'.[48] The occupation of Tonkin, Ferry later acknowledged, 'was first and foremost revenge for the Egyptian affair', an attempt to restore French prestige in the aftermath of the Egyptian humiliation. Beyond 'the legitimate growth in our influence which will flow from a firm and energetic policy [and] the honour of opening one of the richest countries in Asia to French trade', the Ferry government never had very clear objectives in Indochina. There was no overall conception or prearranged plan behind French expansion in Tonkin, Ferry admitted to the Chamber in November 1884: 'Events have more often determined our policy than our policy has shaped the course of events.'[49] Napoleon III had made much the same confession twenty years before.

Popular support for colonial expansion during the 1880s was even less consistent than official policy. Enthusiasm for the trans-Sahara railway and the Tunisian protectorate vanished as quickly as it had arisen. Parliament had approved the Tunis expedition unanimously in April 1881 and ratified the Treaty of Bardo with only one dissenting vote in May. When the expedition ran into difficulties and had to be reinforced with metropolitan conscripts, however, euphoria gave way to recrimination as Ferry's enemies attacked him for burdening France with another Mexico.[50] In November the government was decisively defeated on a vote of confidence. Though Freycinet deliberately trimmed his Egyptian policy to suit the cautious mood of the Chamber, his defeat was even more decisive. 'We have a duty', Clemenceau proclaimed during the Suez debate, 'not to risk the army lightly . . . in adventures which could lead to disaster and national ruin.' Many of his colleagues clearly believed him.[51]

Ironically, the loss of Egypt made French expansion elsewhere in the world much more popular for a time.[52] The British occupation 'reawakened the memory of ancient rivalries which time had faded' and allowed colonial enthusiasts to tap the 'old and inexhaustible vein of Anglophobia running through public opinion'.[53] In November 1882 the Duclerc government was forced by popular demand to submit de Brazza's treaty with the Batéké of the Congo for Parliamentary ratification, not least because of Brazza's rivalry with H.M. Stanley.[54] The explorer's continuing popularity made it essential for the Ferry government to defend his gains at the Berlin Conference two years later.[55] The Madagascar campaign owed much of its support to Anglo-French missionary rivalry on the island, especially when the arrest of an English missionary in June 1883 threatened to provoke another Tahiti-style incident. Ferry was soon being criticized for not asserting French rights to Madagascar vigorously enough. The final vote on the Tonkin Estimates in May 1883 coincided with news of Rivière's death in a battle with the Black Flags outside Hanoi. Parliament approved the Estimates unanimously, and by December 1884 it had voted funds totalling well over 100 million francs for the expedition.

By 1885, however, opposition to the government's colonial policies was again on the rise. Ferry himself had never had any illusions about the fickleness of the public or its representatives in Parliament. 'My great fear is the Chamber,' he told Waddington, now ambassador to London, in December 1883: 'If we can't give the deputies reports of success [in Tonkin], they will create the same shambles that they did with Egypt.'[56] As the costs of the Tonkin campaign mounted and the Chinese war dragged on without a decisive victory, the deputies grew increasingly restive. In November 1884 the Chamber itself had called for the occupation of northern Tonkin. But when the Minister of War, who opposed the new policy, resigned in January 1885, Ferry's majority slipped to 55. Two months later, a motion critical of the government's Tonkin policy was defeated by fewer than 30 votes.[57]

The governments of the Third Republic also found their military agents in Tonkin and the Western Sudan difficult and often impossible to control. Marine officers wasted no time asserting their independence along the Upper Senegal. Lieutenant-Colonel Borgnis-Desbordes of the *artillerie de marine* fought his first engagement, despite orders to the contrary, two months after he took up his command. During his second campaign, again ignoring his instructions, he led an 'offensive reconnaissance' across the Niger. On his return to Paris, he persuaded the Ministry of Marine and Colonies to approve his plans for the immediate occupation of Bamako. 'Once in the Sudan I can thumb my nose at everybody,' Desbordes wrote home at the start of his third campaign, 'and it will take a brave man to stop me from doing whatever I think best.'[58] In similar fashion, Commandant Rivière stormed the Hanoi citadel two weeks after his arrival in April 1882, despite orders to avoid *les coups de fusil*.[59] When he received reinforcements in February 1883, he ignored repeated warnings 'not to drag the government into complications' and attacked Nam Dinh south of Hanoi. 'Since the government . . . was foolish enough to send me 500 men, I set out to accomplish on my own what it lacked the nerve to make me do,' he told a friend in Paris: 'They will now be forced to carry on.'[60] Despite new instructions to take no further action, he then led a sortie against the Black Flags who were besieging Hanoi. The engagement cost the French 50 men, including Rivière himself, thus making the parallel with Garnier complete.

Both Desbordes and Rivière were well placed to disregard their instructions. The former's insubordination was initially covered by the governor of Senegal, General Brière de l'Isle of the *infanterie de marine*. After Brière's departure in 1881, Senegal had six governors or acting governors during the next two years, making Desbordes ever more indispensable as the government's chief Sudanese expert and the only man 'capable of conducting operations in the Upper Senegal'.[61] Though the 'Admirals' Government' in Cochinchina had come to an end in 1879, the colony's first civilian governor, Le Myre de Vilers, was himself a former naval officer and inclined to behave like one. He was the one who first suggested sending Rivière to Hanoi, arguing that 'the fruit is ripe and the time has come to pick it'. He then excused the storming of the citadel as the understandable action of an officer 'whose first concern must be the honour of the flag and the security of the troops under his command'. Le Myre's successor, Charles Thomson, used similar arguments when excusing the capture of Nam Dinh.[62]

More significantly, local independence was also a function of metropolitan policies. Having committed themselves to the military occupation of Tonkin and the Western Sudan, governments had to accept the consequences of their decisions. On occasion they did so quite willingly. Desbordes had little trouble convincing Jauréguiberry to speed up the advance to the Niger in 1882. Ferry did not withdraw from Tonkin after Rivière's death but poured men and money into the conquest instead. For a time, central government became just as aggressive as its local agents, ordering the occupation of Langson in December 1884 and giving the Tonkin expeditionary force permission to invade China.[63]

Like Napoleon III before him, Ferry was to pay a high price for his adventurism. When news of the French retreat from Langson reached Paris at the end of March 1885, the government was immediately forced to resign amid demands for its impeachment, and Ferry himself was almost lynched by a mob outside the Palais Bourbon.[64] Ferry's colonial policy became a central issue in the subsequent elections, which produced the most anti-colonialist Parliament in the history of the Third Republic. Even colonialists had to accept the justice of the electorate's verdict.[65] For the next three years, Indochina remained the target of fierce attacks from Left and Right in Parliament. The combined Estimates for Tonkin and Madagascar were approved in December 1885 by a majority of four votes. The Tonkin Estimates were initially defeated in February 1888 and finally passed by a majority of nine only after the government had reduced them by a token 200,000frs. The Estimates did not secure their first more or less comfortable majority until November 1888.[66]

In the political climate after the Langson débâcle, there could be no question of continuing Ferry's policies. The new Brisson government included several opponents of Indochinese expansion, among them the Ministers of War and Marine.[67] A cease-fire with China was already on the point of signature when Ferry was overthrown, and the Sino-French treaty of 9 June 1885 brought the war formally to an end. A treaty with

Madagascar in December ended that war as well. Freycinet's 'chief preoccupation' when he became Prime Minister again in January 1886 was 'the liquidation of our colonial policy. Overseas undertakings must henceforth be subordinated to the state of our finances and our European interests'.[68] Even recent conquests were proving difficult to consolidate. In the Western Sudan, the headlong rush to the Niger and the suspension of work on the Senegal railway left the French with a precariously over-extended line of forts and no effective means of supplying them. By 1886 officials in the Colonial Department were debating the possibility of evacuation and the Minister himself was talking of 'a crisis whose end is not yet in sight'.[69] In Indochina, the occupation of Hué in July 1885 sparked off a national resistance movement which was to take more than two years to suppress. Poorly housed and badly fed, the Tonkin expeditionary force, 35,000 strong by the summer of 1885, suffered terribly from the ravages of cholera and other epidemics. Perhaps as many as 5,000 men died of disease in 1885 alone.[70]

The upheavals of 1885 also took a heavy toll on French morale. 'France is experiencing her worst crisis since 1851,' wrote the editor of the *Année Politique* in 1886: 'Her national integrity is not threatened, but her moral stature has been diminished. The country's weariness is matched only by the discouragement of her leaders. The whole of France seems exhausted.'[71] In the years to come, the Republic's moral stature was still further diminished by the Grévy scandal and her political stability undermined by the rise of *Boulangisme*. And if national integrity was never threatened, Boulanger's revanchism and the consequent growth of Franco-German tension did make the prospect of another European war seem less remote by 1887 than at any time since 1871.

Yet the anti-colonialist reaction of 1885–89 was less profound than it appeared. The ferocity of the assault on Ferry reflected more than simple revulsion against his colonial policies. The Right still hated him for his attacks on religious education. The Left would not forgive him for his reluctance to introduce social and constitutional reforms. Since colonial expansion was the only issue on which Right and Left could unite against the *opportuniste* Centre, however, the anti-colonialist majority in the 1885 Chamber could never have formed an alternative government. Clemenceau made that quite clear during the Tonkin debate in December 1885.[72] A third of the Radicals voted for the Estimates in 1885, and their continued support was crucial for the retention of Tonkin. By 1889 the survival of both the moderate Republic and its colonial empire was assured. Boulanger's flight to Belgium effectively destroyed his movement, and the Republican centre regained control of Parliament in the 1889 elections. Opposition to colonial expansion was also losing its electoral appeal; fewer than 100 successful candidates included a reference to it in their *professions de foi*.[73]

III

During the three decades after 1890, a renewed expansionist wave extended the second French colonial empire to its final territorial limits. 'If you drop a perpendicular from the frontier of Tunisia through Lake Chad to the Congo,' the Under-Secretary for Colonies, Eugène Etienne, told the Chamber in May 1890, 'then you could say that most of the territories bounded by this perpendicular and the sea . . . are either French or are destined to pass under French influence.'[74] With the Anglo-French agreement of 1898 and the symbolic meeting of three expeditions – from Algeria, the Western Sudan and the Congo – at Lake Chad in 1900, that objective was substantially realized. By 1896 Madagascar had been conquered and annexed, and Laos added to French Indochina. During the decade before 1914, France secured British and German recognition of its primacy in Morocco, which became a French protectorate in 1912. Finally, as a result of the Allied victory in the First World War, France regained the Congolese territories ceded to Germany in 1911 and obtained large parts of German Togo and the Cameroons. It also acquired, for the first time, a mandatory empire in the Middle East.[75]

The impetus behind French expansion after 1890 came from the metropolis rather than the periphery, though this shift of initiative was admittedly gradual. For a decade after 1888 successive administrations tried vainly to end 'the era of conquest' in the Western Sudan and to stop the *officiers soudanais* from turning the colony into their own private military preserve. To break their stranglehold, Paris eventually had to break up the Sudan itself: 'There was no other way to suppress this West African "State within the State".'[76] On a smaller scale, military insubordination along the Algero-Moroccan border created similar problems for the government during the early years of the twentieth century.[77] But the very excesses of the *officiers soudanais* made Paris that much more determined to ensure that the conquest of Dahomey in 1892–94 did not produce another military empire. Central control became all the more essential as the intensification of the scramble for territory in West Africa and the Far East increased the risk of conflict with other European powers. At the turn of the century Foreign Minister Delcassé successfully curbed the efforts of Indochina's fire-eating governor-general, Paul Doumer, to invade Yunnan. With the exception of the notorious Voulet-Chanoine expedition, West African treaty-making missions were also kept on the leash. The two African expeditions which did provoke major international crises before 1914 – Marchand's mission to Fashoda and the occupation of Fez in 1911 – were both launched with official knowledge and approval. France gained its post-war mandates through its efforts on the Western Front, not in the Middle East or West Africa. Its military contribution in the Middle East were negligible. Even in Togo and the Cameroons, its troops were outnumbered by those of its British ally.

The growth of international rivalries in the colonial sphere also increased the popularity of colonial expansion in France. By March 1890 those who had once condemned the conquest of Tonkin were attacking the government for not mounting a campaign against Dahomey. One commentator described the Chamber's delight over Etienne's speech in May as 'the glorification, I was going to say the revenge, of colonial policy'.[78] The Anglo-German agreement of June 1890, widely portrayed as a deliberate snub to France, provoked cries of patriotic outrage which even colonialist newspapers found excessive.[79] 'Obsessed with the desire to "teach England a lesson"', the Chamber overwhelmingly approved the conquest of Madagascar in November 1894. For similar reasons it approved the 'Fashoda strategy', the disastrous attempt to force the British out of Egypt by occupying the Upper Nile. The credits for Marchand's expedition were passed in December 1896 by 477 votes to 18. Even the Socialist leader Jaurès proclaimed: 'It is not a political vote that we shall take but a national one.'[80] Franco-German rivalry over Morocco after 1900 made imperialists out of many continental nationalists who had previously opposed colonial expansion because it would weaken France in any future war against Germany. 'One of the [Tangier] incident's most curious effects,' a prominent colonialist wrote during the first Moroccan crisis, 'has been to arouse an interest in Morocco among political circles which have until now been quite opposed to any sort of colonial enterprise.' After the second Moroccan crisis, the *Comité du Maroc* acknowledged: 'How many people have been converted to the Moroccan cause only by the unexpected, paradoxical but nevertheless formidable popularity which the irritating opposition of Germany won for it!'[81]

But the significance of the empire's new-found popularity should not be overestimated. Public opinion remained susceptible to sudden and violent changes of mood. As soon as the Madagascar expedition ran into difficulties, support for it vanished: 'On all sides, in virtually all sections of society, in most of the press, there were complaints, criticisms, recriminations.' 'One would think we were back in the days of Jules Ferry.' The imperialist passions aroused by international crises lost their fervour when the crises passed. Once the first Moroccan crisis had been settled, the public quickly lost interest in Morocco. '[We] certainly had to fight many bitter battles between 1885 and 1890,' the secretary-general of the *Comité de l'Afrique Française* complained in 1907, 'but the uncompromising hostility of those days was perhaps preferable to the all too frequent indifference with which we now have to contend.'[82] Though post-war Anglo-French rivalries in the Middle East convinced many Frenchmen that Syria must be added to the empire, the costs of its acquisition soon dispelled their enthusiasm. 'Public opinion has been more or less spontaneously alarmed by the prospect of large and costly expeditions,' the *rapporteur* for the Syrian Estimates admitted in 1920: 'People have spoken of a new Mexico, of a new Tonkin, of the possibility of a new Langson, of the disastrous and unlimited expenditure of money.'[83]

Nor were French governments more capable than before of

formulating coherent imperial strategies. If anything, their control over colonial policy grew even weaker after 1890. The Tonkin and Tunisian expeditions had been the subject of frequent, and frequently acrimonious, Cabinet debate during the 1880s. By contrast, the Cabinet rarely discussed African expansion during the 1890s. Though the Bourgeois and Méline governments both approved the Fashoda strategy in 1895–96, the Marchand expedition was not discussed again until the summer of 1898, when France and Britain were on the brink of war. The government as a whole played virtually no part in the negotiation of the Entente Cordiale which finally resolved the Egyptian question. According to the Prime Minister of the day, foreign affairs were 'the business of the President of the Republic and the Foreign Minister' alone. The Fez expedition of 1911 which provoked the second Moroccan crisis was initially approved by three ministers while the rest of their colleagues were out of town. Invariably preoccupied by the Western Front, wartime governments similarly abdicated their collective responsibility for the formulation of French colonial war aims.[84] In the absence of effective Cabinet decision-making, ministries were left to pursue their own policies, often at cross-purposes with one another. The Foreign Ministry negotiated the Anglo-French agreement of August 1890, 'despite its eminently colonial character', without consulting the Under-Secretary for Colonies. As Under-Secretary and later as Minister of Colonies, Delcassé organized expeditions to the Upper Nile against the opposition or without even the knowledge of the Quai d'Orsay.[85]

The political structures of French imperial administration simply added to the confusion. With one brief exception in 1858–60, no single ministry had ever presided over the empire as a whole, and by the early twentieth century the African empire alone was being administered by no fewer than four different ministries. The result, according to one former Minister of Colonies, was that 'bold initiatives, overall views, great projects in the national interest are forbidden to France in Africa'.[86] For most of the nineteenth century, colonies (but not protectorates or Algeria) were the responsibility of a colonial directorate or under-secretariat attached to the Ministry of Marine or the Ministry of Commerce. An independent Ministry of Colonies was not created until 1894, and it remained thereafter at the bottom of the ministerial pecking order, on a par with the Ministry of Public Works.[87] Seven different individuals held the post during the first five years of its existence. Only one of them, Delcassé, had 'a clear policy and the firm intention to implement it'.[88] The Foreign Ministry, of course, enjoyed much higher status, and Foreign Ministers were much less transient than their colleagues at the Rue Oudinot. During the quarter-century after 1894, three ministers – Gabriel Hanotaux, Théophile Delcassé and Stephen Pichon – held office for a total of almost 20 years. Here too, however, ministerial control was sometimes critically deficient. Marcellin Berthelot, who formally approved the Marchand expedition in November 1895, had no experience of foreign affairs and was 'almost paralysed by the work of his new unaccustomed office'. Jean Cruppi, the Foreign Minister who approved the Fez expedition in April 1911, naively believed that the expeditionary force would leave the city once European nationals there had been rescued. Despite his vastly greater experience, Hanotaux often suffered from nervous attacks which seriously impaired his conduct of foreign policy. By January 1897 he seemed on the verge of a breakdown, and President Faure was 'really frightened to see the control of our foreign affairs in his hands'.[89]

The continued weakness of French imperialism's 'official mind' left imperial policy-making as vulnerable as ever to unofficial pressures. Only the source of these pressures changed. Before the 1890s, they had come mainly from the agents of French expansion on the frontiers of the empire. Thereafter, they originated in the metropolis. During the last decade of the nineteenth century, hitherto isolated groups of colonial enthusiasts merged into a single colonialist movement, the so-called *parti colonial*, which was then to exercise a quite remarkable influence over French imperial policies for the next 30 years. The *Comité de l'Afrique Française*, founded in October 1890 to work for 'the union, across the Sudan, of the French Congo, Senegal and Algeria-Tunisia', organized most of the West African expeditions during the 1890s. The *groupe colonial de la Chambre* secured approval for the Madagascar expedition and campaigned unsuccessfully for the incorporation of Siam into a Greater Indochina. Colonialist pressure was largely responsible for the Fashoda strategy. After its failure, a small group of colonialist leaders devised the 'Egypt-Morocco barter' which became the basis of the Entente Cordiale and the French protectorate over Morocco. During the First World War, the colonialists gained a preponderant influence over French Middle Eastern policy and effective control over the formulation of French colonial war aims.[90]

The colonial party's influence was all the more remarkable given its small size and imperfect organization. The total strength of the colonialist movement before the war was never more than 10,000, and was probably less than 5,000 by 1914. The genuine activists, those whose involvement went beyond formal membership in a colonial society, numbered no more than a few hundred in all. The various colonial societies, well over 50 by 1914, which together comprised the *parti colonial* had few formal links with one another and were often sharply divided on crucial issues such as Algerian native policy. All they had in common was a general belief in the expansion and development of the empire. But the pre-war colonialist movement did have a tightly-knit inner circle of leaders and one unchallenged head, Eugène Etienne, who together determined its objectives.[91] Etienne and his lieutenants were 'men who know definitely what they are about and what they want'. They also knew how to get their way. For example, Etienne was able to persuade Maurice Berteaux, the Minister of War, to approve the Fez expedition in April 1911 because the latter 'was a candidate for the Presidency of the Republic and needed the 40 votes of the colonial party'.[92]

Like the generals and admirals of the July Monarchy and the Second Empire, the *parti colonial* had its allies within the government. Though Colonial Ministers were often short-lived and occasionally quite ignorant of colonial affairs, most of them were at least colonialists and belonged at one time or another to the *groupe colonial de la Chambre*. Foreign Ministers after 1894 were usually imperialists as well. Once out of office, Hanotaux joined several colonial societies, including the *Comité de l'Afrique Française* and the *Comité de l'Asie Française*. Delcassé and Pichon were both founder-members of the *groupe colonial*. The ties between the colonialist movement and the permanent officials at the Foreign and Colonial Ministries were even stronger. Those who supervised African expansion at the Rue Oudinot during the 1890s, as well as the head of the African department during the First World War, were all members or supporters of the *Comité de l'Afrique Française*. So too was Delcassé's chief adviser on Moroccan affairs in 1904, Paul Révoil. Similarly, all the officials at the Quai d'Orsay responsible for Middle Eastern policy during the First World War were members of the *Comité de l'Asie Française*.[93]

The French public's nationalism also worked to the colonialists' advantage. On the one hand, it prevented the occasionally violent opposition to colonial adventures from turning into a sustained and well-organized anti-colonialist movement. Right-wing attacks on colonial expansion lost their force once the defence of French rights overseas came to be seen as a patriotic duty. And as the Right gradually became reconciled to the Republic, so it became reconciled to the Republican empire. Left-wing anti-colonialism was similarly tempered by nationalism. Even Clemenceau, the scourge of the Opportunists over Tunisia, Egypt and Tonkin, was careful not to attack the principle, as opposed to the abuses, of overseas expansion. 'We want nothing better than to support . . . the expansion of French interests in the world,' he told the Chamber during a debate on the Senegal-Niger railway in 1883: 'We [simply] do not want French money to be spent for nothing. . . .' Two decades later Jaurès himself was still proclaiming: 'If we have always fought against warlike policies of colonial expansion, against the policy of military expeditions and violent protectorates, we have always supported, and we are always ready to support, the peaceful expansion of French interests and civilization.'[94]

On the other hand, French nationalism enabled the colonialists to rally massive public support behind their objectives whenever they succeeded in presenting colonial issues as matters of national prestige. The colonial party played its nationalist card with great effect over Madagascar in 1894, Fashoda in 1895–96, and Morocco in 1905 and 1911. A resurgence of Anglo-French rivalry in the Middle East after 1914 allowed it to do so again. 'In our day to day political life the *parti colonial* remains in the background,' the chief French negotiator on the partition of the Ottoman empire told his British opposite number in 1918, 'but there are issues on which it truly represents the national will. When one of these issues, like that of Syria, arises, it comes suddenly to the fore, and has the whole country behind it.'[95]

The key to the colonial party's influence thus lay in its ability to exploit two fundamental characteristics of French expansion after 1815: the incoherence of offical policy-making and the fervent nationalism of French society. But a third characteristic, the French public's general indifference to empire, withstood all attempts to change it. Colonialists often insisted on 'the need to undertake the colonial education of the country'. From time to time they tried to persuade themselves that their efforts were bearing fruit and that 'the colonial idea is penetrating all strata of public opinion'. By 1914, however, they had to admit that 'the colonial education of the French people has as yet not even begun'.[96] The empire's contribution to the war effort and its potential contribution to post-war economic recovery did seem to make imperialism genuinely popular once more. 'Over the past few months I have noticed a complete transformation of public opinion in favour of our colonies,' the deputy for Oran wrote in March 1920. When the *groupe colonial de la Chambre* reformed after the 1919 elections, it had almost 200 members, making it the largest single group in Parliament. But the empire's new-found popularity proved as illusory as the plans for its economic development. By the mid-1920s colonialists were again having to admit that 'public opinion takes scarcely any interest in colonial affairs except when they involve some appearance of scandal'.[97]

Though the colonialists and their allies in the government were able to turn empire-building into something more than a series of isolated and unco-ordinated enterprises after 1890, they failed to overcome public indifference to the empire or to convince Frenchmen, including French businessmen, that it was more than peripherally important to the survival and strength of the metropolis.[98] In a sense, their failure was inevitable. Colonies were never as important to France in the nineteenth century as they had been in the eighteenth. They were not vital to its economic prosperity, accounting for only some ten per cent of foreign trade in 1914, compared with 30 per cent in 1787. Nor were they vital to France's survival as a Great Power. No matter how intense colonial rivalries occasionally became, Frenchmen and their governments never forgot that the future of France depended on its position in Europe and that continental priorities, in the last resort, always took precedence over colonial ones. Given the peripheral importance of the empire, imperial expansion was, unsurprisingly, the product of peripheral forces. Before the 1890s most of these forces originated on the imperial frontiers. Thereafter they came from the metropolis, but they were never fully incorporated into the mainstream of French political or economic life. The completion of the second French colonial empire remained the work of a few, occasionally supported by public opinion but rarely understood by governments as a whole. Gabriel Charmes' conclusion would not have been much less accurate had he written it in 1923 instead of 1883.

NOTES

1. G. Charmes, 'La politique coloniale', *Revue des Deux Mondes*, 1 Nov. 1883, 58.
2. On West Africa, see G. Hardy, *La mise en valeur du Sénégal de 1817 à 1854* (Paris, 1921); P. Marty, *Etudes Sénégalaises (1785–1826)* (Paris, n.d.), 93–217. On Indochina, see H. Cordier, 'La reprise des relations de la France avec l'Annam sous la Restauration', *T'oung Pao*, 2nd ser., IV (1903), 285–315; idem, 'Bordeaux et la Cochinchine sous la Restauration', *T'oung Pao*, 2nd ser., V (1904), 505–60; IX (1908), 176–213.
3. Guernon-Ranville (Minister of Public Instruction), Diary, 17 April 1830, cited in G. Esquer, *Les commencements d'un empire: La prise d'Alger*, 2nd ed. (Paris, 1929), 199.
4. Guizot to Lagrené, 9 Nov. 1843, cited in G. Taboulet, *La geste française en Indochine* (Paris, 1955), I, 351. On West African policy, see B. Schnapper, *La politique et le commerce français dans le Golfe de Guinée de 1838 à 1871* (Paris, 1961), 13–86.
5. Ibid.; F. Guizot, *Mémoires pour servir à l'histoire de mon temps* (Leipzig/Amsterdam ed., 1864), VI, 270–5: 'Rien ne nuit davantage à la grandeur des peuples que les grandes entreprises avortées, et c'est un des malheurs de la France d'en avoir, plus d'une fois, tenté avec éclat de semblables, en Asie et en Amérique, dans l'Inde, à la Louisiane, au Canada, pour les abandonner ensuite et laisser tomber ses conquêtes dans les mains de ses rivaux.'
6. J.F. Cady, *The Roots of French Imperialism in Eastern Asia* (Ithaca, NY, 1954), 83.
7. Cowley to Malmesbury, 31 Oct. 1858, cited in W.E. Echard, *Napoleon III and the Concert of Europe* (Baton Rouge, LA, 1983), 187.
8. Ministre de la Marine et des Colonies [henceforth MMC] to Faidherbe, Instructions, 9 Nov., 8 Dec. 1854, Archives Nationales, Section Outre-Mer [henceforth ANSOM] Sénégal I 41/c, 41/a. MMC to Ministre des Affaires Etrangères [henceforth MAE], 2 Nov. 1855; Cintrat, Note, 20 March 1857, cited in H. Cordier, 'La politique coloniale de la France au début du Second Empire', *T'oung Pao*, 2nd ser., X (1909), 49–50; XII (1911), 41–4.
9. Walewski to Napoleon, 16 July 1857, cited in Taboulet, *La geste française*, I, 413–4; H. Galos, 'L'expédition de Cochinchine: La politique française dans l'Extrême-Orient', *Revue des Deux Mondes*, 1 May 1864; R.S. Thomson, 'France in Cochinchina: The Question of Retrocession, 1862–65', *Far Eastern Quarterly*, VI, 4 (1947), 364–78.
10. M. Emerit, 'La crise syrienne et l'expansion économique française en 1860', *Revue Historique*, CCVII (1952), 211–32.
11. Discours prononcé par Sa Majesté l'Empéreur, 14 Feb. 1867, *Annales du Sénat et du Corps Législatif*, 1867, annexe I, 3. On the Mexican adventure, see C. Schefer, *La grande pensée de Napoléon III* (Paris, 1939); A.J. Hanna and K.A. Hanna, *Napoleon III and Mexico* (Chapel Hill, NC, 1971).
12. Discours..., *Annales*, 1861, annexe I, 3; 1862, annexe I (27 Jan. 1862), 1–2; 1864, annexe I (5 Nov. 1863), 2.
13. C. de Rémusat, *Mémoires de ma Vie* (ed. C. Pouthas) (Paris, 1960), III, 195–6.
14. Guizot, *Mémoires*, VI, 156; VII, 69.
15. Guizot to Bugeaud, 24 April 1846, *Mémoires*, VII, 217.
16. The recommendations of the *commission de la Cochinchine* (April–May 1857) were based on a report submitted to the Emperor by Abbé Huc, a French missionary with considerable influence at Court. The vicar-apostolic to north Cochinchina, Mgr Pellerin, also returned to France for a preaching tour in support of Huc's proposals. Pellerin was later appointed the expedition's political adviser. Taboulet, *La geste française*, I, 403–11.
17. L.M. Case (ed.), *French Opinion on the United States and Mexico, 1860–67. Extracts from the Reports of the Procureurs Généraux* (New York, 1936), No. 506. The monthly reports of the *procureurs généraux* were the regime's principal source of information on the state of public opinion.
18. Budget commission report, 3 June 1862, 9 May 1865, *Annales*, 1862, annexe I, 345; 1865, annexe IV, 136–7.
19. Caen, 10 Oct. 1866; Dijon, 9 July 1867, Case, *French Opinion*, Nos. 656, 699.

20. G. Bapst (ed.), *Le Maréchal Canrobert: Souvenirs d'un siècle* (Paris, 1909), I, 399; Bugeaud to Minister of War, n.d., cited in H. d'Ideville, *Le Maréchal Bugeaud d'après sa correspondance intime* (Paris, 1882), III, 155–6. The standard work on French expansion in Algeria is C.-A. Julien, *Histoire de l'Algérie contemporaine*, Vol. I (Paris, 1964).
21. Faidherbe, Memorandum, 1 Oct. 1858, ANSOM Sénégal I 45/a. Faidherbe had served in Algeria for a total of six years between 1844 and 1852.
22. A.S. Kanya-Forstner, *The Conquest of the Western Sudan: A Study in French Military Imperialism* (Cambridge, 1969), 28–33.
23. MMC to La Grandière, 16 May 1867, Taboulet, *La geste française*, II, 513. For a general account of French activities in the Far East, see Cady, *Roots*.
24. Rémusat, *Mémoires*, III, 197, 428.
25. Minister of War to Bugeaud, Instructions, 19 Jan. 1841, cited in C. Schefer, 'La "Conquête Totale" de l'Algérie, 1839–1843', *Revue de l'histoire des colonies françaises*, IV (1916), 59. See too La Grandière to Director of Colonies, 30 July 1867, Taboulet, *La geste française*, II, 656: 'Il est difficile, sinon impossible, croyez-le bien, de diriger les événements à la distance qui nous sépare . . . M. de Chasseloup-Laubat [the previous Minister of Marine and Colonies] le comprenait et . . . me laissait une initiative qui sera toujours indispensable à un Gouverneur dans ma position.'
26. Minister of War to Bugeaud, 19 Jan. 1841, Schefer, 'La "Conquête Totale"', 51; Guizot, *Mémoires*, VII, 56.
27. Rémusat, *Mémoires*, III, 196–7; Guizot to Bugeaud, 21 Sept. 1841, 23 Aug. 1845, *Mémoires*, VI, 387; VII, 194–6.
28. Chasseloup-Laubat, Note, 14 Feb. 1862, Taboulet, *La geste française*, II, 523: 'Je voudrais créer pour mon pays un véritable empire dans l'Extrême-Orient. Je voudrais que notre civilisation chrétienne pût avoir dans cette nouvelle conquête un établissement formidable d'où elle rayonnerait sur toutes les contrées où tant de moeurs cruelles existent encore . . . Le magnifique édifice que je rêve, je ne le verrai pas achevé, mais je suis heureux d'en avoir jeté les fondements.'
29. Kanya-Forstner, *Conquest*, 40, 42–5.
30. F. Garnier, 'Voyages d'exploration en Indochine', April 1869, cited in A. Masson, 'L'opinion française et les problèmes coloniaux à la fin du Second Empire', *Revue française d'histoire d'outre-mer*, XLIX (1962), 426–7.
31. MMC to Dupré, 12 Sept. 1873, Taboulet, *La geste française*, II, 700–1. See too: MMC to governor of Senegal, Instructions, 19 July 1876, ANSOM Sénégal I 61/a: 'La France s'efforce en ce moment de concentrer ses forces et ses ressources dans le but de reconquérir la situation qu'une guerre malheureuse lui a fait perdre en Europe; elle ne peut s'épandre au dehors, prendre d'engagement onéreux, inscrire à son budget des dépenses qui réduiraient ses moyens de défense.'
32. Preface to *Les affaires de Tunisie*, January 1882, cited in P. Robiquet (ed.), *Discours et opinions de Jules Ferry* (Paris, 1897), V, 522.
33. Dupré to MMC, 22 Dec. 1872, 17 March, 19 May, 16 July, 11 Sept. 1873, cited in M. Dutreb, 'L'Admiral Dupré et la conquête du Tonkin', *Revue de l'histoire des colonies françaises*, XVI (1923), 12–16, 22, 24–5, 26, 33–6.
34. Dupré to Garnier, Instructions, 10 Oct. 1873, Taboulet, *La geste française*, 705–7; Garnier to Millot, draft, n.d. [December 1873], cited in D. Brötel, *Französischer Imperialismus in Vietnam* (Freiburg, 1971), 19.
35. MMC to Dupré, 7 Jan. 1874, Taboulet, *La geste française*, II, 738; MAE to MMC, 7 Sept. 1877, Ministère des Affaires Etrangères, *Documents Diplomatiques: Affaires du Tonkin*, $1^{\grave{e}re}$ partie, 1874–1882 (Paris, 1883), No. 24. For details of the 1874 treaty, see ibid., No. 2.
36. E.g. P. Leroy-Beaulieu, *De la colonisation chez les peuples modernes*, 2nd ed. (Paris, 1882), viii: 'Notre politique continentale, sous peine de ne nous valoir que des déboires, doit être désormais essentiellement défensive; c'est en dehors de l'Europe que nous pouvons satisfaire nos légitimes instincts d'expansion . . . La colonisation est pour la France une question de vie ou de mort: ou la France deviendra une grande puissance africaine ou elle ne sera dans un siècle ou deux qu'une puissance européenne secondaire.'

37. Gambetta to Caraman, 23 Aug. 1871, cited in Brötel, *Französischer Imperialismus*, 86. On Gambetta's imperialism, see ibid., 86–91; J.P.T. Bury, 'Gambetta and Overseas Problems', *English Historical Review*, LXXXII (1967), 277–95; C.-R. Ageron, 'Gambetta et la reprise de l'expansion coloniale', *Revue française d'histoire d'outre-mer*, LIX (1972), 165–204.
38. See J. Valette, 'L'expédition de Francis Garnier au Tonkin à travers quelques journaux contemporains', *Revue d'histoire moderne et contemporaine*, XVI (1969), 189–220.
39. Preface to *Les affaires de Tunisie*, cited in Robiquet, *Discours*, V, 526, 524.
40. A. Duponchel, *Le Chemin de Fer Trans-Saharien, jonction coloniale entre l'Algérie et le Soudan* (Montpellier, 1878), 218. See too: P.-L. Monteil, 'Contribution d'un vétéran à l'histoire coloniale', *Revue de Paris*, 1 Sept. 1923, 110: 'En 1879 l'opinion publique fut brusquement orientée vers une idée assez utopique en elle-même, imprécise dans sa réalisation, vague dans les conséquences qui pourraient en surgir, mais qui, en raison même de toutes ses données assez chaotiques, passionna les masses. . . .'
41. *Bulletin de la Société des Etudes Coloniales et Maritimes*, 5, 1881, 61.
42. On West Africa, see C.W. Newbury and A.S. Kanya-Forstner, 'French Policy and the Origins of the Scramble for West Africa', *Journal of African History*, X, 2 (1969), 253–76. On Jauréguiberry and Indochina, see K. Mulholland, 'Admiral Jauréguiberry and the French Scramble for Tonkin, 1879–83', *French Historical Studies*, XI (1979), 81–107. On Gambetta's colonial policies, see n. 37 above. The fullest account of French Tunisian policy is J. Ganiage, *Les origines du protectorat français en Tunisie* (Paris, 1959).
43. By far the fullest account of French involvement in Indochina during the late nineteenth century is C. Fourniau, 'Les contacts franco-vietnamiens en Annam et au Tonkin de 1885 à 1896', Thèse de Doctorat d'Etat, Université de Provence 1983, 4 vols. The period up to March 1885 is dealt with in Vol. I, 389–442.
44. Ganiage, *Origines*, 624–67. Gambetta's conversion was due to the combined pressure of the senior ambassadors, especially Saint-Vallier in Berlin, and the Quai d'Orsay's political director, Baron de Courcel.
45. B. Lavergne, *Les deux présidences de Jules Grévy, 1879–1887. Mémoires de Bernard Lavergne* (Paris, 1966), 77: 'Aujourd'hui [June 1882] qu'irions-nous faire en Egypte? Est-ce que ses affaires nous regardent? Voulons-nous la conquérir? Non! Et si nous ne voulons pas la conquérir, avons-nous la prétention d'aller y établir l'ordre? Qu'est-ce que cela nous fait, à nous, qu'il y ait du désordre en Egypte?'
46. MMC to governor of Cochinchina, draft instructions, encl. in MMC to MAE, 26 Sept. 1881; Freycinet to Jauréguiberry 16 March 1882; Jauréguiberry to Duclerc, 15, 31 Oct. 1882; Duclerc to Jauréguiberry, 22 Oct., 14 Nov. 1882, *Affaires du Tonkin*, Nos. 93, 105, 134, 135, 137, 139; [A. Billot], *L'affaire du Tonkin* (Paris, [1888?]), 11–12; Lavergne, *Deux présidences*, 96.
47. Kanya-Forstner, *Conquest*, caps. 4–5.
48. Gambetta to Ferry, 13 May 1881, cited in G. Hanotaux, *Histoire de la France contemporaine* (Paris, 1908), IV, 665. See too: Courcel, Souvenirs inédits, ibid., 651: '[Gambetta] m'écouta avec une attention soutenue . . . pendant que je développais les avantages, la nécessité d'une action prompte en Tunisie, l'honneur qui en rejaillirait, l'espèce de baptême diplomatique qu'en recevrait cette République qu'ils avaient l'intention d'instituer. . .'; Saint-Vallier (Berlin) to Barthélemy Saint-Hilaire, 26 Jan. 1881, *Documents Diplomatiques Français*, 1er série, III, No. 349: 'l'Europe nous observe pour nous juger et savoir si nous sommes encore quelque chose; un acte de fermeté, d'énergique volonté . . . et nous reprenons notre rang dans l'estime des nations; une nouvelle preuve de faiblesse, et nous achevons de nous reléguer au rang de l'Espagne.'
49. Ferry, Preface to *Le Tonkin et la Mère-Patrie*, April 1890, Robiquet, *Discours*, V, 555; Exposé des Motifs, 26 April 1883, *Affaires du Tonkin*, 2e partie, 1883–1884, No. 183, annexe; speech to the Chamber, 26 Nov. 1884, Robiquet, *Discours*, V, 415–16.
50. Lenglé, speech to the Chamber, 11 April 1881, Ganiage, *Origines*, 670: 'Nous ne voulons pas donner l'argent de la France et le sang de ses soldats pour les Jeckers de la Tunisie.'; Rochefort, 'Le secret de l'affaire tunisienne', *L'Intransigeant*, 27 Sept. 1881, ibid., 675: 'Nous comparions la guerre de Tunisie à celle du Mexique . . . Jecker a été

fusillé par la Commune. Nous nous demandons s'il méritait plus la mort que les pandours qui . . . vont voler des millions sur les cadavres.'
51. *Journal Officiel de la République Française* [*J.O.* hereafter], *Débats Parlementaires, Chambre*, 29 July 1882. The government was defeated by 416 votes to 75.
52. Charmes, 'La politique coloniale', 49: 'Après avoir été longtemps fort décriée en France, la politique coloniale y est devenue depuis quelques mois réellement populaire. . . Ses premières manifestations ont coincidé avec l'abandon fait par les pouvoirs publics de notre politique traditionnelle en Egypte. . . Le lendemain même où l'Egypte nous échappait, nous avons trouvé l'heure favorable pour aller nous établir au Tonkin et à Madagascar.'
53. *Bulletin de la Société des Etudes Coloniales et Maritimes*, 6 (November 1882), 349; Ferry to Waddington (London), 26 June 1884, Archives du Ministère des Affaires Etrangères [AE hereafter], Papiers d'Agents, Waddington 4. In November 1882 the *Société des Etudes Coloniales et Maritimes* created a special *Comité de défense des intérêts français menacés par l'Angleterre*.
54. See J. Stengers, 'L'Impérialisme Colonial de la Fin du XIXe Siècle: Mythe ou Réalité', *Journal of African History*, III, 3 (1962), 474–7. See too Charmes, 'La politique coloniale', 60: 'S'il y a eu, depuis quelques années, un mouvement d'opinion énergique et universel dans notre pays, c'est celui qui s'est produit en faveur de l'entreprise de M. de Brazza au Congo. Pour la première fois dans notre histoire contemporaine, on a vu tous les partis depuis l'extrême droite jusqu'à l'extrême gauche s'enflammer du même zèle pour une même cause.'
55. Ferry to Courcel, 1 Dec. 1884, cited in G. de Courcel, *L'influence de la Conférence de Berlin sur le droit colonial international* (Paris, 1935), 95: 'L'opinion même la plus ombrageuse approuvera les arrangements de Berlin à une condition: c'est qu'il n'en ressortira pas indirectement une victoire de l'Association [Indépendante du Congo] sur M. de Brazza. M. de Brazza est populaire, il a un gros parti, on lui a confié quelque chose de l'honneur national. Il nous faut un arrangement qui flatte l'amour-propre du public français.'
56. Ferry to Waddington, 9 Dec. 1883, AE PA Waddington 4.
57. Robiquet, *Discours*, V, 467–8, 488–93, 508–9.
58. Kanya-Forstner, *Conquest*, 87–94; 'Au vieux Soudan. Lettres inédites du Général Borgnis-Desbordes', *Bulletin du Comité de l'Afrique Française*, *Renseignements Coloniaux*, 6, June 1910.
59. Governor of Cochinchina to Rivière, Instructions, 17 Jan. 1882, *Affaires du Tonkin*, 1ère partie, No. 102, annexe II: 'Toute ma pensée peut se résumer en cette phrase: Eviter les coups de fusil; ils ne serviraient à rien qu'à nous créer des embarras.'
60. Governor of Cochinchina to Rivière, 17 June, 27 July, 9 Sept. 1882, Taboulet, *La geste française*, II, 781–4; Rivière to Madame de Caillavet, 8 May 1883, 'Lettres à Madame A. de Caillavet', *Revue des Deux Mondes*, 1 Feb. 1926, 632.
61. Governor of Senegal to MMC, 1 June 1882, ANSOM Sénégal I 99/a, Correspondance du Gouverneur.
62. Le Myre de Vilers to Minister of Commerce and Colonies, 21 Dec 1881, Taboulet, *La geste française*, II, 763–4; Le Myre de Vilers to MMC, 5 May 1882, *Affaires du Tonkin*, 1ère partie, No. 112; Thomson to MMC, 2 April 1883, ibid., 2e partie, No. 174, annexe: 'Le recul au Tonkin serait aujourd'hui la perte absolue de notre prestige dans l'Extrême-Orient et la ruine complète de notre autorité en Cochinchine.'
63. Fourniau, 'Contacts', I, 452, note 1.
64. G. Hanotaux, *Mon Temps*, cited in Fourniau, 'Contacts', I, 454, note 1: 'Je voyais sur le pont de la Concorde le chapeau haut-de-forme s'avançant au-dessus de la foule qui s'écriait: "à l'eau, à l'eau." Je n'en doute pas, seule sa vaillance le sauva.'
65. E.g. P. Leroy-Beaulieu, 'Les devoirs de la Chambre nouvelle et la politique coloniale', *Economiste Français*, 14 Nov. 1885: 'L'administration précédente a montré une activité incohérente et déréglée sur le terrain colonial . . . Le corps électoral a donc eu grand'raison de blâmer sévèrement la conduite de nos expéditions du Tonquin et de Madagascar.' The new Chamber had more than 180 Conservative deputies and a similar number of Radicals and *Extrême Gauche*, giving the opponents of colonial expansion a clear majority.

66. See E. Schmieder, 'La Chambre de 1885–1889 et les affaires du Tonkin', *Revue française d'histoire d'outre-mer*, LIV (1966), 153–214.
67. Six members of Brisson's Cabinet had voted against Ferry on 30 March 1885; Brisson himself had abstained. Brisson's Minister of War, General Campenon, had resigned from Ferry's government over its Tonkin policy in January 1885. His Minister of Marine and Colonies, Admiral Galiber, was a friend of President Grévy and a harsh critic of the Tonkin expedition. Lavergne, *Deux présidences*, 165–6.
68. *Le Télégraphe*, 11 Jan. 1886, cited in Fourniau, 'Contacts', II, 1157. *Le Télégraphe* had very close ties with Freycinet.
69. Pérard, note pour le Sous-secrétaire, April 1886, ANSOM Sénégal IV 84/a; MMC to governor of Senegal, Instructions, 5 April 1886, ANSOM Sénégal I 74/a.
70. Fourniau, 'Contacts', I, 577–85, 599–600.
71. Cited ibid., I, 459.
72. *Journal des Débats*, 26 Dec. 1885: 'M. Clemenceau a déclaré très nettement que dans le cas du rejet des crédits demandés par le gouvernement, ni lui ni ses amis ne se chargeraient de former un autre ministère. Pour justifier ce refus anticipé, il a montré du geste les 180 députés de la droite, complices empressés de tout vote qui peut discréditer la République.'
73. C.M. Andrew and A.S. Kanya-Forstner, 'The French "Colonial Party": Its Composition, Aims and Influence, 1885–1914', *The Historical Journal*, XIV, 1 (1971), 100.
74. *J.O., Déb. Parl. Chambre*, 10 May 1890, 750.
75. On this final phase of French expansion, see C.M. Andrew and A.S. Kanya-Forstner, *France Overseas: The Great War and the Climax of French Imperial Expansion* (London, 1981).
76. Binger, Note pour le Ministre, n.d., AMSOM A.O.F. VII. See too Kanya-Forstner, *Conquest*, caps. 7–9.
77. C.M. Andrew, *Théophile Delcassé and the Making of the Entente Cordiale* (London, 1968), 261–3. See too: J.J. Cooke, 'Lyautey and Etienne: The Soldier and the Politician in the Penetration of Morocco, 1904–1906', *Military Affairs*, XXXVI, 1 (1972), 14–18.
78. 'Pas Perdus', *Le Figaro*, 11 March 1890.
79. On the significance of the Anglo-German agreement and the French reaction to it, see A.S. Kanya-Forstner, 'French African Policy and the Anglo-French Agreement of 5 August 1890', *The Historical Journal*, XII, 4 (1969), 628–50.
80. *La Politique Coloniale*, 12 Sept. 1895; *J.O., Déb. Parl. Chambre*, 8 Dec. 1896. On Fashoda, see: C.M. Andrew and A.S. Kanya-Forstner, 'Gabriel Hanotaux, the Colonial Party and the Fashoda Strategy', *Journal of Imperial and Commonwealth History*, III, 1 (1974), 55–104.
81. R. de Caix, 'L'incident allemand-marocain'; 'Le traité de Fez', *L'Afrique Française*, April 1905, 155; April 1912, 122.
82. *La Politique Coloniale*, 12 Sept., 8 Aug. 1895; *L'Afrique Française*, Nov. 1907, 404. See too: *La Dépêche Coloniale*, 5 July 1910 (report on Etienne's speech to the *Comité bordelais des conseillers de commerce extérieur*): 'M. Etienne regrette . . . qu'en France l'attention du grand public ne s'attache à une question que lorsqu'elle arrive à l'état aigu, et que la foule se désintéresse des événements dans toutes les circonstances où la persistance, l'esprit de suite sont nécessaires. C'est ce qui est arrivé pour le Maroc, comme pour toutes les autres colonies.'
83. Georges Noblemaire, *J.O., Déb. Parl. Chambre*, 25 June 1920, 2450–1.
84. Andrew and Kanya-Forstner, 'The French "Colonial Party"'; idem, 'The French Colonial Party and French Colonial War Aims, 1914–1918', *The Historical Journal*, XVII, 1 (1974), 79–106.
85. Kanya-Forstner, 'French African Policy', 649–50; Andrew and Kanya-Forstner, 'Gabriel Hanotaux', 61–4.
86. Adolphe Messimy (Minister of Colonies, 1911), cited in *J.O., Doc. Parl. Chambre*, 1920, No. 807, 1099. The Ministry of Colonies administered the tropical African empire. The Tunisian and Moroccan protectorates were the responsibility of the Quai d'Orsay. The Algerian departments came under the Ministry of the Interior, and the military territories in the Sahara under the Ministry of War.

87. *La Dépêche Coloniale*, 2/3 Nov. 1898. As late as 1920 the Ministry was still being described as 'la cendrillon des ministères'. *J.O., Déb. Parl. Chambre*, 29 June 1920. On the history of the colonial under-secretariat, see F. Berge, *Le sous-secrétariat et les sous-secrétaires d'état aux colonies: Histoire de l'émancipation de l'administration coloniale* (Paris, 1962).
88. *La Dépêche Coloniale*, 29 June 1898.
89. Andrew and Kanya-Forstner, 'Gabriel Hanotaux', 73, 82; idem, 'The French "Colonial Party"', 124.
90. For details, see Andrew and Kanya-Forstner, 'The French "Colonial Party"'; 'French Colonial War Aims'.
91. The colonialist leaders generally belonged to several colonial societies at the same time, thus helping to compensate for the movement's lack of any formal organization. Etienne himself belonged to 20 societies and was a patron of another six. On the composition of the *parti colonial* and the affiliations of its leaders, see C.M. Andrew, P. Grupp and A.S. Kanya-Forstner, 'Le mouvement colonial français et ses principales personnalités', *Revue française d'histoire d'outre-mer*, LXII (1975), 640–73.
92. *The Times*, 27 Jan. 1896; *Les carnets de Georges Louis*, II (Paris, 1926), 110, citing Victor Bérard.
93. For details see C.M. Andrew, 'The French Colonialist Movement during the Third Republic: The Unofficial Mind of Imperialism', *Transactions of the Royal Historical Society*, 5th ser., XXVI (1976), 157–8 and notes 40–43.
94. *J.O., Déb. Parl. Chambre*, 3 July 1883, 23 Nov. 1903.
95. Picot to Sykes, 11 Sept. 1918, Public Record Office, FO 800/221, Sykes MSS.
96. *La Dépêche Coloniale*, 4 April 1912, 9 July, 2 Feb. 1914.
97. Roux-Freissineng, *La Dépêche Coloniale*, 6 March 1920; A. Lebrun, 'Nos colonies au travail', *L'Afrique Française*, November 1927, 446. On the membership of the *groupe colonial*, see C.M. Andrew and A.S. Kanya-Forstner, 'The *Groupe Colonial* in the French Chamber of Deputies, 1892–1932', *The Historical Journal*, XVII, 4 (1974), 837–66.
98. See C.M. Andrew and A.S. Kanya-Forstner, 'French Business and the French Colonialists', *The Historical Journal*, XIX, 4 (1976), 981–1000. Cf. J. Marseille, 'Les relations commerciales entre la France et son empire colonial de 1880 à 1913', *Relations internationales*, No. 6 (1976), 145–60; idem, *Empire colonial et capitalisme français: Histoire d'un divorce* (Paris, 1984), pt. I.

Scottish Missions and Education in Nineteenth-Century India: The Changing Face of 'Trusteeship'*

by
Andrew Porter

'Ethics have always been the first refuge of the British imperialists, and . . . it is reasonable to suppose that this was because theology was as vital to the imperial process as surplus capital or high velocity guns.'[1] With this observation, Ronald Robinson turned again to questions of trusteeship which had preoccupied him both in the late 1940s as a civil servant and during the 1960s as chairman of the Cambridge Conferences on Development.[2] Sufficient time has passed since that latest remark for the silence which followed it to have become remarkable, if not deafening. Inattention may reflect the fact that other theologies and alternative services are all the rage. Devotees are more likely to be found prostrate before the relics of Decolonization than cultivating odours of sanctity redolent of Sir Reginald Coupland.[3] With theological studies themselves less fashionable than they used to be, and Robinson's own reservations about the 'Liberal Anglican school of commonwealth history' widely shared,[4] it is perhaps not surprising that few have acknowledged the broad hint that here is still a significant and rewarding field for historians of British expansion.

Robinson has developed this theme at some length.[5] He has argued that 'since the eighteenth century the theology of the British pro-consuls had been defined in terms of "Trusteeship"',[6] and has stressed the periodic redefinition of ideals associated with the term, the importance of collective conviction or personal ideals as a determinant of policy, as well as the fact that Exeter Hall and the overtly religious sectors of the British public had no monopoly of ethical concern for those experiencing the pressures of British expansion and the extension of colonial rule. He has focused closely on the twentieth-century African empire, the sterility of the old morality evident between the wars, the work of the empire's new theologians, and the evangelical enthusiasm of born-again proconsuls led by Andrew Cohen.

For more general consideration, two of Robinson's points stand out. There is his wistful reflection on the current neglect of questions about ethical or moral preoccupations in politics, 'which used to and perhaps should still fascinate historians'.[7] And there is a gauntlet thrown down in his suggestion that 'until the role of moral force in the imperial process is more sharply defined, it is not easy to be sure of the role of high velocity guns or surplus capital'.[8] This essay attempts to contribute to that clearer definition.

Despite much partiality, practical shortsightedness, the fickleness of supporters and surrenders to more pressing realities, the idea of 'trusteeship' – of a responsibility to contribute to the protection, welfare and advancement of non-Europeans caught up in the growth of British influence and control – has been deeply rooted in British culture since the late eighteenth century. Yet ever since Eric Williams sighted the humanitarian Jericho and sounded a fanfare in *Capitalism and Slavery*, generations of trumpeters have circled the citadel. Cohorts of warriors have been slowly demolishing its traditional historiographical defences, here a buttress, there a rampart. The old South African tower has recently been largely destroyed.[9]

Nevertheless, the varied sources of a broadly humanitarian commitment, its continued adaptation and capacity for generating enthusiasm, the nature, extent and influence of its supporters throughout the nation, continue to invite examination.[10] Older writers sensed something of this variety even when their emphases lay elsewhere. G.R. Mellor focused on the activity of British policy-makers and officials, but attributed to unofficial groups, 'the ad hoc societies', a vital role in keeping the idea of trusteeship alive. The existence of 'missionary societies at home and the missionaries afield' helped repeatedly to recall officialdom to its obligations.[11] His point has substance, not only at the level of widespread domestic agitation as analysts of the anti-slavery movement have shown, but also in the minutiae of day-to-day living. Once Hope Waddell and the missionaries came as regular guests to King Eyo's weekly dinners in Calabar, the trading captains and consuls rarely turned them into riotous drinking bouts.[12] This essay, however, is not concerned primarily with the role of missions as watchdogs or lapdogs of imperial governments, affecting the intensity with which principles were officially applied. It looks instead at their understanding of and influence on the practical thrust of 'trusteeship' and their contribution to major shifts in the interpretation of British obligations. Not only is it true that 'no consecutive history even of the idea of trust exists'.[13] There is also no connected study of the place of Christian missionary activity in the history of imperial expansion. The two themes are at many points inseparable: the study of either one may help to deepen understanding of the other.

I

Britain's presence in India has always loomed large in debates about trusteeship, and the emergence of the concept of 'trusteeship' itself is conventionally dated from the late eighteenth century. Edmund Burke's denunciations of Warren Hastings in the 1780s were of central importance in defining standards which might govern Britain's administration of its colonial peoples. For 25 years before the renewal of the East India Company's charter in 1813, evangelicals also fought for the inclusion among government's obligations of the duty to promote, or at least to facilitate, the propagation in India of Christianity.

It has recently been argued, however, that the view of government's benevolent functions which was developing at this time, embodying as it did notions of a responsible 'trusteeship' or the 'humanitarian ideals of the later eighteenth century', 'owed less to new ideologies appropriate to a changing society than to a new urgency in acting on old principles.' Anti-slavery sentiments, for example, had a number of deep roots. 'Slavery was an unnatural despotism . . . never . . . domiciled in the English tradition' and vulnerable to very traditional legal arguments. 'The principles of protection of property and access to an impartial law' were similarly 'very old axioms', which 'can be related more convincingly to . . . the "possessive individualism" of the seventeenth century than to any ideology of industrial capitalism of the future'.[14]

Like many persuasive arguments, this one is capable of extension. A similar point might be made about the missionary strategy of the period, notwithstanding authoritative emphasis on, for example, William Carey's modernity.[15] In India, as in the West Indies, missionaries struggled like evangelicals at home for the right to preach freely and for control of their own pulpits or places of worship. East India Company chaplains were exhorted like lethargic parochial clergy to extend their customary activities to wider audiences. Acquisition of the vernacular languages was seen as vital to the effective dissemination of the Christian message not only through a revived emphasis on preaching but by that most traditional of vehicles, the religious tract or pamphlet. Consequently the British and Foreign Bible Society and the Religious Tract Society operated with equal determination in Berkshire and Bengal. At this point, of course, the missionary task began to embrace that of education.[16] Not only was the spread of literacy recognized as an essential aid to the teaching of Christianity, but there was an obvious need for the training of native preachers and teachers to take up the missionary baton. Even acknowledging the new geographical scope and urgency being attached to Christians' missionary obligation, it has to be said that there were few periods in the church's history in which such methods had not been adopted. In matters spiritual as well as secular the late eighteenth- and early nineteenth-century exponents of 'trusteeship' were often elaborating earlier ideas and practices rather than breaking new ground.

A more significant divide (no less so for having been extensively written about) is marked by the emerging commitment in the 1820s and 1830s among those concerned with India's future to the country's progressive transformation through the expansion of Western higher education, using English as the medium of instruction. The early development of this perception of Indian needs and approach to the practicalities of reform and conversion, as well as something of the interplay between secular motives and religious concerns in those chiefly involved in India's government, is well illustrated in the career of Charles Grant, Scotsman, evangelical, and East India Company director.[17]

This was not, however, a development confined to India. During the 1820s and 1830s a much more aggressively 'constructive' interpretation of 'trusteeship' began to make itself widely felt. The possibility of rebuilding or transforming non-European societies was accepted by many as preferable to more conservative or protective conceptions of imperial responsibilities. The roots of this change are varied and often difficult to disentangle. Nevertheless, great importance was clearly attached on all sides to education, and especially to higher or English-medium education, as the means of providing the leaders such reconstructed societies required. This widespread association of Western education and effective leadership generally reflected the prejudices of metropolitan commercial and professional classes; but it was also a response to the demands of indigenous groups anxious to take advantage of opportunities provided by western contact. In the West Indies, the foundations of a new society were to be laid by emancipation; in West Africa reform would be carried forward on a wave of legitimate trade. In New Zealand and South Africa settler ambitions were to be balanced and tamed by the similar reconstitution of native societies. In each case this breakthrough to an understanding of trusteeship appropriate to an expanding metropolitan society offered openings to individual evangelicals and missionary bodies anxious to ensure that Christianity provided an essential moral and cultural cement.[18]

In India parallel developments occurred more or less simultaneously within both the official world and the missionary fraternity. The effective lead was provided by the missionaries, above all those of the newly-arrived Church of Scotland. Taking his cue in part from the example of Indians' willingness to pay for higher English-medium education at the Hindu College in Calcutta, Alexander Duff established a central institution there, and was followed by his countrymen in Bombay (1832), Madras (1837) and Nagpur (1844). Having previously made only limited, tentative moves in this direction, other denominations now followed suit. Within the administration, under the pressure of financial economy, the perceived need for an efficient administrative class, and mingled utilitarian or evangelical influences, the same view became dominant during Lord William Bentinck's governor-generalship (1828–35).[19]

Even when the expansion of private Indian-controlled schools is taken into account, the limitations of this strategy for change were clearly considerable, in the number of Indians educated, the distribution of schools and colleges, and even more in the number of conversions thereby achieved by the missionaries.[20] Nevertheless, the commitment continued to shape educational policy and remained central to the missionary enterprise. Notwithstanding the limited encouragement given to elementary vernacular education under the grant-in-aid system of 1854, it continued to be a major ingredient of the prevalent understanding of Britain's responsibilities for more than 50 years.[21]

The policy always had its critics, but it was not until the 1880s that general doubts as to its wisdom surfaced. Then the missions were seriously divided. The operations of the Wesleyan Methodist Missionary Society were the target of a critical campaign mounted by the Rev. Hugh Price Hughes; a far-reaching committee of enquiry in 1890 was unable to do more than paper over the cracks of controversy.[22] Equally important and certainly more symbolic was the simultaneous challenge in the Scottish churches to their educational missions.[23] In 1887 the General Assembly of the Free Church decided to dispatch a deputation to examine its Indian missions. As a result of this, the church through its Foreign Mission Committee decided on a fundamental shift of resources into direct vernacular evangelism. In the formal language of the Minute, it was seen 'as necessary, while in no way sanctioning anything that may tend to impair the efficiency of the educational work, specially to foster the evangelistic operations, . . . to limit to the present amount the resources spent on the educational institutions, and to devote to the evangelistic side whatever increase of contributions may be received, and any saving that may be effected in connection with educational work. . . .'.[24] Similar strains were felt in the Church of Scotland. Although these were less forcefully expressed, a similar enquiry advocated closure of the Institution in Bombay, self-support for educational institutions elsewhere and diversion of funds to evangelism.[25]

For the Government of India, disillusionment was prompted notably by the growth of political activity among Western-educated Indians, especially after the formation of the Indian National Congress in 1885. Again government action largely duplicated changes in missionary policy as it had done in the 1830s. Despite the immense labours of Lord Ripon's Education Commission in 1882–83 there was little immediate action. It was eventually Lord Curzon, as Viceroy from 1898, who took serious steps first to control what was seen as an indiscriminate expansion of poor-quality and ultimately subversive English education, to control the supply of graduates, and then to inject greater vigour and efficiency into the chaotic organization of primary vernacular schools.[26]

The onslaught on India's educational missions caused ripples throughout the missionary world. Historians, however, have gone little further than to remark, for example, how Scottish missionaries in Nyasaland held 'disappointingly modest' ambitions in the educational sphere when compared with their West African predecessors of the 1840s.[27] It is therefore worth asking what prompted this reversal of missionary policies. Although the policies of the late nineteenth-century governments of India have been widely scrutinized, the broad coincidence of developments at that time in both missionary and government circles has gone unremarked, despite parallells in this further redefinition of the components of Britain's 'trusteeship' as striking as those of the 1830s. Enquiry into the missionary dimension is in fact germane to discussion of general questions important to the imperial historian. To what extent did Britain's imperial establishments share a fundamental unity of outlook or susceptibility to similar pressures for ideological change? How important have been different metropolitan and peripheral factors in prompting such changes? Of what significance for the rhythms of redefinition are the interplay or relative autonomy of missions and governments?

II

Old warriors long went on fighting the battle for educational missions. The Very Reverend Dugald Mackichan, principal of the Free Church's Wilson College in Bombay through the 1890s, gave no ground to his critics even 30 years on. In the Chalmers Lectures for 1926 he not only dismissed their misconceptions of such work, but claimed that the educational commitment lay at the heart of his church's tradition and achievement. Despite contrary claims, Alexander Duff had not perverted the Assembly's intentions, but had 'from the beginning' acted 'in obedience to the specific instructions he had received when he set forth on his mission'.[28] Such claims, however, were both partial, neglecting factors at home and in Calcutta which undoubtedly affected Duff's organization of the new mission, and disingenuous, ignoring the distinct character imparted by Duff's own emphasis on English higher education.

There was nothing remarkable in the Church of Scotland's genuflection towards educational activity as an essential adjunct of missions when its Assembly decided to establish its work in India in 1824. Recent research has shown very clearly how the pattern of church expansion in Scotland and the intimate links between parish school and parish church shaped the thinking of the different parties within the church when it came to foreign missions. Thomas Chalmers reasoned from the universality of human nature to identity of methods at home and abroad:

> If schools and bibles have been found to be the engines of civilization to the people of Britain it is altogether a fair and direct exercise of induction when these schools and bibles are counted upon . . . as equally powerful engines of civilization to the people of other countries.

Leading Moderates like John Inglis, whose Assembly motion, figuratively speaking, set Duff on his way, felt

> it cannot be doubted that a man of an understanding mind, habituated to thought and reflection, has an advantage over others, for estimating both the evidence of Christian doctrine, and its accommodation to human wants. . . . We should, therefore, do injustice to the hope which we entertain of the universal prevalence of the gospel, if we did not make a fair allowance for the corresponding disadvantage under which others labour. It is obvious that whatever shall tend to remove such an obstruction to the success of the gospel, must have the effect to facilitate its progress in the world.[29]

Such sentiments were perfectly compatible with developing practice everywhere in the mission field, both where Scots worked alongside others, as in the London Missionary Society, or alone, for example, in the Glasgow and Edinburgh Missionary Societies which, like the LMS, had been founded in the boom years of 1795–96. This congruence of Scottish theorizing and local needs helps to explain the persistence in the 1820s of 'metropolitan' traits in a man like Dr John Philip, at odds with colonial administration and settler practice in South Africa.[30]

Priority given to the use of English, however, was exceptional, both in India and elsewhere. Occasionally it was inescapable, for example in Freetown (Sierra Leone) where missionaries were faced with forming an entirely new community from freed slaves of diverse origins. The Fourah Bay Institution was to provide the coping stone of an entirely new system built from scratch. In India, however, even in the very few schools where English experiments were being made (chiefly belonging to the SPCK and CMS), a strong preference for the vernaculars or Persian remained and achievements in English were limited.[31] Scottish movement towards the English and higher education strategy owed little either to the fundamental popular enthusiasm for missionary expansion mounting at home or to local example in India. Metropolitan influence in this direction reflected rather that of a particular group of ministers within the Scottish church crucially placed to work out the practical details for the implementation of the General Assembly's decision in principle for an Indian mission. As author of the plan of 1825–26 and convenor of the church's Foreign Mission Committee, John Inglis was especially important, together with Alexander Brunton and the evangelical Alexander Thomson, all three already closely involved with education and missionary schemes in Edinburgh and the Highlands.[32]

Equally significant, however, was Duff's own assessment of local conditions and his personal drive. Instructed to establish a higher institution outside Calcutta for the training of native vernacular teachers, he was instead rapidly convinced that 'in regard to education elementary English schools are best adapted to the present circumstances'.[33] With the expansion of Calcutta's commerce and European population the demand for English was considerable, whereas Indians seemed to him unlikely to attend a new vernacular training college. Duff's plan was to multiply the numbers of English-speaking Indians in the expectation that, especially if commercial demand had peaked as he suspected, there would soon be candidates enough anxious to train as English-medium teachers for 'an Institution of a Higher order' to thrive. To assist the economic and efficient use of money, time and energy, a central site in Calcutta was also to be preferred, particularly in a climate where travelling was difficult. The novelty of the methods to be used was justification enough for his intrusion where many other missionaries were already at work.[34]

Within six months Duff was reporting that 'hitherto . . . [the school] has proved successful, if not triumphant' in attracting and holding pupils, especially those of the higher castes.[35] Before long his perception of the value of English schools was, he claimed, attracting 'unanimous consent' and not only sympathy but growing practical interest at the highest levels of government.[36] In the course of 1832 Duff began to press on the home committee the need for the most advanced classes to be removed to a new central building, open to all and designated a College.[37] New premises were approved for 1837, and with continued success both in attracting pupils and in the public examinations, the division between School and College was finally accepted at home and formalized in 1840–41.[38]

III

Notwithstanding the confident optimism of the 1830s, there were always difficulties in sustaining Duff's missionary programme. For all the speed with which Duff implemented his plans and others imitated his example, the policy rested on uncertain foundations. The first of these was finance. There was little idea in Scotland of the costs involved. In 1825 the Church's Assembly envisaged as adequate a parochial collection perhaps once every five years, and Duff himself wanted to be rid of such concerns with all their 'secular tediousness'. 'Let me, if possible, have little or nothing to do with money-management'.[39] However, notwithstanding precarious prosperity and still undeveloped habits of giving by a missionary public, the innocence or foolhardiness of the China Inland Mission and later 'faith' missions which dispensed with formal financial machinery was not yet envisaged. Duff in fact tailored his educational plans to take account of social and economic conditions in Calcutta. Others were still more sensitive to the general possibility that commercial collapse like that of 1832 in India or bad harvests at home could seriously threaten the missions by reducing income. Even at the end of the century such slumps were still cause for worry.[40]

If a steady income and missionary volunteers were to be forthcoming, publicity and propaganda were essential to keep up enthusiasm and, as Duff put it, to 'enkindle a more lively interest among the people of Scotland.' Rather therefore than annual reports, which 'must always lie beyond the reach of the great body of the people', Duff advocated a regular and impressive periodical.[41] It was a commonly adopted solution at this time, but brought its own difficulties above all in deciding what to publish.

Duff's particular strategy accentuated this problem in ways which ultimately left the Scottish missions vulnerable. It was essentially the policy of a minority within the Church, with relatively weak appeal to the larger body of churchgoers who preferred the image of the missionary as preacher. Whether this popular view was based, as many missionaries often suspected, on no more than romanticism and ignorance, or on consciously-held and decidedly 'evangelical' beliefs, made little difference. In the Scottish church it meant there was a gulf between the now-predominant missionary method with its emphasis on higher and

English schooling, and the preferences of the rank and file at home who were relied upon for financial support. This was particularly true in the Free Church of Scotland, the refuge of the more populist and evangelical of Scottish Christians after the great Disruption of the Church in 1843, but also the church to which all Scottish missionaries in India at the time adhered.

The missionaries' correspondence shows a clear awareness of the dilemma posed by their need to inform and enthuse the Church at home about their work while at the same time avoiding undue emphasis on their methods which might offend common prejudices. Duff had reservations about providing details of teachers employed and schools set up, knowing them as yet 'attended with little benefit and considerable expense'. John Anderson in Madras raged against those at home 'who itch for romance and premature success' and who criticized educational work for its 'secularity'. 'I am afraid these spiritual folks are foes to all machinery . . . when it does not tally with what they are wont to call doing a thing on principle. . . . let those who brand us as secular send forth their preaching missionaries. Experience and the sun will speedily bring them to reason. . . .'[42] The problem was persistent and tiresome. 'With all deference to the Christian public at home,' wrote Mackichan from Bombay in 1893 regarding similar accusations, 'we ought to tell them that we are more likely to know what is important in the interests of the work to which our lives are given. . . .'[43]

On one hand, people at home had to be acquainted with the magnitude of the task facing missionaries. On the other, such analyses left vulnerable to criticism missionaries committed to methods readily agreed to be slow and costly. As Duff put it, 'ask for quality, and you cannot have it without both trouble and expense'.[44] Some missionaries were prepared to say that support not based on full recognition of the problem was not worth having, but this was not a common view.[45] Persuading subscribers to overlook their reservations about method, to back the missionaries' judgment and to face trouble or expense, could be achieved in three ways: by evident success in producing converts both in numbers and of a quality satisfactory to all parties; by placing an optimistic gloss on information from the field, so generating metropolitan anticipation; and by identifying obstacles to missionary success which might somehow be removed. Publicity was of course crucial to all three.

In mid-nineteenth-century India claims to success were hard to sustain, although everywhere much was made of such baptisms as there were and of positive signs observed in the behaviour and atmosphere of the schools. Although Duff's early results won round many evangelicals at home during the 1830s,[46] mission secretaries in Scotland must often have despaired at the unwillingness of missionaries in their letters home to relay even the straight narrative detail of their daily existence. Duff did his best, struggling to balance his 'mortal aversion . . . to the ceaseless monotony of an ordinary journal' with the fact that 'I scorn the idea of *dressing up common facts* into *interesting stories*, for the sake of producing an *effect*. . .'. Clearly he wanted support from home, but he was reluctant to dissemble or arouse what he knew to be false hopes. 'Human intercourse is usually composed of materials of no rare occurrence: there generally is little romance in real life. Conversations with Natives . . . are *almost* always *mere* conversations.'[47] Clearly Bengal's humours only enhanced the solemnity of the Kirk.

Where dramatic breakthroughs were wanting and routine material was provided, it was still often found unsuitable or lay beyond the ingenuity of honest men to cast in a positive light. Missionaries frequently relayed detail which was not thought fit for circulation to wider audiences – about illness, the press of routine administrative business which distracted them from their central tasks, or the lack of support and of basic supplies. There was little to be done, for example, with the glum report from Poona that 'Nothing has occurred in our field of labour since I last wrote to you . . . we still behold from day to day, only a field of dry bones'.[48] Indeed, in taking extracts from the Indian correspondence of the 1830s and 1840s, secretaries avoided passages which in any way highlighted the monotony and thanklessness of missionary labours, which suggested that there was room for improvement in adapting existing activities to Indian realities, or which might imply to vigilant eyes a neglect of spiritual priorities.

It was comforting to hear about the weakness of 'Brahmanical power & intolerance', to know that in Poona 'Pure priestly influence over the body of the people is dwindling away every hour', and that 'the power of the Marathi Sirdars . . . is utterly broken, & themselves are fast sinking into insignificance'. It was far less reassuring, and so not for general circulation, that in a centre of modernity and strategic missionary importance like commercial Bombay, 'a race of moneyed men has sprung up, – their wealth has raised them to power; – and that power they are anxious to extend & perpetuate. Hence the system of caste & clanship is more rigidly kept up here than in other places, and we have greater difficulty in obtaining scholars of the middle ranks. . .'.[49] Duff's plans to teach Political Economy were rejected out of hand, despite his plea that it would contribute vitally to the undermining of 'the all comprehending framework of superstition in this land' by challenging received views on marriage, employment and labour. Nor was it desirable to highlight the anxiety of Aitken's pupils in Poona to begin the study of chemistry.[50]

Other combinations of activity might be even more dispiriting or offensive to metropolitan readers. With the growing enthusiasm for women's education it was wise to let them know how 'The Female Schools have been attracting considerable notice . . . [and] that under the care of the Lady who is on the way out to take charge of them, they will make very great progress & be very great blessings to many'. It would not do, however, to repeat the full story of how the

> grown up women are becoming much more familiar than formerly, . . . [in the reading class] When I edge round my chair a little to see them, and as it were to pay the greater attention to them,

though they seem to feel and blush from the novelty of their position, they think not of running away & hiding themselves from observation, as they would lately have done.

Here, as in other letters, evidence of missionaries encouraging women's interest in other subjects such as arithmetic and sewing, together with Mitchell's search for a seamstress, was also put quietly aside.[51] Victorian Scots could spot impropriety and secularism a long way off.

In such ways the information available at home about the realities of missionary enterprise was sorted, censored and sanitized for consumption by the majority in the churches. Missionary publication became an art form in its own right. It was often bland and comfortable, often remote from reality because of the conflicting interests it attempted to reconcile. It soon revealed an inbuilt tendency to cater for metropolitan prejudice, and in the middle years of the century proved its worth as a means of generating resources for work overseas. In the Free Church, despite the immense loss of property and assets in the Disruption, the fabric and operations of the church were gradually rebuilt both at home and abroad. The Church of Scotland found new ministers, fully restoring its missionary establishment in India by the end of the 1840s. Mission funds certainly underwent fluctuations, but none so serious as to provoke major shifts in strategy. However, as a prime method of upholding before the home audience the missionary strategy established in the 1830s, the limitations of publications like the *Record* of the Free Church were revealed once the mid-century emphasis on rebuilding gave way to a renewed concern with what had been achieved.

Well aware that the work of the schools and Institutions or Colleges should not appear too prominent, missionaries in the field always affirmed that they used every available means to promote the Christian message, and that preaching and the vernaculars were not neglected.[52] Yet to financial supporters at home, many of whom were culturally attuned (increasingly so in matters of education) to the idea of payment by results and certainly expected some visible return for their sacrifices, it was clear that results measured in terms of converts did not materialize. Moreover, despite efforts to present a balanced picture of the work, the missionary Colleges of the Presidency towns dominated the scene.

There was therefore a pronounced tendency to deflect criticism and so avoid questioning of the basic strategy by pinning the blame for lack of achievement on, for example, government. Frequently this had to be done circumspectly, for missionaries also welcomed the patronage of officials both for its own sake and for its presumed effect on Indian regard for the missions. They wanted private subscriptions to their funds, needed official assistance and protection, and always lived in hope of government funds for their schools. Nevertheless, for many years criticism of government for creating obstacles to missionary success was common, and was widely seen as plausible. Indignation centred, first, on the government's support in its own colleges for a secular or 'irreligious' education, and later on its indiscriminate support under the grant-in-aid system set up in 1854 of numerous rivals alongside the missionary institutions.[53] Experience of the Mutiny only intensified the Christian activists' criticism of government for not doing enough to promote the missions' conception of true education.

Traditional missionary practices thus remained everywhere more or less intact, not least within the Free Church where Duff's influence seems to have increased in the 1860s when, having retired from the field, he acted as convenor of the Foreign Mission Committee.[54] However, as the Mutiny faded into the distance, as the influence of the founding missionaries like Anderson (d. 1855) and Wilson (d. 1875) and eventually Duff himself (d. 1878) fell away, and as government 'neutrality' on religious matters persisted, the pressure to rethink missionary policies and so to reinterpret the practical expression of 'trusteeship' grew steadily.

IV

The eventual erosion of the 'English school tradition' was related in part to the continuing pressure from within India for work in the vernacular. Some Scottish colleagues could find an essential role for vernacular schools even while admiring Duff's achievements. 'Just as well might we think that the Colleges of Scotland without its parochial schools, could have elevated and enlightened the popular mind, as think that we can do without vernacular schools in India'.[55] The need to establish branch schools as feeders to the central Institutions, the employment in them of native Indian teachers, a feeling that country districts should be worked in association with the great urban centres, all contributed to their continuing vitality. They thus remained potential competitors for mission funds with the English schools. Even if their results were unspectacular, they seemed to some missionaries a desirable additional activity, for example to Aitken in Poona who found his English school attended not by Hindus as hoped, but by 'the half-caste population in the Camp bazar'. Given 'the amount of instrumentality which has been at work for a number of years in India, & contrast with it the amount of success', Aitken wrote, this wider range of activities and deeper commitment was both essential and a corrective to the unreflective metropolitan celebration of Calcutta's or Madras's achievements.[56]

Later in the century, the failure of native congregations in Bengal to recruit new members led William Miller to the conclusion that the need was for 'more evangelistic work alongside of our Education institutions whose direct object would be to give the Gospel to the people & *nothing else*. . . '.[57] The famines of the mid-1870s drew the Scottish missions like others into new areas of activity, for example with orphans. In some districts village preaching and itineration kept up over a period seemed to arouse new interest in the mission and open new opportunities after long periods of insignificant progress. This occurred in Madras, where Adam

Andrew and his assistants in the late 1880s found more and more of the lowest castes approaching the mission for assistance; they were responding, Andrew thought, to the preaching of recent years. As a result of Andrew's vernacular aptitude and interest, a completely new field of work was taken up by the Free Church's Madras mission.[58]

Debate about the employment of medical missionaries operated in a similar direction. There was widespread agreement that to establish them in many of India's larger cities would be superfluous, Western medicine there being already comparatively well-known and accessible. Discussion focused on the wisdom of setting up elsewhere either central hospitals or village dispensaries plus a travelling doctor, but in both cases vernacular competence and work by the medical missionary was seen as crucial.[59]

It was this tendency of missionary effort to press inland away from the large port cities, combined with the feeling of some missionaries that results under the 1830s strategy were increasingly incommensurate with the effort expended, that continually injected new life into Scottish vernacular work. Eventually this led to radical conclusions. Despite great personal disagreements with Andrew, James Peattie, secretary to the Mission Council in Madras, concluded from his work that

> the true solution of the caste-question lies here. Raise the non-castes; give them brain-power enough to take their place in the battle of life with the caste-man; infuse Christian principles into their lives, and soon a change will be perceptible in Hindu society. Hindus cannot, in agriculture, do without the Pariahs, and hence if the Pariahs were Christianized a great effect would be made on rural Hinduism. Education has not done much yet for the great bulk of the 35 millions of the Madras Presidency.

Vernacular education and evangelizing 'among the lower rural classes' was 'the grand lever' for the transformation of Indian society.[60] The work of other missions in Travancore and Tinnevelly taught the same lesson. Duff had represented his College as a mine laid under Hinduism; Peattie's conclusion implied that the explosives had been faulty and the mine itself misplaced.

Even as in India missionary effort seeped into new vernacular channels, and Duff's strategy ceased to command its old allegiance, the central Institutions continued to dominate the scene, making little concession to novel practices and theoretical misgivings. The result seems to have been a loss of impetus and co-ordination, the growth of internal conflict and inefficiency. The distraction of missionaries in the Institutions from their central tasks had always been seen as a danger; now the extension of work into the countryside seemed sometimes quite incompatible with efficient administration, and conflicts developed over the division of funds within the missions. In Madras, Andrew eventually gave up trying to settle financial priorities within the local Mission Council. He complained instead direct to Edinburgh of a system which had become steadily more anomalous, of 'supervision run mad', of 'a waste of energy . . . liable to produce friction amongst the various subordinate agents. . .'.[61]

Most indicative, perhaps, was resistance among the missionaries themselves to learning the vernaculars. Dr Walker, the Free Church's medical missionary at Conjeveram and Walajabad was still incompetent after five years. Certainly the linguistic difficulties were great. But Walker's failure was also attributable, so it was thought, to the fact that senior missionaries in Madras who were hardly more qualified shrank from applying the rules. Although the Foreign Missions Committee at home finally attempted to remedy the general problem in 1892 by restricting responsibility and refusing promotion for those failing in the local languages, there still remained possibilities for evasion.[62] The spirit of Duff, who had never acquired a vernacular himself, lived on. It was a serious liability in a country where by the 1880s the spread of private schools and the transfer of government schools and colleges into local hands was proceeding rapidly, causing the missions to lose their once-commanding lead.

V

New developments in India and evidence of the inability of the system there to cope adequately with them undoubtedly contributed to metropolitan rethinking and revision of missionary strategies after 1885. Change in the metropole, however, also played its part. By 1870 it was widely accepted that an elementary education for the whole population was essential. More important still were changes in the religious climate of Scotland itself and the related problem of maintaining missionary societies' income even at a level to finance existing undertakings. There was a limit to which even the most constructive and judicious editing of missionary publications could put a favourable gloss on either the small numbers of Indian converts – estimated at 3,359 after 50 years – or the perceived lack of energy and self-support in the Scots' Indian congregations. The convenor of the Free Church's Foreign Mission Committee, Professor Thomas Lindsay, expressed the extensive disquiet when in 1886 he questioned further grants to Madras, on the ground that they would 'intensify what seems to many of us the fundamental error in a good deal of our past work in India, so far as a native church goes – building the pyramid from the top instead of from the bottom – training men for the pastorate & not providing first of all congregations to which they must be pastors'.[63]

Not only had Duff's methods not worked out as anticipated. Lindsay sensed that many doubted their scriptural justification, and his correspondence shows how strongly Scottish beliefs had shifted against the traditional educational mission. Fund-raising, whether directly by the church or by external groups, often seemed to depend for its success on being linked to evangelism and vernacular work in the villages.[64] For missions to survive it was also necessary that they should be able to recruit well. As fashions changed among the theological students on whom they chiefly depended, the Scottish churches felt obliged to consider a retreat from the customary patterns of missionary work. After all, 'It would be a grand thing for Western India to get the very flower of these Volunteer Students and lead the way in self-devotion'.[65]

Throughout the evangelical world there was among ordinary churchgoers a strong current of feeling hostile to the formal bureaucratic and often costly nature of traditional missionary activity. Among the Wesleyans, for example, it took the form of attacks on the high living standards of Indian missionaries. In the Church Missionary Society the arguments focused above all on the Niger mission, but in India too the society's involvement in secondary and higher education was carefully reviewed and economies sought.[66] Demands for new methods were widely voiced, methods which it was claimed would not only bring greater success, but would conform to the ideas of a revivified evangelical theology stressing peripatetic evangelism as the missionary's first duty rather than any unduly prolonged struggle for the conversion of particular individuals. Missions, whether organized within the churches as in Scotland or by voluntary lay societies such as the CMS, had to respond to this new current of thinking if they wished to survive and expand; otherwise, men and income were likely to be diverted to new, less structured and more directly evangelistic rivals. After a spate of attacks on the Indian missions at the Bombay Decennial Conference in January 1893, Lindsay correctly anticipated a bad financial year ahead: 'I fear a good deal of the money that ought to come to us will be sent to the China Inland [Mission] & Salvation Army'.[67] His fellow-convenor in the Church of Scotland was of similar mind, and both dreaded the additional impact of outcries over issues large or small – ritualism, Sunday labour on mission premises, even 'the letting of part of Madras premises to a licensed grocer'.[68]

Disillusionment and criticisms of missionary practice, reinforced by changing theological fashions which reawakened the old evangelical preference for missionary preaching, contributed significantly to the decline of the missions' income. The Scottish churches at home did not suffer in the same way: sufficient funds were found to make the 1870s and 1880s the greatest period of church-building Scotland had ever known.[69] However, by 1880 the Church of Scotland was faced with foreign mission expenditure in excess of income by 46 per cent; windfall gains from unpredictable legacies seemed the only way of narrowing the gap.[70] The Free Church was slightly better off, but from 1884 revenue from the home congregations – regarded as the real test of financial soundness – remained static for the rest of the decade. Throughout the 'eighties the Foreign Mission Committee struggled with overdrafts on current accounts.[71]

While income faltered or fell, the demands of the schools rose steadily. The Free Church's Madras mission was therefore directed in 1884 to prevent increases in expenditure. This had no effect. Spending on scholarships, for example, rose from Rs.35 in 1883 to Rs.909 in 1889, and total outlay on the mission more than doubled between 1883 and 1891.[72] It was impossible to escape the fact that an arguably bankrupt strategy was absorbing an increasing share of resources at a time when new openings were appearing (not only in India but also in Africa and China).

One suggested solution to the problem, even while continuing the struggle for funds at home, was to press Indian presbyteries and mission congregations into making financial self-support a reality. Despite the efforts of the Free Church in this direction, in India and elsewhere lack of numbers and great poverty weighed heavily against success.[73] So, too, the Scots, like other European missionaries, were almost everywhere reluctant to face the surrender of control which was seen as the natural corollary of native self-support. In these circumstances falling revenues at home precipitated a change of missionary direction in India. It was impossible for educational missions to escape severe scrutiny. Demands for retrenchment were followed from 1885 by visitations from Scotland and detailed reviews of their operations.

For the Free Church, Thomas Lindsay, Professor of Ecclesiastical History at Glasgow and Convenor of the Foreign Mission Committee, spent 13 months from September 1888 touring India as a Deputy of the General Assembly, accompanied for half that time by the Reverend J.F. Daly. Lindsay's progress was regularly charted in the Free Church *Monthly*, while behind the scenes efforts were made to influence the outcome of his investigations and revive the popularity of educational missions. Lindsay sent home for publication frequent 'Notes on Missionary Travel', signalling his general commitment to 'a new departure in India in evangelistic work carried on in the vernacular', and his co-Deputy spoke similarly to the Church's annual Assembly in May 1889, well ahead of the formal report on their investigations.[74] For the traditionalists, George Smith – old India hand, secretary to the Foreign Missions Committee, biographer of Duff, Wilson and Hislop, and committed to educational missions – quoted speeches by Lindsay which seemed more favourable to the educational cause. He wrote privately to missionaries in India urging them to write fully for the *Monthly*, in order to assist 'the right understanding of our Educational Missions'.[75]

The pressures for a new strategy, however, were too deep-rooted to be deflected now by such tactics, especially when the Deputies' investigations confirmed more than a decade's growing suspicions. For Lindsay

> The one thing which really overwhelmed me when I was in India was the great disproportion between what was spent on higher education & on evangelistic work. That was burnt into me . . . if our people saw what I saw our mission funds & our mission sympathies would largely cease.[76]

Although Lindsay was a liberal-minded scholar, he was no uncritical enthusiast in matters of reform. When he finally reported to the Church in 1890, his comments on educational missions showed his anxiety to carry their supporters with him. He recognized that education and evangelism were often necessarily and significantly intertwined. At the same time, while unequivocal in arguing for a shift of resources into evangelism, because such 'work in India had hitherto been starved', he rejected the idea that effective evangelism could be carried out on the cheap.[77] However, his recommendations spelt the end of the Duff tradition involving the pre-eminence of the central Institutions, the bias towards higher education, and insistence on the medium of English. Lindsay reinforced his standpoint after his return by sharing his platform at the Assembly in 1890 with Adam Andrew. Andrew, it was reported, home on furlough from his work with the pariahs of Madras, 'corroborated Professor Lindsay's views on the necessity of evangelistic work'.[78]

The Free Church met considerable resistance from many missionaries in India to its attempts to redistribute funds and reorganize administration. The battle of the prints also continued. Changes were made in the format of the *Monthly Record* to back up the drive for funds, not only allowing the greater use of illustrations but giving more prominence to editorial introductions and summaries at the expense of direct quotation from missionaries' letters.[79] Supporters of the new direction like Andrew saw advantage both in dispatching frequent reports for the metropolitan audience, and in careful scrutiny of what colleagues were submitting for publication, as means of protecting their own work and checkmating local opposition. The party of resistance suspected Lindsay as convenor of restricting publicity for their educational work in the interest of current fashions.[80] In both the Free Church and the Church of Scotland new organizational efforts at home during the 1890s paralleled the changes in the field, and were quite successful in winning congregational support for local missionary associations.[81] Eventually the change of emphasis in India and the revival of home support for the churches' missions were accomplished. By 1900 there had evolved a new symbiosis between metropolitan belief and provision and missionary practice in India. There is no room here to explore in detail either the practical implementation of the Scottish churches' change of direction, or the extent to which Christian missions in general held back even if only temporarily their work in schools and colleges. It is above all their ideas and intentions which have been the concern of this essay.

VI

The progress of any wide-ranging missionary enterprise can rarely be fully explained by reference to its work only in a single field. African disasters could easily dash Indian hopes, just as both were susceptible to fluctuating metropolitan fashions or fortunes. The reforms pushed through in the Scottish missions in the 1890s did not prevent current expenditure, demands for volunteers and plans for expansion again outrunning income. Nevertheless, the prominence of India in Scottish missionary endeavour was everywhere recognized. It is clear that resolution of the growing conflict over 'educational' missions was seen as central to the recovery of the Free Church and Church of Scotland missions from the severe crisis of funding and confidence which they experienced in the two decades after 1875. This crisis was pre-eminently metropolitan in origin, the product of financial pressure, shifting religious enthusiasms and desire for greater success in converting the heathen. Its solution, by the redirection of efforts into more direct evangelism and work in the countryside felt to be in line with both a revised theology and some very traditional prejudices, was of considerable significance for the manner in which prominent sections of both the expatriate British community in India and those at home interested in Indian development envisaged their contribution to India's future.

In so far as it represented a greater commitment to India's rural peasantry and to the poorer classes of society, redirection of missionary effort moved along paths which matched the growing concern of government after 1875 with issues such as famine relief, rural indebtedness and the plight of the landless. The Government of Madras, for example, quite willingly assisted missionary work among the pariahs.[82] It reflected, too, a general loss of confidence within missionary circles in the likely emergence of sufficient numbers of highly-educated Hindus as satisfactory and influential leaders of united Christian communities. This no longer seemed probable in many older mission fields, while in the newer areas the possibility was either inevitably distant, or irrelevant if, as some assumed, the Second Coming was imminent. A continuing, perhaps increasingly important role for the missionary, and the postponement of a self-financing, self-propagating and certainly self-governing Indian church, was the result. In parallel fashion the Government of India set its face against the devolution of significant power to Indians. Curzon's reforms were directed towards greater administrative efficiency, 'good government' to quieten critics and make political concessions unnecessary; they were to open the way for a measure of material progress in the long term under British rule.

In religious or ecclesiastical matters, as in civil or secular affairs, the implications of 'trusteeship' in India were explicitly redefined. During the 1880s and 1890s education was a subject of concern to both missionaries and administrators. The educational policies of the 1830s and 1840s no longer held out good prospects at an acceptable cost either of Christianization or of incorporating collaborating groups into the structures of the Raj.[83] Reform and retrenchment at the highest levels, combined with the more purposeful diffusion of effort and resources towards elementary vernacular education held out an economical alternative, on the one hand exploiting potential sources of new converts, and on the other cultivating the conservatism and relative content of broader sectors of the population.

Missionaries, like administrators, moved to take more account of Curzon's 'voiceless millions who can neither read nor write'.[84] These parallel movements nevertheless reflected both their commitments to often widely different goals and responses to very disparate pressures. Conversion rarely loomed large on the administrator's horizon; unlike Indian Civil Servants, missionaries relied very largely on metropolitan direction and money from home; and domestic reactions to Indian practice – arguably one of the most generally important influences on levels of giving to missions – could crucially affect missionary operations world-wide. By comparison Indian government was both self-sufficient and self-contained.

It is, of course, not surprising to find such variety underlying the general commitment to notions of 'trusteeship': 'that doctrine equipped [imperialists] with a Gladstone bag of ethics which could pack almost any principle without bulging'.[85] The multiplicity of principles stressed by Robinson found its natural expression in many and changing practices. This essay has drawn attention to the conjunctures of the 1820s/30s and 1880s/90s, to the emergence and eventual redefinition of a broad agreement on Indian education policies, and to the place of the missionary experience within that change in the application of trusteeship ideas.

It will of course be necessary for a better understanding of the shift in attitudes to explore further both the metropolitan dimension in educational thinking and the parallel evolution of government and missionary strategies. At least until the links between the thinking of governments and of missions have been more fully explored, some historians may prefer to see in the congruence confirmation of their belief that missions function simply as an arm of the colonial state. Others will be tempted to see both parties reacting simply and simultaneously to inescapable realities, choosing the policy of 'elite filtration' as the only practical course in the 1830s, and similarly responding in the 1880s to its evident failure, whether judged by Christian or by secular criteria. Nevertheless, it seems so far plausible to suggest that at least on the missionary side developing ideas of trusteeship display neither the uncomplicated correlation with colonial circumstances nor the subordinate relationship to colonial government which these analyses require. In considering not only why Scottish missions in particular should have played such an important role but also why they did so when they did, a range of metropolitan factors remote from the centres of imperial or colonial power may well, it seems, have exerted decisive influence. The evolution of trusteeship ideas was no more directed by a narrowly official class than the ideas themselves were the creation of an official mind.

Just now, values and assumptions conducive to a single-minded concentration on economic calculation dominate much of the writing – 'radical', 'realist' or 'revisionist' – on British expansion and imperial policy. Correctives are required, reminders needed that there is life outside the bankruptcy court, and fantastic idealism amid the stupidity, greed and dross. The experience of Duff and his successors perhaps provides one such, another illustration of how 'schoolboy, utopian, theorist-enthusiasts' may at times have been quite as influential as any 'collection of hard-faced, systematic imperialists'.[86] Ronald Robinson's work has always pointed to the variety of imperial relations while holding fast to a bundle of general axioms, and as a result has often provoked the majority of us who may be either too impressed with empire's detail or alternatively too detached from it. For that stimulation, not to say entertainment, it will continue to be both necessary and influential.

NOTES

* My work in the Scottish missionary archives at the National Library of Scotland was made possible by a grant awarded from the Irwin Fund of the University of London. In Edinburgh I benefited greatly from the kindness and hospitality of Dr Ged Martin. For comments on the manuscript I am very grateful both to my fellow editor, Dr R.F. Holland, and to Professor Peter Marshall.

1. R.E. Robinson, 'Andrew Cohen and the Trnsfer of Power in Tropical Africa, 1940–1951', in W.H. Morris-Jones and G. Fisher (eds.), *Decolonisation and After. The British and French Experience* (London, 1980), 57.
2. See the contributions to this volume by Ronald Hyam and D.K. Fieldhouse; also R.E. Robinson, 'The Trust in British Central Africa Policy, 1889–1939' (unpub. PhD thesis, University of Cambridge, 1951).
3. Roy Bridges, for example, reviewing *The Cambridge History of Africa Vol 6, c. 1870–c. 1906* in *Journal of Imperial & Commonwealth History* (XV, 3, May 1987, p.326), noticed that on East Africa 'after a reign of close on 50 years, Coupland is finally dislodged as an authority worth citing in the bibliography'.
4. *Africa and the Victorians* (2nd ed., 1981), 'Explanation', xiv; see also his 'Oxford in Imperial Historiography', in Frederick Madden and D.K. Fieldhouse (eds.), *Oxford and the Idea of Commonwealth* (1982), 30–48.
5. In three articles: 'Andrew Cohen and the Transfer of Power'; 'Sir Andrew Cohen: Proconsul of African Nationalism (1909–1968)', in L.H. Gann and P. Duignan (eds.), *African Proconsuls* (Stanford, 1978), 353–64; 'The Moral Disarmament of African Empire 1919–1947', *Journal of Imperial and Commonwealth History* VIII, 1 (Oct. 1979), 86–104.
6. 'Andrew Cohen and the Transfer of Power', 57.
7. 'Moral Disarmament', 86–7.
8. Ibid., 86.
9. Martin Legassick's article, 'The Frontier Tradition in South African Historiography', circulated in 1970–71 and published in Shula Marks and Anthony Atmore (eds.), *Economy and Society in Pre-Industrial South Africa* (London, 1980), 44–79, and 'The Imperial Factor in South Africa in the Nineteenth Century: Towards A Reassessment' by Atmore and Marks, *Journal of Imperial and Commonwealth History* III, 1 (Oct. 1974), 105–39, led the way.
10. See, for example, Christine Bolt and Seymour Drescher (eds.), *Anti-slavery, Religion and Reform: Essays in Memory of Roger Anstey* (Folkestone, 1980); and Seymour Drescher, *Capitalism and Antislavery: British Mobilization in Comparative Perspective* (London, 1986).
11. G.R. Mellor, *British Imperial Trusteeship 1783–1850* (London, 1951), 417.
12. Hope Waddell, Diary, entries for 5 and 21 Jan. 1850, National Library of Scotland (hereafter NLS) MS7740, fos. 66, 70.
13. 'Moral Disarmament', 87.
14. P.J. Marshall, 'The Moral Swing to the East: British Humanitarianism, India and the West Indies', in Kenneth Ballhatchet and John Harrison (eds.), *East India Company Studies. Essays presented to Sir Cyril Philips* (Asian Research Service: Hong Kong, 1986), 89–90.

15. Stephen Neill, *A History of Christian Missions* (2nd. rev. ed., 1986), 224.
16. Kenneth Ingham, *Reformers in India, 1793–1833: An Account of the Work of Christian Missionaries on Behalf of Social Reform* (Cambridge 1956); E.D. Potts, *British Baptist Missionaries in India, 1793–1837* (Cambridge, 1967); M.A. Laird, *Missionaries and Education in Bengal 1793–1837* (Oxford, 1972).
17. A.T. Embree, *Charles Grant and British Rule in India* (London, 1963).
18. See, for example, J. Gallagher, 'Fowell Buxton and the New African Policy, 1838–42', *Cambridge Historical Journal*, X (1950); J.F.A. Ajayi, 'Henry Venn and the Policy of Development', *Journal of the Historical Society of Nigeria*, IV (1959), 331–42; J.B. Webster, 'The Bible and the Plough', ibid., (1963), 418–34; Andrew Porter, '"Commerce and Christianity": The Rise and Fall of a Nineteenth-century Missionary Slogan', *Historical Journal*, 28, 3 (1985), 597–621. Cf. Stanley Trapido, '"The Friends of the Natives": Merchants, Peasants and the Political and Ideological Structure of Liberalism in the Cape, 1854–1910', in Marks and Atmore (eds.), op. cit. (1980), 247–74.
19. Laird, 237–62; John Rosselli, *Lord William Bentinck. The Making of a Liberal Imperialist 1774–1839* (London, 1974), esp. 208–25. See also E.T. Stokes, *The English Utilitarians and India* (Oxford, 1959); John Clive, *Thomas Babington Macaulay* (London, 1973), esp. Chs. XII and XIII; J.F. Hilliker, 'British Educational Policy in Bengal 1833–1854', (unpub. PhD thesis, University of London, 1968).
20. For statistics, see Anil Seal, *The Emergence of Indian Nationalism* (Cambridge, 1968), 18–19, 22, 26, Tables 1–4; Aparna Basu, *The Growth of Education and Political Development in India, 1898–1920* (Delhi, 1974), Ch. 5, esp. 105–6. The standard account of government education policy to 1885 remains B.T. McCully, *English Education and the Origins of Indian Nationalism* (New York, 1940).
21. R.J. Moore, *Sir Charles Wood's Indian Policy, 1853–1866* (Manchester, 1966), 120–3; S. Srivastava, 'Some Aspects of Education and Educational Administration in the Madras Presidency between 1870 and 1898: A Study of British Educational Policy in India' (unpub. PhD thesis, University of London, 1978), esp. Chs. 2 and 3.
22. G.G. Findlay and W.W. Holdsworth, *The History of the Wesleyan Methodist Missionary Society* (5 vols, 1921), I, 134–60; J. Gelson Gregson, *Apostolic Missions for the Present Day* (1887); *The Missionary Controversy. Discussion, Evidence and Report* (Wesleyan Methodist Missionary Society, 1890); D.P. Hughes, *The Life of Hugh Price Hughes. By His Daughter* (1904), Ch. XIII.
23. See T.G. Gehani, 'A Critical Review of the Work of Scottish Presbyterian Missions in India, 1878–1914, with Special Reference to their Social, Economic, Educational and Organisational Activities' (unpub. PhD thesis, University of Strathclyde, 1966), 192–211.
24. Minute 91, 16 Dec 1890, Free Church of Scotland, Foreign Mission Committee (hereafter FMC) Minutes, Vol. 8, 285, NLS Dep 298/113.
25. Church of Scotland, Minutes of the Foreign Mission Committee 1887–1891, 203–5, 250, 296, 308–11, 426–7, 430, NLS Dep 298/10.
26. Basu, *passim*; D. Dilks, *Curzon in India* (2 vols, London, 1969–70), I, 244.
27. John McCracken, *Politics and Christianity in Malawi 1875–1940* (Cambridge, 1977), 180.
28. D. Mackichan, *The Missionary Ideal in the Scottish Churches* (London, 1927), Ch. VII and 113 n.1.
29. W.J. Roxborough, 'Thomas Chalmers and the Mission of the Church with Special Reference to the Rise of the Missionary Movement in Scotland', (unpub. DPhil thesis, University of Aberdeen, 1978), quotations from 298, 314.
30. Andrew Ross, *John Philip (1775–1851) Missions, Race and Politics in South Africa* (Aberdeen University Press, 1986).
31. Potts, Ch. 6; Laird, 93–100, 237–62.
32. Laird, Ch. 7 esp. 198–200; D. Chambers, 'The Church of Scotland's Nineteenth Century Foreign Missions Scheme: Evangelical or Moderate Revival?', *Journal of Religious History* 9, 2 (1976), 115–38.
33. Duff to Inglis, 23 Aug. 1830, NLS MS7530 F. 35.

34. Ibid., fos. 26–38, and 9 Nov. 1831, f. 82.
35. Ibid., 23 Dec. 1830, f. 50.
36. Ibid., 5 Oct. 1831, 14 Jan. 1832, fos. 79, 99.
37. Ibid., 12 Sept. 1832, fos. 112–14.
38. Laird, 202–22.
39. E.G.K. Hewat, *Vision and Achievement 1796–1956. A History of the Foreign Missions of the Churches united in the Church of Scotland* (1960), 34, 36; Duff to Inglis, 17 Aug. 1831, NLS MS7530, f. 78, and 1 Oct. 1830, fos. 41–2.
40. Rev. James Charles (St Andrew's Church, Calcutta) to Inglis, 19 Dec. 1832, ibid., f. 124; Samuel Tomlinson to Dr George Smith, 10 June 1892, NLS MS7820, fos. 175–6.
41. Duff to Inglis, 19 March and 27 May 1831, NLS MS7530, fos. 57, 61.
42. Ibid., 5 Oct. 1831, f. 79; Anderson to Convenor FMC, 14 Nov. 1839, NLS MS7532, fos. 345–50.
43. Mackichan to Prof. T. Lindsay (Convenor FMC, FCS), 21 April 1893, NLS MS7820, f. 264.
44. To Inglis, 19 Nov. 1831, NLS MS7530, f. 86.
45. Robt. Hamilton to Alexander Brunton (Convenor FMC, FCS), 9 June 1840, NLS MS7532(2), f. 381.
46. Chambers, 'Evangelical or Moderate Revival?', 120.
47. Duff to Inglis, 30 July 1833, NLS MS7530, f. 164.
48. James Aitken to Brunton, 30 April 1842, NLS MS7532(2).
49. J. Murray Mitchell to Brunton, 1 Oct. 1841, NLS MS7532(1), f. 179.
50. Duff to Inglis, 12 Sept. 1832, NLS MS7530, fos. 112–3; Aitken to Brunton, 16 June 1841, NLS MS7532(1), f. 156.
51. Mitchell to Brunton, 29 Sept. 1841, 31 Dec. 1842, ibid., fos. 175, 195.
52. Even, e.g., Duff to Inglis [n.d., but early 1833], NLS MS7530, f. 149; Anderson to Convenor FMC, 14 Nov. 1839, NLS MS7532, fos. 345–50.
53. Moore, Ch. 6.
54. Duff's ideas and personal interventions decisively affected, for example, development of the Lovedale Institution and the Kaffraria mission from 1864 onwards: see Sheila M. Brock, 'James Stewart and Lovedale: A Reappraisal of Missionary Attitudes and African Response in the Eastern Cape, South Africa, 1870–1905', (unpub. PhD thesis, University of Edinburgh, 1974), Chs. 1–3.
55. Mitchell to Brunton, 31 Dec. 1842, NLS MS7532(1), f. 195.
56. Aitken to Brunton, 26 Aug. 1840, 30 March 1842, ibid., fos. 59, 246.
57. Miller to George Smith (secretary, FCS FMC), 24 April 1883, NLS MS7838, f. 79.
58. For the development of Andrew's work with the pariahs of Chingleput, see the correspondence for 1884–93, NLS MSS 7845–6.
59. See the FCS correspondence with J.T. Morton, who wished to finance medical missionaries in India, from 1888–91, NLS MSS 7773–4, 7845–6.
60. Peattie to Lindsay, 30 March 1893, NLS MS7846, f. 251.
61. Andrew to Lindsay, 2 Dec. 1891, 20 June 1893, NLS MS7845, f. 174, 7846 f. 310.
62. On Walker, see Lindsay to Peattie, 10 Dec. 1892, NLS MS7775, f. 314; and Andrew to Lindsay, 20 June 1893, NLS MS7846, f. 310; on the operation of the new language rules see, for example, John Stewart to George Smith, 7 June 1893, ibid., f. 305.
63. Lindsay to G.M. Rae, 21 Oct. 1886, NLS MS7772, at f. 585.
64. Lindsay to Mackichan and to Hector, 1 March 1893, NLS MS7775, fos. 426, 432.
65. Lindsay to Mackichan, [n.d. but ?26 Sept.] 1893, ibid., f. 618; cf. Reports of the Schemes of the Church of Scotland 1883, p. 100.
66. The literature on the Niger crisis is voluminous: in addition to the articles by Andrew Porter in *Journal of Imperial and Commonwealth History* V, 1 (1976), VI, 1 (1977), and VII, 2 (1979), see most recently C.P. Williams, 'From Church to Mission: An Examination of the Official Missionary Strategy of the Church Missionary Society on the Niger, 1887–1893', W.J. Shiels and D. Wood (eds.), *Studies in Church History 23: Voluntary Religion* (1986), and 'The Ideal of the Self-Governing Church: An Examination of the Official Policies of the Church Missionary Society. . . from c. 1850–c. 1910', (unpub. PhD thesis, University of London, 1986). For the CMS in India,

see, e.g., correspondence between W. Gray (CMS Secretary) and A. Clifford (Sect., Calcutta Corresponding Committee) in 1888–89, CMS Archives G2 I1/L12, University of Birmingham.
67. Lindsay to Peattie, 28 Feb. 1893, NLS MS7775, f. 422; and to Mackichan, 1 March 1893, ibid., f. 426.
68. J. McMurtrie to A. Hetherwick, 15 June, and to D.C. Scott, 31 Aug., 26 Oct. 1893, NLS MS7534, fos. 852, 895, 908; Lindsay to Mackichan, [n.d. but ?26 Sept] 1893, NLS MS7775, f. 618.
69. Andrew L. Drummond and James Bulloch, *The Church in Late Victorian Scotland 1874–1900* (Edinburgh, 1978), 162–4.
70. Andrew C. Ross, 'Scottish missionary concern, 1874–1914: A golden era?', *Scottish Historical Review* LI (1972), 57 and App. I.
71. G. Smith, 'Fifty Years of our Foreign Missions' Revenue', *Free Church of Scotland Monthly Record*, May 1885, 162–3, and figures printed annually in the June issues.
72. Surveyed in Lindsay to Miller, 24 Jan. 1891, NLS MS7774, f. 413.
73. For example, Free Church of Scotland, Foreign Mission Committee Minutes, Jan–Feb 1883, June 1884, Vol. 7, 189, 193, 283.
74. *Free Church of Scotland Monthly*, March 1889, 79; see also July 1889, 'Notes on Missionary Travel VII'. For Daly's speech, ibid., 207.
75. George Smith, 'Rev. Professor T.M. Lindsay, D.D.', *Monthly* (Nov. 1889), 333–4; Smith to Hector, 31 Dec. 1890, NLS MS7774, f. 380.
76. Lindsay to Hector, [n.d. but ?early Sept. 1890], NLS MS7774, f. 280.
77. *Free Church of Scotland Monthly*, July 1890, 205.
78. Ibid.
79. Lindsay to McCulloch, 8 March 1892, NLS MS7775, fos. 33–4.
80. Andrew to Smith, 30 Nov. 1893, NLS MS7846, f. 328; Lindsay to Peattie, 28 Feb. 1893, NLS MS7775, f. 422.
81. Ross, 'Scottish missionary concern', 59–60, 65–6. Ross is, however, concerned to argue for what he sees as the continuing paucity of support for missions, which he suggests was due to the inhibiting effects of the ecclesiastical connection with Scottish missions.
82. Srivastava, 56–7; FCS Madras correspondence, *passim*.
83. For the incorporation argument, see A.J. Roberts, 'Education and Society in the Bombay Presidency 1840–58' (unpub. PhD thesis, University of London, 1974).
84. Quoted in Judith M. Brown, *Modern India. The Origins of an Asian Democracy* (Oxford, 1985), 139.
85. 'Andrew Cohen and the Transfer of Power', 57.
86. R.E. Robinson, 'Conclusion', in A.H.M. Kirk-Greene (ed.), *Africa in the Colonial Period. The Transfer of Power: The Colonial Administrator in the Age of Decolonization. Proceedings of a Symposium held at St. Antony's College, Oxford, 15–16 March 1978* (Oxford, 1978), 180.

The Giant that was a Dwarf, or the Strange History of Dutch Imperialism

by

H.L. Wesseling

It is not necessary in these pages to call attention to the writings about imperialism by Jack Gallagher and Ronald Robinson. It is true that only one of their articles was actually published in the *Journal of Imperial and Commonwealth History*, but the *Journal* itself can be considered as a running commentary on the various ideas launched by this outstanding duo. Concepts such as informal and peripheral imperialism, ideas about local crises and sub-imperialism, collaborationist and even excentric theories of imperialism, have all in one way or another influenced, stimulated and indeed dominated recent debate on British imperialism. It is only a slight exaggeration to suggest that the entire debate on British imperialism since the early 1950s has been a discussion of the various propositions put forward by the philosophers from the *Baron of Beef*.[1]

Of course, these ideas have also influenced the interpretation of European imperialism in general. In fact many British historians are in the strange habit of simply writing 'imperialism' when actually they are referring only to the British variety. This is to some extent understandable. After all, Britain was the imperial power *par excellence*. For that very reason, however, Britain was not the most typical imperial power; rather, it was atypical. Therefore theories about British imperialism cannot by simple extrapolation be transformed into general theories, and discussions in other European countries on imperialism have accordingly followed different lines and focused on different questions.

In France Henri Brunschwig's *Mythes et réalités de l'impérialisme colonial français, 1871–1914*, which appeared in 1960, just one year before *Africa and the Victorians*, set the tone for the debate on French imperialism.[2] Brunschwig does accept that, in the case of France, there has been a definite 'imperialist' period; roughly 1880–1914. Indeed, this could hardly be denied. But while traditional in this respect, he is original in his interpretation of this phenomenon. After a careful examination of the economic interests of French colonialists, as well as of the economic balance sheet of French imperialism, he reaches the conclusion that to explain it in economic terms would be a myth. The empire did not pay, there was no link between protectionism and imperialism, and most of the French imperialists had no economic motives or interests. Consequently, there must be a different explanation. According to Brunschwig, this is to be found in the rising tide of nationalism in the French Republic, deeply wounded by the defeat of 1870. Thus, his book is basically a refutation of the economic theory of imperialism.[3]

H.-U. Wehler's theory of German imperialism follows a rather different train of thought.[4] Though he stresses the economic background of imperialism, yet he agrees that for Germany, too, the empire was not very profitable. In his view, the link between economics and empire must be sought on a different level. He emphasizes the economic problems of the new *Reich* (with its rapid and unbalanced economic growth) as well as its social problems (its lack of legitimation because of its creation *von oben*, by force). He considers Bismarck's bid for colonies as a shrewd political move intended both as part of a general, more or less anti-cyclical, economic policy, and of a social policy seeking to unite the Germans around issues of foreign policy and thus to overcome internal tensions. Wehler's emphasis on the domestic rather than on the diplomatic motives of German imperialism – that is, in German historiographical jargon, on the *Primat der Innenpolitik* – and on the continuity of German history forms part of the general debate on the course of German history since 1870. Therefore the historiography on German imperialism has a character very much of its own, dominated by political issues and characterized by an almost exclusively Eurocentric approach.

Italian imperialism was also studied from a special perspective, that of the 'new imperialism' of the fascist era. Jean-Louis Miège in a general survey emphasizes its political and ideological dimensions, comparing it in this respect to Spanish imperialism (*Hispanadad* and *Italianitá*).[5] The interpretation of Portuguese imperialism was for a considerable time dominated by Hammond's theory of an 'uneconomic imperialism'.[6] Gervase Clarence-Smith has recently challenged this view and made a strong case for an economic interpretation of Portuguese imperialism.[7] Jean Stengers has described the extraordinary case of Belgium, where imperialism was the one-man show of King Leopold II, and analysed the singular nature of the King's imperialism.[8] Thus, since the 1960s, we find new theories, revisions and debates on imperialism in all the European countries involved, but not in the Netherlands. Let us now see how this silence is to be explained.

I

The absence of the Dutch in the international debate on imperialism is striking. Until very recently there has been no discussion at all of the Dutch case. In the many volumes on comparative imperialism and on the theory of imperialism, and indeed, even in most of the international bibliographies, we do not find any discussion of it. What is even more surprising is that the same is true for Dutch historiography. Of course there are scores of studies on Dutch expansion and Dutch colonial policy but none of the authors discusses this subject within the conceptual framework of imperialism.

How is this to be explained? To a certain extent ideological factors may have played a role in this. The traditional self-image of the Dutch makes it very difficult for them to consider themselves as an imperialist nation. From the nineteenth century onwards the Dutch have made a sharp distinction between, on the one hand, the great powers and their abject but inevitable game of power politics and, on the other hand, their own small and peaceful nation cultivating a policy of neutrality, mutual respect and the promotion of trade and progress. In this context it was possible and even logical to distinguish between Dutch colonial and European imperialist policies. Thus the prime minister who presided over the final stage of the Aceh War, Abraham Kuyper, found it 'an utter absurdity' to call the Dutch policy in Indonesia imperialist. That was a contradiction in terms as imperialism was by definition a monopoly of the great powers.[9] Now Kuyper was a man of the Right, but Dutch Marxist authors and politicians have also argued that the economic preconditions for imperialism required by their theory were, in the Dutch case, not fulfilled and thus that Dutch imperialism could not and did not exist.[10] It was not so much ideological reasons but rather conceptual problems that made Dutch politicians and political analysts hesitate to speak of a Dutch imperialism.

The fact that the Netherlands were not discussed in the historical debate on imperialism may, however, have a different explanation. There are two particular contributory factors. The first is a rather practical one. From its very beginning up to the present, the debate on imperialism has first and foremost been a debate on the partition of Africa. As is well known, the Netherlands were practically the only West European power not to take part in the scramble for Africa. Instead in 1872 they sold their last possessions on the Gold Coast to England. As they did not play a role in the scramble the Dutch have received little mention in the debate.

The second reason is of a conceptual nature. However exactly it is defined, the concept of imperialism has strong associations with the idea of expansion and territorial aggrandizement. Historically it is also closely connected with the concept of an 'age of imperialism'. According to this there was one period in European history (1880–1914) in which this expansion took a very spectacular form. This is, of course, rather obvious in the case of France, Germany, Italy and Belgium; but the British advocates of continuity and informal empire also could not and did not deny that during the 'age of imperialism' a huge formal empire was acquired by the British. In the Dutch case, however, the general pattern of the nineteenth century is not one of expansion but of contraction.

The Dutch seaborne empire of course had its heyday in the seventeenth century. In the eighteenth century it had already lost its paramountcy in Asia to the British. The great days of the British East India Company came and those of the Dutch East India Company (VOC) were over. In 1799 the once so glorious Company was dissolved. Shortly after this the Netherlands became part of the French imperial system, and during the days of Napoleon all Dutch possessions were taken over by the British. When finally peace was restored the Dutch regained part of their former possessions, essentially those in Indonesia.

When in 1816 the Indies reverted to the Netherlands, Dutch domination was virtually restricted to Java. Even on that island, as the long and bloody Java War of 1825-30 demonstrated, their mastery was not undisputed. Moreover, Dutch influence on the economy was limited since trade was entirely dominated by Britain whose Industrial Revolution allowed it to exchange textiles for tropical products. Holland had no such industry as yet and thus Dutch ships frequently sailed for the East in ballast. In order to change this, in 1824 a trading company, the *Nederlandse Handel Maatschappij*, was founded with the support of the dynamic King William I. Improvement in the financial position of the colony, however, had to wait until 1830, when Governor-General Van den Bosch introduced the Cultivation System. This brought great economic changes to Java and put an end to the financial burden the colony placed on the Netherlands because of the deficit in its finances. The Cultivation System was in fact a tax in kind: the population had to devote a proportion of its time to the colonial government and to cultivate a proportion of its land – in principle one fifth – with products suitable for export to Europe, above all coffee, tea, sugar and indigo. These had to be delivered to the government. For this labour the population received a certain wage, the so-called *plantloon*, which was unilaterally determined by the government and bore no relation to the value of the products. Nevertheless it was sufficient to allow the land-rent to be paid. The land-rent had been inherited from the era of British rule under Raffles. The original intention of Van den Bosch had been to replace it entirely by the Cultivation System but this was found impracticable.

The Cultivation System flourished until 1870. Thereafter it still remained in existence – the last remnants were dismantled only in 1915 – but became steadily less important. It had made Java an important producer and exporter of tropical produce and was initially an object of international praise and admiration. This, however, was not to last very long. As early as the 1840s criticism of this system, so out of tune with the liberal spirit of the times, had begun. It became steadily more insistent and reached its peak in 1859 in the famous novel by 'Multatuli' about the abuses of the Cultivation System, *Max Havelaar*. This book was to influence public opinion decisively. When in 1860 the liberals came to power, the system was gradually demolished to make way for a system of free labour and private enterprise made possible by the 1870 Agrarian Law of Minister De Waal. By an irony of history in those years when the conservatives, in principle supporters of the system, also had their criticisms of the excesses of the Cultivation System, its proceeds reached their highest point as a result of price rises on the European market. The liberal theoreticians argued that private entrepreneurs would take over the task, but this argument proved false as these entrepreneurs preferred the protection of the government above truly free enterprise, for which in

Java the social conditions were not as yet present. Equally Dutch capitalists preferred to invest in American railways or Russian bonds rather than Netherlands Indies enterprises which they found too risky. Thus the frequently repeated theory that the Cultivation System was obsolete and disappeared spontaneously, as it were, because entrepreneurs took over its function was a myth of liberal historiography, as Fasseur has demonstrated.[11] Rather it was the victim of liberal ideological criticism and repeated complaints and scandals about nepotism or favouritism in the awarding of the very lucrative sugar contracts. In other words, the explanation of its disappearance has to be sought in political, not economic, factors.

In 1870 there began a new period of economic development and territorial expansion as a consequence of the opening of the Suez Canal and of De Waal's Agrarian Law which allowed the settlement of European planters. However, there were many economic problems, arising not least from the impact of the 'Great Depression' of 1873–96. In the same years there was also the bloody struggle over territorial expansion in Aceh (north Sumatra). Expansion in the form of punitive expeditions and administrative extension had been a constant feature of Dutch colonialism in the nineteenth century, but the Aceh War was different because of its scale and intensity. It lasted for a very long time – from 1873 to 1903 – and its number of casualties at approximately 100,000 is unmatched in Dutch military history. What, then, were the causes of this long conflict? Was it an act of jingoistic imperialism? Certainly not. The war was very unpopular, as much with the ever-prudent Dutch government as with the protesting Dutch taxpayer and the public at large. Nor can the reasons be found in economic motivation. There was no need of markets or raw materials, let alone capital investments on these far-away shores. Some historians have smelt petroleum behind the drawn-out conflict. But this penetrating odour cannot be traced before about 1895 when the war had already been long under way. The causes of the Aceh War, then, lay in diplomatic factors. Fear of American intervention and later of England, Germany and Japan forced the Dutch government to plant the flag and to have it respected in areas which they would rather have left alone. As a small country with limited abilities to react the Netherlands could not permit dangerous vacuums to exist on the fringes of its colonial sphere, but on the other hand could not allow major military operations either. Therefore the war dragged on for about 30 years until General Van Heutsz in 1903 brought it to an end. No wonder the conqueror of Aceh was received in Holland as a hero in 1904. The reception of this Dutch Kitchener can be seen as the first clear demonstration of an imperialist mentality in Holland. Widespread criticism of the Boer War (1899–1902), which was seen as a struggle by those of Dutch stock, was in no way alien to this mood.

The introduction of the *Korte Verklaring* ('Short Declaration') in 1901 by the colonial government of Batavia is a clear indication of a systematic policy of effective occupation. This declaration – to be signed by almost all regional Indonesian rulers and princes – meant a legalized and uniform subjection to Dutch colonial rule. In the same year, too, a new colonial policy was introduced that became renowned as the 'Ethical Policy'. Its background is to be found in a famous article by C. van Deventer in the journal *De Gids* of 1899. Van Deventer claimed that the Netherlands had a 'Debt of Honour' – the article's title – to the Indies. He calculated the debt at 187 million guilders, the sum that Holland had earned from the Cultivation System. Van Deventer's idea that the millions should be given back was not taken up in this form, but it was accepted that an active policy had to be followed to increase the prosperity and improve the position of the Indonesians. This policy was officially introduced in the 1901 'Speech from the Throne' in which was stressed the 'moral duty' which the Netherlands, as a Christian nation, had towards Indonesia. This policy was manifested in the improvement of education, public health and agriculture and the appointment of Indonesians to local administrative bodies. This happened for the most part simultaneously with a more active interest in the Netherlands Indies on the part of the Dutch business community.

By 1904 a period of economic growth began that lasted until the crisis of the 1930s. Important parts of the so-called 'Outer Possessions', such as Sumatra's east coast, southern Borneo and tin islands like Banka and Biliton were integrated into the economic system. Minerals such as tin and petroleum became increasingly important. Nevertheless, until the Second World War, although the proportions of individual commodities changed, three-quarters of the export trade consisted of agricultural products. Tobacco increased, coffee became less significant and rubber took up a major place. In these years the idea arose that the Netherlands was permanently bound to its overseas empire and its prosperity could not exist without it. B.C. de Jonge, Governor-General from 1931 to 1936 declared, 'We have ruled here for three hundred years with the whip and the club and we shall still be doing it in another three hundred years'.[12] It was thus very quickly forgotten that the Dutch had only entered most of the areas thirty years previously, let alone ruled them. These later developments, interesting as they are, are not of so much importance for the question of whether or not there was in Dutch colonial history, as in other countries, 'an age of imperialism' between approximately 1880 and 1914.

II

What we do see in this period is the expansion of Dutch authority in the Archipelago. But the nature of this phenomenon is open to debate. It can be interpreted as the consolidation of what had hitherto been a tenuous colonial authority. Certainly this process was a protracted one which continued throughout the century and was far from new in the 1880s. Such continuity contradicts the concept of an 'age of imperialism', with its implications of novelty or innovation. These are probably the main reasons why implicitly or, in some cases, explicitly historians have hesitated to speak of a Dutch imperialism.[13]

Only very recently has it been argued that the Dutch case is after all roughly analogous to others, that the Netherlands followed more or less the general pattern and that a Dutch imperialism can be incorporated into the general debate on imperialism. The Utrecht historian Maarten Kuitenbrouwer has developed this argument in an interesting and well documented book.[14] In this treatment he not only pays attention to the development of Dutch colonial policy, but also deals with Dutch international policy in general (for example, its diplomacy with regard to the partition of Africa) and Dutch public opinion (for example, the agitation about the South African Wars of 1881 and 1899–1902). On the basis of a rich documentation he offers a fine analysis of the interaction between domestic, foreign and colonial policy. What interests us most here, however, are his conclusions.

Kuitenbrouwer argues that the Netherlands was definitely an imperialist power and that its behaviour did not differ much from the general European pattern of imperialism. The first argument is of course essentially a matter of definition. According to the two definitions of imperialism Kuitenbrouwer offers, Dutch imperialism already existed in the seventeenth century.[15] More important is his conclusion that the Netherlands followed the general European pattern. Dutch actions in the period c. 1880–1914 were comparable with those of other powers during this age of imperialism. Kuitenbrouwer follows in his argument the suggestion made by Raymond Betts in his book *The False Dawn* that the age of imperialism was characterized by two elements, 'contiguity' and 'preemption'.[16]

In general these are not very useful concepts, nor do they illuminate our understanding of Dutch expansion in particular. 'Contiguity' is supposed to signify that power expanded from existing possessions to neighbouring territories. In such a very general form this is, of course, a truism, applicable to all forms of expansion of power in all periods of history. What is much more characteristic of the age of imperialism, however, is that often expansion did *not* follow this pattern; instead, quite unconnected and most unexpected territories were annexed. After all what contiguity brought the French to Madagascar, the British to Egypt, the Germans to New Guinea or the Italians to Adowa? Generally speaking, contiguity was both much more a characteristic of the previous period, and was indeed characteristic of the Dutch in Indonesia in the period of imperialism, 1880–1914. That, however, does not make the Dutch case a replica of the others, but rather illustrates how different it was from them.

The second characteristic according to Betts (and Kuitenbrouwer) is 'preemption'. Betts – following William Langer – understands by this what in imperial Britain was called 'pegging out claims for the future' and in Germany was known as the *Torschlusspanik*: that is to say the claiming of territories without any real need to have them and only in order to prevent others from taking them. Here Betts is surely right. This often irrational behaviour is indeed typical of the imperialist period – and this explains, incidentally, why there often was no contiguity. But I do not think Kuitenbrouwer is correct in arguing that this was also typical of the Dutch. What Kuitenbrouwer calls the preemptive aspect of the Dutch expansion is something very different. He understands by it the introduction of effective occupation in areas that belonged to the Dutch sphere of influence in the Archipelago but where its authority was not actually present. This was done with the aim of removing from the other powers all excuses or pretexts for intervention. To any devotee of bridge-playing this use of the term appears quite appropriate, more so than the way in which it is employed by Betts and Langer. In bridge, the term 'preemptive' is used for actions that are tactically aggressive but strategically defensive. That is indeed what the Dutch expansion in the Archipelago amounted to and therefore in this case the term 'preemptive imperialism' is very suitable. But it does not make Dutch behaviour more like that of the others; on the contrary. The confusion comes from the fact that the term is used in two different senses. 'Consolidation of the existing', as Kuitenbrouwer calls the Dutch form of preemption is a policy of the 'haves'. It is something very different from the *Torschlusspanik* or annexation-fever of the colonial 'have nots' that was so typical of most of the other imperialists. Thus the question remains whether in Dutch colonial history we can distinguish an imperialist period, different in nature from previous and/or later periods. Was the late nineteenth century such a period? Do we see a new colonial policy, new incentives, new results?

A new policy there was not. The imperialist ambition was more openly confessed and public opinion was more aware of the importance of empire, but it was essentially the same policy as in previous periods and the ambitions were not aimed at securing any larger territory than before. Nor do we find in the Netherlands new incentives for colonialism. There were no new economic or political problems that demanded novel forms of imperialism. An imperialist ideology and mentality came only after 1900, and this as the result not as the cause of imperialism. The same colonial policy was indeed executed with more energy and thus there was a greater amount of imperialist activity. Yet this had nothing to do with changes in Holland: it was associated with the changing international situation.

Imperialist activities could be initiated at various levels. They could come from private initiatives, local government officials, the colonial government, an imperialist pressure group, the cabinet and elsewhere. Imperialist actions, however, were always the result of a chain of decisions and that, like every other chain, was only as strong as its weakest link. That is to say, imperialist actions could be initiated but they could also be stopped or misfire at every level. As Fasseur has demonstrated, in the case of the Netherlands Indies the chain consisted of three links: the man on the spot, the Governor General at Batavia and the Ministry at The Hague.[17] In general imperialist ambitions slackened with every step to a higher level. Traditionally The Hague frustrated imperialist ambitions in the East. There was only one exception to this rule, which was when lack of action could create an unclear situation offering to other states the possibilities or a pretext for intervention. Then for a short moment prudence and parsimony had to give way to 'affirmative action'. The novelty in the last quarter of the nineteenth century was that there were more of these situations, or at least there was more fear of them arising. Thus if Dutch imperialist activity increased in this period it was the result of changing circumstances, not changing policies. Dutch imperialism was not a matter of action but of reaction. It was – and this seems to be unique – almost exclusively a function of international politics. In short, the only reason for Dutch imperialism was the imperialism of others.

Did this result in new acquisitions or annexations? Was the age of imperialism one of territorial expansion in the Archipelago? This is a delicate and difficult matter because the answer to the question as to whether new possessions were acquired depends on what one considers to have been already-existing possessions. There is, of course, no doubt that in 1914 the Dutch effectively controlled a much greater part of the Archipelago than they had done, for example, in 1815. This extension of effective control was a continuous process that went on from the very beginning right to the end of the colonial period. The question is whether this was a form of territorial expansion. Effective control was something much debated in theory but very difficult to assess in practice. In any case, it was not the real criterion in the definition of what were colonial possessions. Much more important was the official or silent recognition by the other powers.

It is debatable whether the entire Archipelago was accepted as a Dutch sphere of influence. There was no international official recognition of its exact borders. The Treaty of London was on a few points open for discussion and of course the other powers were no party to this. On the other hand the protection of England, the *arbiter mundi*, was an important asset and in actual practice the other powers never questioned the right of the Dutch to pacify or punish whatever part of the Archipelago they wished as long as other powers' ambitions and claims were reasonably discussed and respected. This the Dutch were always willing to do, as the treaties with Britain, Germany and Portugal demonstrate. There were no great disputes about this. As a matter of fact, one finds in Dutch colonial history quite a few respectable statesmen, Cabinet ministers and governors-general who suggested selling or giving away huge parts of the Archipelago, like Borneo or New Guinea – or, indeed, everything but Java and Sumatra – to some foreign power. This never happened but it is also true that in 1914 – after a century of 'imperialism' – the Dutch colonial possessions in Indonesia did not exceed the limits of the Dutch sphere of influence of 1815. Nor did they when the Dutch left in 1949. If the same had happened in the case of

France, England, or Germany, Hobson would never have published *Imperialism: A Study*, and historians would not be discussing the subject today.

III

What conclusions should be drawn from this? Let me say first that in my opinion the important question is not whether we should or should not speak of Dutch imperialism. As there are so many definitions of imperialism this would be purely a matter of semantics. Some definitions include Dutch colonialism and some do not. Nor do I subscribe to the idea that if Dutch policy cannot be properly called 'imperialist' it would then by any standard be better or morally superior. Imperialism by any other name would be as bad. Nor finally am I arguing that we should do away with the term altogether. Imperialism is here to stay – at least as a concept.

In fact, the word imperialism is used more often than ever, not only by historians but also, and maybe even more so, by students of international relations. This leaves us with two possibilities. We can either consider it as a historical concept applicable to a specific period in the history of the expansion of Europe. Or we can define it in such a way that it becomes an analytical tool in the study of international relations in general or of power politics *tout court*. The latest theory of imperialism put forward by Ronald Robinson, the so-called 'excentric theory' of imperialism or the 'Robinson model Mark IV' – because there are three previous ones – belongs to the last category. In this model imperialism is conceived of in 'terms of the play of international economic and political markets in which degrees of monopoly and competition in relations at world, metropolitan and local levels decide its necessity and profitability'.[18] While older Robinsonian models, like the 'imperialism of free trade', the 'periphery' and the 'collaborationist' theories, explained several aspects of the transition from imperialism to empire, then to independence, the new model is a convertible: it can be used both to explain some specific problems of the history of European expansion and as a universal theory. It analyses imperialism in terms of a struggle between big and little brothers, of asymmetry of power and of changing terms of collaboration. Thus formulated history becomes a rather abstract thing. All power relations have some asymmetry and all history is the history of collaboration – as well as of conflict – between human beings. Perhaps it is better, therefore, to reserve the term for one particular episode in world history: that of the expansion of Europe. Then the concept of imperialism can be used as an analytical tool to distinguish specific periods in the history of European expansion and specific forms of interaction between European and non-European factors. What do the British and the Dutch cases tell us about this?

The first question, then, is the old one of periodization. Is it useful to distinguish a specific stage in European expansion, the last quarter of the nineteenth century, and label it imperialist? Both the Dutch and the British cases seem to suggest that this is not true. Continuity is much more important. In the case of Britain, however, there is the undeniable fact that, for whatever reasons, a very considerable and even extraordinary territorial expansion took place in that period. Therefore for Britain one can still defend the thesis of an 'age of imperialism'. This was not the case in Holland. In Dutch colonial history the main transition was the one from old to new colonialism that took place around 1900. It was this new colonialism characterized by a systematic *mise en valeur* and an active rôle on the part of the state that brought a new dimension to Dutch colonialism.

This was not an exclusively or uniquely Dutch phenomenon. The new colonialism that came into being around the turn of the century was something of a rather more general nature. The only difference was that in the other European countries it received less attention because by that time they were still fully engaged in the territorial partition of the world that was going on and continued until 1914. Holland was not so engaged. Then came the Great War in which most European powers were involved. Again Holland did not participate, with the result that 1914–1918 is not such a watershed in Dutch history as it is in other countries. Only after 1918 did it become clear that a new period had begun, that of full colonialism. For this reason Thomas August has argued in a recent article in *Itinerario* that the 1920s and 1930s should be considered as the real age of imperialism.[19] It would surely be very unhelpful to do this because it would make the term even more confusing, but one can agree with the idea that the heyday of colonial rule was not in the nineteenth but in the first half of the twentieth century. Economically, socially and administratively colonialism was only then fully established, while at the ideological level a colonial consciousness also came into being.

The interesting thing is that, due to its particular position, in the case of the Netherlands this transition became visible round about 1900. There are indications that in France and Germany as well the transition to 'the highest stage of colonialism' – if not of capitalism – took place around this time. It would be interesting to look deeper into this and to consider whether the traditional *caesura* of 1880 should not be replaced by one around 1900.

So much for periodization. The other issue is the one of typology or morphology. What general patterns and what specific national articulations can be found in European imperialism? What similarities and dissimilarities can be distinguished? Here it seems that although there were, of course, many important and obvious differences between Britain and the Netherlands, there is an essential similarity between the two of them in their attitude towards the new imperialism. Both were essentially displeased with what was happening. In their own and very different ways, both were happy with the world as it was and would have preferred things to stay as they were. In other words, as far as the overseas world was concerned, both were satisfied powers. This explains why their reaction to the new imperialism was ambiguous. On the one hand, they showed a very real imperialism in the sense of a more systematic and officially accepted policy of economic exploitation. On the other hand, for them the new world of imperialism was also full of new problems, of growing competition and possible conflicts. The age of imperialism was an age of new possibilities but also, and more important, of new dangers. It was not an age to be welcomed; but it could not be evaded. In their attitude towards the new imperialism no two powers showed greater similarities than Britain and the Netherlands: defensive rather than offensive, reluctant rather than enthusiastic. In short, their attitude was one of reaction rather than action. In both cases there was more continuity than discontinuity, and what discontinuity there was derived from a change in circumstances, not in policy. The famous words from the Cambridge *Book of Proverbs*, 'informal if possible, formal if necessary', seem applicable to the Netherlands too.[20]

There was of course the important difference that has already been mentioned. The British – reluctantly or not – acquired an immense new empire. The Dutch did not even think about it. Their sole concern was to keep what they had, which was a great deal. No colonial empire was considered to be more attractive, profitable and worthwhile than the Indies. From Germany to Japan the Indies were looked at avariciously. Yet the Netherlands was one of the smallest and most vulnerable states of Europe. This makes the position of the Netherlands unique: it was a colonial giant but a political dwarf. Therefore Dutch imperialism was after all *sui generis*. It followed to some extent the general pattern of European imperialism, introducing a more active and systematic colonial policy after 1900 than before. It was comparable to a large extent with Britain in so far as its attitude towards imperialism was concerned. Yet due to its unique position it had to follow a very specific policy. In the colonial field it protected its sphere of influence, demonstrated great *souplesse vis à vis* its neighbours, developed the economy of the Indies and, all importantly, kept them open for foreign trade and investment. In international politics it followed a policy of strict neutrality and almost perfect aloofness.

As the age of imperialism proceeded, diplomacy became a subject of mass politics and also of the mass media. The tone of the public debate changed, in the Netherlands as elsewhere. Racist attitudes towards the Indonesians were openly admitted, a brutal policy of mass extermination of the Achinese was publicly advocated. Jingoistic feelings of hatred against the British because of the South African War were vigorously demonstrated. Many a Dutchman felt humiliated by his country's lack of power and brooded upon its glorious past in the seventeenth century. Nevertheless, in practice all this did not influence Dutch foreign policy at all. Diplomacy remained in the hands of the 'Western establishment', and they knew all too well that in a world full of dangers a small nation can only walk on tiptoe. It is in this realism that there lies the answer to a question perhaps even more puzzling than the one posed by Paul Kennedy: Why did the *Dutch* Empire last so long?[21]

NOTES

1. The Baron of Beef, a well-known hostelry close to St John's College in Cambridge.
2. H. Brunschwig, *Mythes et réalités de l'impérialisme colonial français, 1871–1914* (Paris, 1960).
3. The recent book by J. Marseille, *Empire colonial et capitalisme français. Histoire d'un divorce* (Paris, 1984) offers much new data and throws a new light on the economic aspects of French imperialism.
4. H.-U. Wehler, *Bismarck und der Imperialismus* (Cologne, 1969).
5. J.L. Miège, *L'impérialisme colonial italien de 1870 à nos jours* (Paris, 1968).
6. R.J. Hammond, *Portugal and Africa, 1815–1910. A Study in Uneconomic Imperialism* (Stanford, 1966).
7. G. Clarence-Smith, *The Third Portuguese Empire, 1825–1975. A Study in Economic Imperialism* (Manchester, 1985).
8. J. Stengers, 'King Leopold's Imperialism' in R. Owen and B. Sutcliffe (eds.), *Studies in the Theory of Imperialism* (London, 1972), 248–75.
9. As quoted in M. Kuitenbrouwer, *Nederland en de opkomst van het moderne imperialisme. Koloniën en buitenlandse politiek, 1870–1902* (Amsterdam, 1985), 195.
10. Cf. H. Roland Holst, *Kapitaal en arbeid in Nederland*, 2 vols. (Amsterdam, 1902).
11. C. Fasseur, *Kultuurstelsel en koloniale baten* (Leiden, 1975), *passim*.
12. Quoted by L.H. Palmer, *Indonesia and the Dutch* (London, 1962), 35.
13. Cf. I. Schöffer, 'Dutch Expansion and Indonesian reactions: some dilemmas of modern colonial rule (1900–1942)' in H.L. Wesseling (ed.), *Expansion and Reaction. Essays on European expansion and reactions in Asia and Africa* (Leiden, 1978), 78–100; C. Fasseur, 'Een koloniale paradox. De Nederlandse expansie in de Indonesische Archipel in het midden van de negentiende eeuw (1830–1870)', *Tijdschrift voor Geschiedenis* 92 (1979), 162–87; H.L. Wesseling, *Myths and Realities of Dutch imperialism: some preliminary observations*. Paper presented to the Second Indonesian-Dutch Historical Conference, Ujung Pandang, 22–30 June 1978.
14. Kuitenbrouwer, *Nederland en de opkomst van het moderne imperialisme* (see note 9).
15. Cf. ibid., 8–9.
16. R. Betts, *The False Dawn. European Imperialism in the Nineteenth Century* (Oxford/Minneapolis, 1976), 81.
17. Cf. Fasseur, 'Koloniale paradox' (see note 11).
18. R. Robinson, 'The Excentric Idea of Imperialism, with or without Empire' in W.J. Mommsen and J. Osterhammel (eds.), *Imperialism and After. Continuities and Discontinuities* (London, 1986), 286.
19. T August, 'Locating the Age of Imperialism', *Itinerario*, X, 2 (1986), 85–97.
20. Cf. J. Gallagher and R. Robinson, 'The Imperialism of Free Trade', *Economic History Review*, Second Series, VI, 1 (1953), 1–15.
21. Cf. P. Kennedy, 'Why did the British Empire Last So Long?' in P.M. Kennedy, *Strategy and Diplomacy, 1870–1945. Eight Studies* (London, 1983), 197–218.

Decentralized Violence and Collaboration in Early Colonial Uganda

by

Michael Twaddle

Historians of colonial Uganda are no strangers to violence. Indeed, the Protectorate itself was to a very large extent conceived in the violence which erupted between two politico-religious groupings of Ganda chiefs emerging from an unusually bloody succession war. This war started when Mwanga II was overthrown by a conspiracy of palace musketeers in September 1888. Subsequently, not only did religious groupings introduced earlier in the nineteenth century by a diversity of Muslim and Christian emissaries to the courts of Mwanga's father and grandfather, Mutesa I and Suna, become tragically murderous but elements of class warfare emerged dramatically too. This happened when the leading followers of the Muslim claimant to the Ganda throne killed off most of their slaves, 'because their loyalty could not be relied upon'.[1] Into this maelstrom at the start of 1890 marched Carl Peters in pursuit of a German empire in the heart of Africa. Then came Frederick Jackson, Ernest Gedge and Frederick Lugard on behalf of the Imperial British East Africa Company (IBEAC) – Jackson and Gedge on the very heels of Peters, Lugard at the end of the year. During the earlier succession war (1888–90), the Roman Catholic and Anglican Protestant politico-religious groupings had emerged essentially in response to the seizure of power at the kingdom's centre by the Muslim king, Kalema. By the very end of 1889 both Catholic and Protestant Ganda chiefs were uneasily allied against both this particular king and Muslim Ganda generally under the banner of a restored and now ostensibly repentant Mwanga II. Militarily, however, Mwanga's position was markedly precarious. Should either Catholic or Protestant Ganda chiefs and their followers and slaves withdraw support from each other at any time, the Muslim revolution in Buganda would almost certainly be assured of an instantaneous triumph over the grouping remaining at Mwanga's side.[2]

It was at this time that Mwanga's supporters sent their first requests for help to the IBEAC's pioneer column then marching into the East African interior under the leadership of Jackson and Gedge. Jackson responded by marching away from Buganda instead of towards it, and by dispatching a crumpled IBEAC ensign to raise the Buganda Christians' flagging morale. Only when Carl Peters opened Jackson's mail at what is now Mumias in western Kenya did Jackson and company then hurry on to Buganda; but by the time they reached there Peters had concluded a treaty with Mwanga in the German interest, a treaty negotiated essentially with the Catholic politico-religious grouping's support. Jackson and Gedge huffed and puffed, and did obtain the support of the smallest of the four politico-religious groupings then struggling for primacy within Buganda – the Anglican Protestant circle associated with the Church Missionary Society. But Jackson and Gedge had insufficient rifles and men of their own to make any really decisive contribution to resolving the Ganda succession war one way or the other. All they were able to do was to persuade the European Christian missionaries then resident in Buganda to put pressure on their converts to send a joint Catholic-Protestant commission of enquiry to the East African coast, in the hope that this would in time demonstrate within which particular imperialist sphere of influence – German or British – the leading European countries wished the kingdom of Buganda to fall in future.

It was with this very uncertain and fraught political atmosphere still prevailing that Frederick Lugard marched into Buganda at the close of 1890. Lugard had only a small fraction of the logistical support accorded to *Reichskommissar* Wissmann, his nearest counterpart in the more southerly German imperialist sphere in eastern Africa, and all he and his immediate associates in the infant IBEAC administration in Buganda could do was to play the various contending factions off against one another. This Lugard did with such skill that his name is still popularly reviled within Roman Catholic circles in Buganda today. To start with, Lugard organized both Catholic and Protestant groupings into a largely successful military expedition against their Muslim opponents. Then he marched off westwards to recruit Sudanese soldiers left unemployed by the recent collapse of the Turko-Egyptian empire in what is nowadays southern Sudanese border territory with Uganda and Zaire; these Muslim mercenaries Lugard thenceforth employed to underpin the IBEAC position in Buganda and in the region immediately to the west of it. Unfortunately, however, upon returning to Buganda from this enterprise, Lugard issued precision rifles to Protestant Baganda. These the Protestants turned upon their erstwhile Roman Catholic allies. Unsurprisingly, Roman Catholic missionaries were incensed by Lugard's action in issuing rifles only to Protestants. For a number of years the White Fathers were to complain bitterly about all this to the French government. As it happened, the Catholic missionaries' leader, Cardinal Lavigerie, had increased their political influence in France at this time because of his role in rallying Catholic support for the Third Republic, and Catholic missionaries in Buganda were therefore able with French government support to cause much diplomatic embarrassment to successive British governments until the issue of compensation was settled. However, when Mwanga II eventually raised the standard of revolt against British penetration in July 1897, and a substantial number of Roman Catholic chiefs too revolted alongside Mwanga, Catholic missionaries changed their political tune. For some months they became most enthusiastic supporters of the British colonial connection; that is, until hostilities ceased and Sir Harry Johnston negotiated the Uganda Agreement of 1900. This brought Ganda Protestant chiefs substantial privileges and was to lead to the Buganda kingdom being ruled until 1962 by a Christian oligarchy of chiefs in which Protestants, not Roman Catholics, throughout exercised most considerable power.

Most of these facts are reasonably well known to historians of British expansion from Roland Oliver's study of *The Missionary Factor in East Africa* (1952), Margery Perham's biography of Lugard (1956), and Anthony Low's chapters in the Oxford *History of East Africa* (1963 and 1965). As a result of Andrew Roberts's pioneering article of 1962 in the *Journal of African History* on 'The sub-imperialism of the Baganda', also familiar in outline is the subsequent story of Ganda co-operation with British rule in administering areas of the Uganda Protectorate other than Buganda itself. Indeed, the story of how Baganda chiefs and clerks assisted British colonial administrators in governing areas of Uganda occupied by hitherto politically decentralized peoples, by the so-called 'tribes without rulers' whose social structures were integrated more frequently by ritual mechanisms than by any concentrations of purely political power in the hands of relatively few Africans, was so well established by the time Ronald Robinson came to compose his wide-ranging and seminal article on the 'Non-European Foundations of European Imperialism' that it became one of his paradigmatic examples, along with the earlier and still better-known story of 'Buganda from 1886 to 1900'.[3]

It is not the intention of this essay to repeat what is already published about either of these two Ganda collaborative stories. Nor is it intended to subject Robinson's suggestions on resistance and collaboration to any comprehensive celebration or review. That task has just been accomplished by John Lonsdale in his masterly study of 'The European scramble and conquest in African history' in Volume 6 of the *Cambridge History of Africa* and, less overtly but none the less eloquently, by John Iliffe in the sections of his *Modern History of Tanganyika* dealing with the changing imperatives of collaboration dictated by direct rule and taxation as opposed to initial contact. Rather the intention is a more modest but, in the light of Uganda's subsequent history, none the less salutary one. Historians of colonial Uganda are already aware of the importance of Ganda sub-imperialism in spreading appointive chieftaincy on the Buganda model in a violent as well as in a non-violent manner among hitherto politically decentralized peoples occupying other areas of the Uganda Protectorate.[4] What they, and historians of British expansion more generally, are much less conversant with is the reverse traffic in what may be called 'politically-decentralized violence'. Collaborative arrangements were not only shaped at the higher levels of political negotiation or forged under the pressures of co-ordinated mass resistance. The low-level and diffused yet often persistent violence resorted to by individuals or small communities in response to the activities of the lesser agents of British authority is less easily recaptured, but could be of critical importance for the administrative structures and social patterns of collaboration. It is with that reverse traffic and with some of its immediate and longer-term consequences in Uganda that this essay is principally concerned.

The essay therefore attempts to make two essential points. It argues that politically-decentralized violence had a two-fold importance in the early colonial period in Uganda: it not only forced upon British administrators acceptance of local modifications to Buganda-style client-chieftaincy among 'tribes without rulers' outside Buganda and the western kingdoms, but it also influenced the changing balance of colonial and collaborative power within these politically more centralized societies after 1900. These points it seeks to illustrate by looking in some detail at the Katsonga incident of 1906 and successive sporadic murders among the Gisu (alternatively Bagisu, or Bagishu) people occupying the westerly slopes of Mount Elgon in the far east of the Uganda Protectorate.

I

The principal actors are the obvious ones, given a colonial setting. There was the Protectorate Commissioner, Henry Hesketh Bell, a brisk figure with experience of the West Indies as well as the Gold Coast. There was his deputy, George Wilson, from a rougher background in Australia but probably a more astute manager of protectorate politics. There were the local British protectorate officials, such as Boyle and Cubitt at Jinja, and Ormsby and Coote at Mbale. There was the protectorate interpreter, Abudala Makubire. There was the British protectorate judge, Morris Carter. There were the two local European missionaries, the Reverend J.B. Purvis of the Protestant Church Missionary Society (CMS) and Father Speare of the Roman Catholic Mill Hill Mission (which followed the White Fathers to Uganda in 1895), together with their respective spiritual superiors. Just offstage there was Semei Kakungulu, the 'very useful pioneer and imperialist, notwithstanding his black face'.[5] Kakungulu had conquered and organized Bagisu and many other hitherto politically decentralized peoples in eastern Uganda into a Bantu kingdom during the very first years of the twentieth century while at the same time ostensibly extending British protectorate authority over them. By 1906 he had just been promoted to be President of the Busoga Lukiko [or chiefly council], not (as Kakungulu himself believed) as a genuine promotion, but as simply the most convenient means to hand of getting rid of this particular over-mighty African subject from an area where local British officials considered he had built up excessive power for himself. However, many of Kakungulu's earlier chiefs and camp followers stayed on in eastern Uganda. So too, of course, did most of the indigenous occupants of the area, among them those responsible for the continuing acts of violence against the remaining Ganda chiefs, clerks, and tax-collectors.

With Kakungulu safely promoted to Busoga, and his remaining chiefs partially bureaucratized in other areas of eastern Uganda, the official British historiography of colonial pacification was rewritten. 'This district is a decidedly composite one', declared Boyle in his annual report for 1905–06:

> There is a complete lack of cohesion, and it is consequently most difficult to administer such people satisfactorily, more especially as it is, in reality, only two years since we took any active participation in administering this district, our influence until then only extending over an area of small dimensions in close proximity to the Government station. The Kakunguru was the real ruler and, although he himself is, I believe, just to the native, his following of freebooters were quite the reverse, and I understand it was most difficult, if not impossible, for an injured native to lay his cause before him for redress. In 1904, we instituted Government Agents, nominated by the Kakunguru, for each sub-district, but we found they were still enriching themselves at the expense of the natives under their care. An example was made of some of those caught *flagrante delicto*, but even this did not stop them, and it culminated in the fracas which caused the Budama expedition [of 1905, against the Jopadhola people]. The system was then modified, and these agents now correspond with and are directly responsible to the Collector, at Mbale, and are paid by means of refunds from the Hut Tax.

This tax, Boyle reported, was now paid with the proceeds of produce rather than from forced sales of cattle of the sort that had prompted the Jopadhola rebellion of 1905.[6] The system of ruling the politically decentralized peoples of eastern Uganda through Ganda agents, Boyle concluded, 'is apparently working well now, and as we gradually substitute good men for bad, we shall I hope get a satisfactory class of Muganda to administer these sub-districts, until we can educate and establish over each tribe chiefs of their own race'.[7] The system itself, in other words, was satisfactory, only the particular Africans operating it needed changing.

Kakungulu's chroniclers also composed their versions of the district's early administrative history with due regard for subsequent experience. To them eastern Uganda immediately north of Busoga in 1906 appeared remarkably similar to Buganda at the time of Mwanga II's rebellion in 1897. Like Buganda at that time, this area was now a kingdom without an effective king. Like Buganda too, it was now to be ruled by chiefs politically divided over matters of religion. However, unlike Buganda, paramount power was henceforth to lie with the reigning British Collector's interpreter rather than with the former king's chief minister. 'When Kakungulu left for Busoga', wrote Paulo Kagwa, 'Makubire made himself Chief Minister Gulemye. Matayo Terwanire became Mugwanya and Yosiya Mayanja became Kisingiri';[8] 'Gulemye', 'Mugwanya' and 'Kisingiri' being respectively Sir Apolo Kagwa, Stanislas Mugwanya and

Zakariya Kisingiri, the three Regents who ruled the Buganda kingdom during the minority of Mwanga's son, Daudi Chwa, in the late 1890s and throughout the 1900s.

The Catholic Agent Matayo Terwanire, however, did not remain in position for long. In October 1906, he was dismissed from his post at Buyobo, 'owing to disobedience' in building a road further into the Gisu hills than Ormsby had ordered.[9] But the administrative division of Bukedi into 'counties' on the Buganda model continued, as too did similar politico-religious divisions among Ganda Agents governing those counties. The paramount influence of Abudala Makubire also continued with the British Collector.

II

One Friday in 1906, Sydney Ormsby was encamped for the night in a rest house at Katsonga, which was situated about four miles from the CMS station at Nabumali. 'That evening a Muganda called Sedulaka Sempa had a quarrel with a Mugishu, a native of the country', reported Archdeacon Walker, secretary of the Church Missionary Society in Uganda, to his counterpart in the British protectorate administration three months later.

> The wife of the native called the people to come and help her as the Muganda was ill-using him. In consequence of this a company of men who had been drinking came rushing up, & one of them speared the Muganda and killed him.
>
> Early the next morning Mr Ormsby, on hearing of the death of the Muganda, ordered his men to seize all the cattle in the neighbourhood. The men herding the cattle offered resistance and the order was then given to fire on them. Seven of the natives were shot, of whom three were women. These were killed outright, and another girl was wounded in the abdomen, also a small child also died owing to its mother having been killed. . . .
>
> Then the houses of all the people within a radius of a mile were set on fire. The sheep and goats as well as 100 to 150 head of cattle were driven off to the Government station at Mubale. Of these 71 have since been returned to the people. In addition to the above cattle, the Government Interpreter took 5 head of cattle and his man Musa took 30.

These details of the Ganda Agent's death and the subsequent official reprisals the Archdeacon was retailing to the Sub-Commissioner concerned, solely 'that the truth might be known and justice established'.[10]

Hesketh Bell, the relatively new Commissioner of the Uganda Protectorate, was concerned when he received news of the Archdeacon's complaint. 'The district seems to be in anarchy, and must be pacified as soon as possible,' he minuted to his deputy at Entebbe. 'The main thing, however, is not to unsettle the district, and "Punitive Expeditions" are to be avoided at all costs. You know the recent pronouncements made in the House of Commons . . .'[11] Judge Carter would therefore leave for Mbale and enquire whether it would be wise to station some troops permanently there. 'Force is the only argument,' commented the Commissioner, 'but it must be applied discreetly and calmly.' Judge Carter would also enquire into the circumstances surrounding the incident at Katsonga about which the archdeacon had complained. 'Mr Carter's report,' the Commissioner predicted, 'will be an ample and final answer to any statements that may come from unofficial sources either here or in England.'[12]

Judge Carter gave Hesketh Bell his report about the Katsonga incident on 27 November 1906.[13] There was no conclusive evidence that the Muganda had been killed because of his own previous cruelty, concluded Carter. Nor was there evidence to suggest that the Collector's Police had not been attacked first, 'except the statements of the natives'. There was, however, evidence that the number of women killed in proportion to men was 'a large one'; but the explanation for that, Carter suggested, might be that 'askaris may not have been able to see clearly owing to the long grass'. Collective punishment, Carter also suggested, was inevitable where primitive peoples were concerned, 'owing to the practical impossibility of securing the individual criminal'. With that Bell agreed. 'In Europe,' he minuted, 'when the Police or Military are called upon to fire upon a mob, innocent people are frequently killed.'[14]

In February 1907, George Wilson forwarded a two-page summary of Carter's 15-page report on the Katsonga incident to Archdeacon Walker,[15] for the perusal of Purvis, the CMS missionary at Nabumali. Purvis was not impressed. Carter's enquiries had been prejudiced from the start, wrote Purvis to his Archdeacon a month later, by the fact that they had been conducted through Ormsby, who was himself the object of those enquiries. They had been further prejudiced by Ormsby's apparent inability to provide Carter with an adequate interpreter of Lumasaba, the language of the Gisu people. 'I cannot look upon any enquiry as "fully" conducted,' commented Purvis, 'as far as my witnesses were concerned, by an interpreter who, intending to ask the question "What is your name?" asked "Your time, when?" '[16] But there was little that either Purvis or his CMS Archdeacon could do now that Ormsby had left Uganda on overseas leave. As Bishop Tucker later put it, attempting to change Carter's conclusions on the Katsonga incident was rather like arguing with a brick wall.[17] A few months later, Purvis himself left Uganda on overseas leave, and later in the year he accepted a clerical position in the north of England.[18]

In December 1906, Judge Carter submitted a second report to Hesketh Bell, dealing with the more obviously administrative aspects of his commission.[19] 'The BAGISHU', he reported, 'were numerous as well as obstreperous. But they were divided into 'a very large number of small tribes', and he considered it most unlikely that any substantial number of those tribes would ever combine to foment rebellion against the British.

He also thought a force of 100 police would be more useful at Mbale than an equivalent number of King's African Rifles; 'the people are most primitive', he declared,

> and in many ways like children and I consider that the mere presence in the district of a body of troops would have little more effect from a disciplinary point of view upon the BAGISHU, than would be the stationing of a regiment in a town in England upon the school children there. It is the schoolmaster wielding his rod on occasion who impresses the children with the advisability of behaving, and the BAGISHU are more likely to be impressed in a similar way by the Collector who uses the police.

So too, though Judge Carter was too judicious to mention it, would be the Liberal Government then in power in Britain, for though finding large punitive expeditions in Africa no longer acceptable, it might be prepared to tolerate any number of small 'police actions'.[20]

Coupled with his recommendation regarding the employment of police around Mbale, Judge Carter also commented upon the custom of employing Ganda Agents in administrative positions in eastern Uganda. 'The Interpreter Abdulla', who had been accused of dishonesty by Purvis, was acquitted of that charge. The presence of Ganda Agents, which had been objected to by Father Speare of the Mill Hill Mission as well as by Purvis, was a more difficult issue to resolve. That these Agents were 'not an unmixed blessing', Carter agreed; yet the 'real question', in his opinion, was whether any substitute could be found for them. 'Both the missions employ them in their work; I am therefore of the opinion that the Government would find it impossible at present, until the chiefs have learnt to exercise authority, to do without the Baganda agents.' But Carter did suggest the desirability of paying them a fixed salary rather than a percentage of tax receipts.[21]

The point about the Ganda being indispensable to British officials locally, Hesketh Bell accepted without question. 'The Baganda Agents are evidently necessary', he minuted briskly. 'When I visit the Mbale district I will see what arrangements can be made for their better supervision.' But the suggestion about salaries he promised merely to 'bear in mind',[22] a place where it would have had very little influence upon the matter at issue if various protectorate officials had not pressed it further.

In January 1907 Alexander Boyle was again addressing himself to 'the vexed subject of the Baganda Agents employed in the Bukedi district', as the whole area of eastern and central Uganda lying immediately north and east of Buganda and Busoga was then known. Boyle too now suggested that 'fixed rates of pay' should be paid to those Agents. The system of percentages, he suggested, was both unfair and injudicious: unfair, because the Agents with the greatest local problems received the lowest financial rewards; injudicious, because it induced 'the agent to put too much pressure on the natives in parts where we do not wish to push matters too hurriedly'.[23] Bell replied that salaries would cost more than percentages,[24] but Boyle persisted,[25] and George Wilson backed him up. 'The work appears to be highly responsible', minuted Wilson to Bell; moreover, it was work in which 'men of the best character and with good intelligence <u>could</u> be used'.[26] In April 1907 Hesketh Bell gave way,[27] and in the following month Alexander Boyle authorized that £392 of protectorate funds should be set aside as 'pay of Baganda Agents in the Bukedi District'.[28]

III

In his report on the Bukedi district for 1907–08, Sydney Ormsby commented that the change had already had 'an excellent effect' upon local administration in the area under his command. Whereas before there had been 'indiscreet methods of collection by which the taxpayers suffered', now that Ganda Agents received fixed rates of pay they were able to devote 'more of their time to the general improvement of the natives than they were inclined to do before'.[29] Now Ormsby was even writing about the inevitability of employing Ganda Agents locally as a longer-term proposition. 'I have great faith in the Baganda' for the purpose of collecting taxes, Ormsby now wrote – 'provided that the right men are chosen and are subject to constant and searching supervision'.[30]

'That no punitive expedition has taken place during the year under review is I think satisfactory proof that the District is getting quieter and the natives more used to our rule,' commented Ormsby elsewhere in the same report. But he did also admit that 'certain police measures among the Bagishu Hill Tribes' had been necessary during the year. They had indeed. During January 1907, a punitive expedition had been dispatched to southern Gisu country as a reprisal for further murders of Ganda Agents which had taken place and as a punitive expedition to end all punitive expeditions in that particular area. 'The Bagishu suffered considerable losses,' Hesketh Bell reported in turn to London in March, 'and it is probable that they have received a lesson which will not require repetition.'[31] It was a vain hope. The Bagisu concerned were evidently prepared to receive no end of a lesson of that sort: local murders of Ganda Agents continued, and 'punitive expeditions' gave way to 'police patrols' later in the year.[32] Yet still the murders of Ganda continued, and the 'general feeling of uneasiness'[33] among Ganda in Bukedi became steadily more acute. 'Baganda Agents . . . report that the Bagishu are becoming very truculent,' reported Coote on 17 October,[33]

> and that all are talking about the success of the clans who killed the Baganda. Some friendly chiefs have come in and corroborated the Baganda statements pointing out that they themselves are being threatened by their unruly neighbours for assisting our Agents, and clans who are at present neutral are rapidly becoming contaminated with this spirit of revolt.

But the political infection had spread even further than Coote realized, as George Wilson was at pains to point out three days later.

On that day Wilson composed an important minute on the Ganda murders around Mbale for the benefit of Alexander Boyle at Jinja and his various subordinates in Bukedi.[34] Wilson pointed out to begin with that those murders had created various complications. First, there was pressure from the Buganda kingdom: 'The Uganda Chiefs are greatly concerned and want to know what we are doing for the proper protection of their countrymen'. Secondly, there was criticism from European missionaries: 'Bishop Tucker is all that moderation and consideration should require in this matter but he reasonably hints that his hands will be forced if this sort of thing goes on'. Thirdly, there was criticism from other quarters which needed little further identification for any even moderately ambitious British protectorate official: 'The critics of the policy of using even the intelligence of aliens in our policy of development of districts mark these down as evidence on their side and could do so with such effect as to precipitate a withdrawal of the Baganda Agents and so annihilate all the good work that has been done in the north of the Central Province'. Finally, if *that* happened, it would amount to 'giving [the western Ugandan kingdoms of] Unyoro, Toro and Ankole a handle to use that will also damage those countries'; this was a prospect which must have appeared all the more immediate because of the Bunyoro rebellion earlier in the same year.[35]

With these four 'complications' in mind, Wilson instructed Boyle to divide the Bukedi district into two: 'Umiro' to be administered from Jinja, the rest from Mbale as before. He also instructed Cubitt 'to proceed instantly and examine the circumstances of the present murders' and then to 'report exhaustively – remembering that his report will be subject to mission enquiries. Absolute candour will be essential'.[36] Purvis's protests at the Carter enquiries during the previous year – not to mention the decentralized violence by local people themselves against the still comparatively new demand for hut tax – had clearly not been completely in vain.

'The Bageshu if not the more populous race in the Province are an exceedingly populous people,' Cubitt reported just over a month later.[37] But they were also an exceedingly divided people fragmented into 'innumerable Sections or Clans', which were 'again divided into smaller Sections, who occupy one Spur or ridge'. Each of these possessed 'an extraordinary conceit or pride in their valour or more powerful witchcraft which each sub-section believes its own':

> You attack Ridge A, the people on B see what is happening, they see the houses burning, the food being looted, but they care nothing. The next day the people from Ridge A come in, you tell them to call in the people on Ridge B, but the people on B refuse to come or obey saying 'Yes, you may have beaten the people on A, but you have not beaten us'. So they too must have their lesson.

But now each of the clans responsible for murdering Ganda Agents had received suitable further 'lessons' from the protectorate police. Somewhat unwisely, Cubitt predicted 'no further trouble'.[38]

Regarding the Ganda Agents employed locally, Cubitt reported that he had 'discovered no serious complaint against them'.[39] But he too had now arranged for their better administrative deployment in future. 'There is a big dividing ridge which runs from Mt Elgon to the Hill behind the Station,' wrote Cubitt:

> this ridge I have utilised as a division for the two head Waganda Agents – one is in charge of the Southern Section with seven 'Bomas' under him, he is known and liked by all those clans; whilst the Northern is under another, who is equally well known and has seven 'Bomas' under him. They have been informed that they will report monthly to the Collector on all matters concerning their districts, and immediately if any signs of unrest or disquiet are brought to their notice by the 'Bomas' under their charge or noticeable in any Clan in their district.

The head Agent in the south was to be Jafali Mayanja, a Ganda Muslim who had fought for Kalema during the Buganda succession war of 1888–90 and then been one of Semei Kakungulu's county chiefs in his short-lived kingdom at Mbale during the earlier 1900s.[40] The head in the northern area was to be Sale Lule, a man with an almost identical *curriculum vitae* but remembered by elderly Ganda during the 1960s principally as having been 'a man of Abudala Makubire' in the 1900s.[41]

Before receiving Cubitt's report, Hesketh Bell had in fact prepared himself for the arduous task of removing Ganda Agents completely from Bukedi. Only a few days before reading his report Bell had minuted: 'It is evident to me that the Baganda are not a success there, & they must be replaced by some other agency'.[42] But after reading Cubitt's report, Bell changed his mind yet again. Ganda Agents did not need removing from the area after all, merely rearranging in yet another administrative pattern.

In August 1908, Bell paid his long-expected visit to eastern Uganda, and in the following month formally reported on it in a special dispatch to London. 'Owing to lack of financial resources and paucity of staff', he wrote,

> the Administration of Uganda has, up to the present, been unable to devote any adequate degree of attention to that part of the Protectorate which lies to the east of the Mpologoma River and Lake Kioga. The whole of this vast territory comprising more than 25,000 square miles and including nearly two millions of people has been suffered to remain in a dormant and expectant condition. Indian traders have penetrated it at their own risks, and now and then we have had to dispatch small military and police expeditions to punish the tribes for the murders of those adventurers.

Yet circumstances had now fortunately forced the British protectorate authorities in Uganda to administer the area. 'Gradually', reported Bell,

> we found the tribes of Bagishu and Bakedi almost unconsciously placing themselves under the orders of any British officer with whom they came in contact, and Pax Britannica has gone on spreading over the country in an ever-broadening wave, until we find today that, whether we wish it or not, we are now bound to develop and turn to proper account the great and promising territory which now almost clamours for proper and adequate administration.

It was a rhetorical smokescreen, of course, but it was marvellous stuff and not surprisingly it was published subsequently as a British Parliamentary Paper.[43] In reality, however, when the first British administrator had been posted to Mbale in 1904, he had not found the politically decentralized peoples of eastern Uganda 'in a dormant and expectant condition', but temporarily organized into a kingdom under the command of that good friend of Great Britain, Semei Kakungulu. As for subsequent developments, these too had not happened 'almost unconsciously', but in response to the continuous murders of Ganda Agents, both before and after the Katsonga incident of 1907. These murders were mostly prompted by the attempt to collect hut tax for the first time among politically decentralized peoples, but the attempt became more rather than less arbitrary when British protectorate officials in the area effectively dismantled their leading African collaborator's kingdom and attempted to organize tax-collection themselves with the aid of Ganda irregulars.

IV

In this analysis lies the burden of Purvis's critique of British protectorate rule published upon his retirement from the Church Missionary Society:

> It was the express wish of the then Commissioner of Uganda that the raw natives in this eastern portion of the district should be 'brought into line' . . . very gradually; and probably to make sure that the Muganda chief [Semei Kakungulu] and his men played square with the native . . . the Government . . . official post was moved from Budaka to Mbale . . . but after some four years' residence in the district I am bound to say, having earnestly and carefully weighed the seriousness of the statement, that during the years of my residence which mark the introduction of [the hut tax] law into Masaba there seems to me to have been less peace, less security of property, and more, very much more, bloodshed than during the period I lived there without direct British administration.[44]

Purvis went on to attack hut tax collection and punitive expeditions explicitly as 'not tend[ing] to idealise British rule in the minds of the natives'.[45] Only by very selective quotation indeed, can Purvis's critique of *British* policy here be transformed into condemnation of Semei Kakungulu and Ganda Agents individually.[46] It was the policy in essence which Purvis attacked, not the persons implementing it.

Admittedly, local peoples did not see it that way at the time or subsequently. However, as this essay has surely also implied, the politically decentralized peoples occupying this particular corner of the Uganda Protectorate were not entirely without influence upon the course of policy during the early colonial period. Through the Katsonga affair and successive violent reactions of a sporadic, decentralized kind against Ganda Agent rule, British protectorate officials were forced to make a number of important adjustments to the various administrative patterns wherein Ganda Agents were deployed in eastern Uganda during the later 1900s.

There is a second point here. Besides forcing local modifications to Buganda-style client chieftaincy, decentralized violence during the later 1900s also affected the overall balance of influence at protectorate level of more centralized African societies. Earlier, Kakungulu's kingdom in eastern Uganda had provided a certain counterweight to the Buganda kingdom, but with Kakungulu's transfer to Busoga this counterweight quickly turned to straw. Thenceforth, the Buganda kingdom was to know no institutional equal within the wider Uganda Protectorate. Decentralized violence against Ganda Agents implementing British hut tax policies in eastern Uganda during the 1900s therefore ultimately reinforced rather than undermined the political centrality of the Buganda kingdom legally established by the 1900 Agreement.

There are two final considerations. If the enhanced institutional primacy of the Buganda kingdom within colonial Uganda was one partial but clear consequence of decentralized violence in eastern Uganda during the 1900s, a still more enhanced Ganda enthnocentricity was another. It has been noted elsewhere that Ganda sub-imperialism provoked ethnic reactions among hitherto politically decentralized peoples subjected to its sway.[47] But it would be foolish to ignore the impact upon the Ganda of the reverse traffic in decentralized violence. When George Wilson wrote that Ganda chiefs were 'greatly concerned' about the continuing murders of their countrymen employed in eastern Uganda 'and want to know what we are doing for the[ir] proper protection',[48] he was only referring to the tip of this particular iceberg of ethnic concern, since every descent group and religious denomination in Buganda had sons and daughters among Ganda abroad.

None the less, though immensely significant, decentralized violence was much less embarrassing to British protectorate officials imperially than violence of a centralized sort. Provided that 'police actions' were employed in preference to 'punitive expeditions', Protectorate Commissioners could and did escape metropolitan censure completely. Decentralized violence was simply too decentralized to be significant in London. But in Uganda it was quite another story.

NOTES

1. See my chapter on 'The ending of slavery in Buganda' in Suzanne Miers and Richard Roberts (eds.), *The End of Slavery in Africa* (Madison, Wisconsin, 1988), and Chapter 3 in my forthcoming biography of Semei Kakungulu.
2. The crucial contemporary evidence is Gedge's diary, the relevant volume of which is at Rhodes House Library, Oxford (Ms Brit. Emp. 290, box 6). For further discussions, see my accounts of 'The Muslim revolution in Buganda', *African Affairs* 71 (1972), 54–72, and 'The emergence of politico-religious groupings in late nineteenth-century Buganda', *Journal of African History* 29 (1988), and references cited therein.
3. In: Roger Owen and Bob Sutcliffe (eds.), *Studies in the Theory of Imperialism* (London, 1972), 118–140.
4. Besides Andrew Roberts's article, see John Tosh. *Clan Leaders and Colonial Chiefs in Lango* (Oxford, 1978) and 'Colonial Chiefs in a Stateless Society: A Case-study from Northern Uganda', *Journal of African History* 14, 473–90; and Joan Vincent, *Teso in Transformation* (Berkeley, 1982).
5. The phrase is that of Father L.J. van den Bergh in a letter to Mill Hill, 14 Feb. 1901; quoted in *St Joseph's Advocate* (Spring 1901).
6. 'Annual Report on the Central Province. 1905–06', encl. Boyle to Entebbe, 7 Sept. 1906, Entebbe Archives [hereafter EA]/SMP/975/06.
7. Ibid.
8. Paulo Kagwa, *Omukwano gwa Kabaka Mwanga* [unpublished Luganda MS in Makerere University Library, Kampala, n.d.], 84.
9. Ormsby to Jinja. 1 Nov. 1906, EA/SMP/261/06.
10. Walker to Boyle, 18 Aug. 1906, EA/SMP/946/06. The day was 18 May 1906.
11. Bell to Deputy Commissioner, 24 Aug. 1906, loc.cit.
12. Ibid.
13. Carter to Entebbe, 27 Nov. 1906, loc.cit.
14. Bell, n.d., on Carter, 27 Nov. 1906, loc.cit.
15. Wilson to Walker, 1 Feb. 1907, copy, loc.cit.
16. Purvis to Walker, 2 April 1907, encl. in Walker to Entebbe, 16 April 1907, loc.cit.
17. Tucker to CMS Committee in London, 9 Aug. 1907, CMS Archives, London G3A7/1907b [CMS Archives on Uganda have been transferred since to Birmingham University Library, but file references remain the same].
18. Millar to CMS, London, 7 May 1907, Purvis to same, 9 Sept. 1907, CMS Archives G3A7/1907a and b.
19. Carter to Entebbe, 27 Dec. 1906, EA/SMP/Confidential/76/06.
20. On Liberal distaste for punitive expeditions, see G.H. Mungeam, *British Rule in Kenya 1895–1912* (Oxford, 1966), 155, 173–80; and R. Hyam, *Elgin and Churchill at the Colonial Office 1905–1908* (London, 1969), 207–17.
21. Carter to Entebbe, 27 Dec. 1906, EA/SMP/Confidential/76/06.
22. Minute by Bell, 5 Jan. 1907, loc.cit.
23. Boyle to Entebbe, 6 Jan. 1907, EA/SMP/82/07.
24. Minute by Bell, 19 Feb. 1907, loc.cit.
25. Boyle to Entebbe, 5 March 1907, loc.cit.
26. Wilson, minute, 14 March 1907, loc.cit.
27. Bell, minute, 6 April 1907, loc.cit.
28. Boyle, 'Special Warrant', 6 May 1907, loc.cit.
29. Ormsby, 'Bukedi District Report 1907–1908', n.d. but stamped 'Received 16 May 1908' at Entebbe, EA/SMP/859/08.
30. Ibid.
31. Bell to London, 18 March 1907, copy in EA/A/39/7/07.
32. See H.R. Wallis, *Handbook of Uganda* (London, 1920), 58, for one list; Boyle [April 1907] in EA/SMP/273/07 for another.
33. Coote to Jinja, 17 Oct. 1907, EA/SMP/1293/07.
34. Minute by Wilson, 20 Oct. 1907, loc.cit.

35. See Edward I. Steinhart, *Conflict and Collaboration: The Kingdoms of Western Uganda, 1890–1907* (Princeton, 1977), 210–55; M. Louise Pirouet, *Black Evangelists* (London, 1978), 103–9; Holger Bernt Hansen, *Mission, Church and State in a Colonial Setting* (London, 1984), 396–399; and G.N. Uzoigwe, *Revolution and Revolt in Bunyoro-Kitara* (Kampala, 1970), *passim*.
36. Wilson, 20 Oct. 1907, EA/SMP/1293/07.
37. Cubitt to Entebbe, 26 Nov. 1907, EA/SMP/1572/07.
38. Ibid.
39. Cubitt to Entebbe, 20 Oct. 1907, EA/SMP/1293/07.
40. Daudi Musoke, *Ebyafayo bya Bugisu* (unpublished typescript in Makerere University Library microfilm section, n.d.), 24.
41. Ibid.; also my interview with Salimu Mbogo at Kachumbala, Mbale, 4 Aug. 1965.
42. Minute by Bell, 30 Oct. 1907, EA/SMP/1293/07.
43. *Report by the Governor on a Tour through the Eastern Province*, Cd 4524, 1909. Only two paragraphs – on local European missionary rivalries, and on personal animosity between Semei Kakungulu and the chief minister of the Buganda kingdom, Sir Apolo Kagwa – were omitted from the original text.
44. J.B. Purvis, *Through Uganda to Mount Elgon* (London, 1909), 359.
45. Ibid., 360.
46. See Vincent, *Teso*, 115.
47. Besides the studies cited in note 4, see also my discussion of ' "Tribalism" in eastern Uganda' in P.H. Gulliver (ed.), *Tradition and Transition in East Africa* (London, 1969); and John Tosh, 'Small-scale Resistance in Uganda: The Lango "Rising" at Adwari in 1919', *Azania* 9 (1974), 51–64, a study of much broader interest than its title suggests.
48. See note 34 above.

Spoils of War:
Sub-Imperial Collaboration in South West Africa and New Guinea, 1914–20

by

Colin Newbury

Ever since Richard Jebb discussed the nature of dominion nationalism and the imperial attachment as a developing alliance, historians have been at pains to explore the local and regional differences which gave rise to distinctive attitudes and policies in the developing nation states of the British Empire.[1] The test of the alliance in war clearly changed as well as strengthened the definition of common interests in foreign policy, defence and international trade. Whether wartime consultation, separate signatures to the peace treaties and the acquisition of colonial responsibilities moved the dominions very far towards distinctive formulation of their interests between 1919 and 1939 is open to question. In Australia, it has been argued, security was sought in a territorial buffer zone to the north in New Guinea, rather than foreign treaty systems and international organizations.[2] Much the same might be said of South Africa in the inter-war period, when the western flank of the Union was extended by the Mandate over South West Africa, and attention was turned inwards on the problems of political control in a developing multi-racial society. For both dominions foreign policy was defensive in style and heavily weighted towards the preservation of the high levels of internal investment and external trade that were part of the legacy of the First World War.

It will be argued here that something more than a territorial imperative for reasons of security emerged from Australian and South African insistence on retention of former German colonies. The short-term effects on the formulation of regional foreign policies in both dominions owed much to their appreciation of the cost of military occupation and their evaluation of the economic potential of the occupied territories. In the longer term, experience showed that neither New Guinea nor South West Africa was likely to benefit the dominions' economies, though sectional interests within the merchant and mining communities of both societies might present their case for special treatment in terms of taxation or transport as a 'national' issue. Even less than imperial Germany were the two sub-imperial powers prepared to make extensive state investments in the infrastructure of the Mandates. But other lessons were learned, especially by the Union's recently-created Department of Mines and by Australian mercantile companies, on the benefits and penalties of colonial monopoly.

The immediate focus of that experience was their treatment of German assets in the two territories in quite distinctive ways which parallel their domestic policies towards German properties and residents. The topic of dominion participation in reparations and the opportunities presented to British and American capital investment in former German colonies has been inadequately explored. Yet it was an important consequence of the Versailles settlement. And it raises questions about the direction and limits to sub-imperial collaboration within the British wartime alliance on the marginal battlefields, where the emphasis was on acquisition, rather than destruction, and even entailed a measure of co-operation with the enemy in a colonial conquest.

I

However xenophobic some colonial responses may have been to the presence of international rivals in Southern Africa or the Pacific from the early 1880s, there was little detailed planning on the eve of the war for military operations in neighbouring territories. The Commonwealth had learned to live with the fact of German New Guinea, after taking over the administration of British Papua in 1906. Australians were more nervous of Japan as an Asian power than of the outpost of a European power. Nor is there any evidence of hostility between the Union and German South West Africa which shared a long, undefended frontier at the Orange River and Bechuanaland.

Trade links between the dominions and either of the German colonies were tenuous and poorly developed in the face of German mercantile and shipping competition. There were some Afrikaner settlers in South West Africa and there was a small number of British traders and planters in New Guinea, but there was little British investment. As a major land and mining enterprise, the British-registered South West Africa Company was almost unique in a colony dominated by a dozen German companies and two-thirds of its capital was owned by Germans.[3] A team of businessmen and engineers from Kimberley made a detailed assessment of the territory's diamond industry in 1913, with a view to market co-ordination, rather than competition. And in 1914, on the initiative of the Union's Ministry of Finance, representatives of the German diamond companies agreed to participate in a production cartel together with Union mines.[4] But although the British consul, E. Muller, forwarded regular reports from Luderitzbucht to Pretoria, none of his observations could be construed as preparation for invasion. In German New Guinea, the company manager and planter, F.R. Jolly, who acted as British consul, sent no reports at all to the Foreign Office.

Once war had been declared on their behalf, the South African, Australian and New Zealand governments were invited by a joint naval and military committee of the Imperial General Staff on 5 August 1914 to attack German possessions to neutralize their wireless facilities. The Colonial Office added the phosphate islands of Angaur and Nauru to the list as a useful afterthought. It was hoped, too, the invitation would have the right 'political effect' on South Africa, where there was a serious division in Botha's Cabinet on the necessity for any participation in the war at all. The dominions were reminded, however, that it would be for the imperial government to dispose of any occupied territory at a peace settlement.[5]

The Australians and New Zealanders accepted at once. Western Samoa was occupied at the end of August; the radio on Nauru was destroyed; and a hastily equipped expeditionary force was landed on New Britain and captured the wireless station. On 17 September 1914 Acting-Governor Haber surrendered German possessions in Melanesia to Brigadier Holmes with full honours of war and an assurance of full pay for officers and officials. Many of the administrative officials agreed to serve at their posts in the central services, but most were shipped out with military personnel to Australia and to Germany. Even so, the terms were considered unduly generous by the Department of Defence in Melbourne and by the Committee of Imperial Defence in London, where application was made for a refund from Germany through neutral channels, before any salaries were paid.[6]

Apart from a few incidents of looting and flogging, the plantation and trading economy of German New Guinea was delivered into Australian hands with a minimum of recrimination. German planters and merchants continued business in co-operation with Australian shippers, under Holmes's military administration. German labour controls were enforced, recruitment expanded, and military expeditions were used to counter resistance. The masters changed, but 'all boys and kanakas . . . were told that the situation was just the same as before'.[7]

By contrast with this easy takeover, operations against South West Africa cost considerably more blood and treasure and a near civil war. Plans for a joint military and naval offensive across the Orange River and along the coast were delayed because of a shortage of arms and lack of co-operation between the newly-created defence department and the naval commander-in-chief at the Cape, Rear-Admiral King-Hall.[8] Rifles were rushed in from the Straits Settlements and Hong Kong, and Swakopmund was bombarded and Luderitzbucht occupied by a small force in mid-September 1914. But the split between Botha's ministry and Hertzog's Nationalist opposition was compounded by the defection of senior staff officers with troops from the Free State and the Transvaal. From 12 October 1914 the Union was under martial law, and what had begun as a 'party quarrel' between Afrikaners developed into a poorly co-ordinated campaign by nearly 11,000 rebels to neutralize South Africa's war effort.

In the end, the *opstand* was put down by Afrikaners, leaving Botha and Smuts free in December 1914 to mobilize 30,000–40,000 men against Major Franke's 6,000 colonial troops and reservists. Despite differences of opinion between Botha and Governor-General Buxton over whether to encourage a revolt by the Rehoboth Bastards (they were told to keep quiet), imperial and colonial co-operation by land and sea was not in doubt from then on. The Union Jack was raised over Windhuk in May with its wireless station still intact. Before the end of Botha's northern campaign against the remnants of German forces, it was also agreed that South Africa would intern 900 officers and men 'with permanent domicile' in the Protectorate and allow 4,000 reservists to return to their farms and homes. Other men of military age and some medical and nursing personnel were repatriated through the Netherlands. According to the terms made with Acting-Governor Seitz, 9 July 1915, a message was sent to the Kaiser announcing that officers were permitted to keep their arms and horses and the reservists their rifles as a protection against former subjects. In all, the Union's campaigns cost more casualties putting down the rebellion than in capturing German territory.[9]

What the South Africans got for their efforts was a massive land area of some 332,000 square miles with a population of 228,000 Africans in a closely administered 'police zone' and the more distant Ovamboland, Okavango and Kaokoveld regions of settlement. Farmers, miners, traders and officials of European origins numbered 14,830, before repatriations in 1919. Money had been poured in by the imperial government to make good the conquest of the Herero and the Bondelswart, and about £15 million had been expended to construct ports and a railway system linking farms, mines and the administrative capital. Current revenues in the last years of German rule came principally from taxes on diamond production and export, bringing gross annual revenue including military expenditure and savings to £2 million for 1914/15.[10]

With a land area of about 90,000 square miles the New Guinea mainland and its archipelago of islands to the east presented formidable topographical obstacles to any imperial power which sought to rule an estimated population of four to five hundred thousand inhabitants. The Germans under the New Guinea Company and the imperial administration of 1900 to 1914 controlled little outside the coastal periphery. At enormous cost they had alienated over half a million acres and held about 150,000 acres in plantations, including the estates of the missions. Total agricultural and mercantile assets were valued at £5 million, serviced and protected by a small colonial state which depended on customs duties, head taxes and subsidies to make up annual budget deficits.[11]

After the partition of the northern Solomons in 1899 which concluded the Anglo-German division of Melanesia, the main attraction of German New Guinea for Australian commercial interests lay in cheaper labour costs than in surrounding British territory and in the carrying trade and agency work for companies importing and exporting through Sydney. Burns, Philp and Co. expanded their plantation investment from Papua and the Solomons into Bougainville and Buka in 1912 and 1913, setting up a subsidiary, the Choiseul Plantation Company, in the hope of both breaking into the local copra trade in competition with Nord-Deutscher Lloyd and escaping from more onerous land regulations in the British Protectorate.[12]

Consequently, when the expeditionary force led the way, Australian mercantilism was not far behind. Burns Philp dispatched their islands inspector, W.H. Lucas, in September 1914 with a cargo of supplies on the *Moresby* and instructions to co-operate with German merchants and replace their agents interned in Australia. Lucas adroitly directed the local carrying trade away from Far Eastern ports to Sydney by using his effective monopoly of transport; and in 1916 the company was accorded all agency work for German planters. In Melbourne, the attorney-general's department conceded that this advantage was not 'trading with the enemy' under Commonwealth legislation. More reluctantly, the Foreign Office, the Board of Trade and the Colonial Office recognized that the Australian company was needed to service the requirements of an occupied territory and was a 'special case' under the Trading with the Enemy (Extension of Powers) Act of 1915. They did, however, raise the question of reciprocal trade advantages for Japanese allies, something which Melbourne chose to ignore.[13] In any case, Lucas had other ends in view and began to make an inventory of companies and plantations for future confiscation. At his head office in Sydney, the company chairman, Sir James Burns, went further and framed a memorandum for the governor-general on Australia's 'natural destiny' in the Pacific and the place of Burns Philp in Melanesia as a mercantile bulwark against foreign competition.[14]

In the meantime, the military administration under Holmes and his successor, Colonel Pethebridge, pursued a policy of pragmatism and economic self-interest which reassured German civilians and encouraged reinvestment of earnings from plantations. By the terms of the capitulation existing currencies and commercial laws were recognized; the exchange rate was fixed at one shilling to the mark; the liquid assets of the German administration – amounting to no more than £25,000 – were taken over; and the local treasury performed the functions of a savings bank and transferred funds to Sydney agents, until a branch of the Commonwealth Bank was set up in 1916. Then German paper currency was withdrawn at the old rate of exchange and the silver-nickel specie of the German period continued at par with the Australian shilling, despite pressure from the Commonwealth to have it devalued. For local trade and payment of labourers' wages, the white man's coin of whatever origin kept its parity in New Guinea; and the fact that the King's head resembled that of the bearded Administrator Pethebridge only confirmed the soundness of the 'new marks'.[15]

As a result of Australian indulgence with the local plantation economy and command of the carrying trade, New Guinea imports and exports rose in value from £225,416 in 1915/16 to £1.2 million in 1919/20, nearly all of which passed through Australian ports. Copra exports doubled 1913 tonnages, though very little was processed in Australia. In practice, this monopoly of trans-shipments proved something of a bottleneck in competition with wartime shipping space for wheat. But the idea that the production of the captured territory might compensate for the high cost of administration took root in the minds of merchants, politicians and the military officials who contributed to the *Rabaul Record* which ran regular features on the attractions of tropical agriculture. Both Holmes and Pethebridge were soon convinced that the future of the territory was to become a British possession. Palm tree plantings doubled under their rule, and indentured labour increased from 17,529 in 1914 to 27,728 at the end of the military administration in 1921. German labour ordinances were consolidated and applied with the usual penal sanctions, standard wages, long contracts of two to three years, deferred pay and restriction of casual work. Employers' rights to inflict corporal punishment were, it is true, suspended at first and then tolerated for most of the military period until the formal abolition of flogging in 1919. But an open market in traded copra was curtailed for the benefit of planters and exporters; and the head tax for unemployed males was extended intermittently, but with measurable effect on recruitment and production.

The growing appreciation of the soldier-administrators and the merchant-shippers that there was a prize of war in the making was matched by efforts of the Sydney Chamber of Commerce to encourage import substitution for goods formerly imported from the Central Powers and, more extensively, by the general review of Australia's commercial destiny in the Inter-State Commission of 1916. The evidence heard was mercantilist and aimed at securing trade once in German hands. It was consistent with the predatory views of the economic conference of Allied Powers in Paris in June 1916; and much of its conclusions had been foreshadowed by William Hughes in his campaign to undermine the foundations of German overseas investment by ending the metal combines in Australia.[16] The presence of Hughes at the Paris conference confirmed the work of the commissioners in Melbourne and made it certain that the occupied colony would become a target for Australian shipping companies and would-be planters. Once it was known, too, that the cost of the military occupation of New Guinea (close on £1 million, 1914–21) was never likely to be covered by local revenues, there was an added incentive for claiming compensation.[17]

This was small beer, compared with the cost of the South West African campaign. By the middle of 1915 the Union government knew that there would be a deficit of £2 million, on top of military expenditure amounting to over £8.7 million for all operations in Africa and abroad. Almost 4,000 reservists and their families had to be resettled; and about one third of the civilian population was living off rations distributed through British and German officials. Exports had ceased to produce any taxes or exchange from abroad during the campaign, when the German administration had financed itself by overdrafts on the banks, by commandeering goods and livestock and by the issue of 'Seitz' notes which were not negotiable outside the Protectorate.

To prevent total collapse, four German banks were allowed to reopen alongside two South African banks which made advances to companies and traders. Credits of 14 million marks held for transmission to Germany were left intact by the occupying force and were used to fund the local Land Bank. The Deutsche Afrika Bank was allowed to obtain £300,000 in remittances through New York which were used by German merchants to pay for imports from the Union 'at considerably enhanced prices'.[18] They soon exhausted this source of currency and were left with marks devalued at 29 to the pound and the unacceptable 'Seitz'.

By these means the white community lived largely on capital and credit, until the export of hides, skins, wool and copper ore revived at the end of 1915. Union banks made advances against 'town and farm properties' to encourage a thriving import trade through Cape Town merchants. But without diamond exports no profits tax was received at all during the year, and a loss of revenue equivalent to £894,000 had to be made up from votes of Union departments. The Administrator, E.H.L. Gorges, expected a continuous deficit.

Reopening the mines for production was, therefore, a priority of the administration in co-operation with German personnel. One of General Botha's first proclamations prohibited casual prospecting in the Luderitzbucht fields, where there were company titles to be respected. Only white labour was employed in the repair of plant damaged during the war. After some argument with Acting-Governor Seitz, the administration managed to recover 75,000 carats of pre-war stock hidden during the evacuation of Windhuk, including a stone of 40 carats worth £5,000.

Copper, too, was encouraged by grants, but labour was in short supply. Of the 5,000 Ovambo employed on six months' contracts by mines, railways and farmers, no more than 2,000 were prepared to work for monthly wages of £1 and food paid by their former rulers. Both the Khan copper mine at Arandis and the Otavi Mine and Railway Company produced concentrates at about half their 1913 levels, but export was uncertain, because the American Smelting and Refining Works at New York made unacceptable demands for treatment charges and because the administration insisted that smelted ore should be sent to England for sale.

Apart from one diamond mine which resumed production towards the end of 1915, the local diamond industry was slow to recover. Output for 1916 amounted to no more than 12 per cent of pre-war production by weight. Parcels were sent to London, but no sales took place, and the mines remained dependent for working expenses on loans from the Union banks. For a territory which earned three-fifths of its ordinary revenue from diamond taxation, the collapse of the market was disastrous, and copper exports did little to help.

The main reason for this fiscal poverty was that the South African government and its military administration were not free to sell diamonds overseas. From January 1915 a War Trade Advisory

Committee under Sir Francis Hopwood sought to stop enemy supplies of bulk and strategic commodities; and from June 1915 a special committee was set up by the Board of Trade for the War Trade Department to monitor the diamond traffic, on the advice of Alfred Mosely, a former Cape diamond merchant and confidant of Cecil Rhodes. Mosely warned that there was a clandestine export in industrial stones through Holland from the six or seven London firms specializing in this branch of the trade whom he tended to brand as suspect because of their German origins. Dutch dealers in industrial stones were 'taking them back in their pockets'.[19]

While they did not accept all of Mosely's allegations, the Board and the War Trade Department agreed that the large stocks of South West diamonds held by the London diamond syndicate should be frozen for the duration of the war, and that the export of rough stones, whether suitable for gems or for industrial purposes, had to be controlled by licence and by the establishment of an expert committee to monitor traffic to Holland. In order to enforce this control, Mosely advised that the Dutch dealers and cutters could be refused South African goods. The Board concluded that centralized control through London was the only effective way of preventing a leakage to Germany through neutral countries. Therefore, the Colonial Office was told that 'our Dominions should prohibit the export of any diamonds cut or uncut except to the United Kingdom'. Because expert advice was needed to decide which types of stones exported to the Continent were suitable for industrial purposes, the Board appointed Mosely and the leading diamond merchants, V.A. Litkie and Ludwig Breitmeyer, head of the syndicate, to monitor the trade. A conference with the War Trade Department and the Order in Council of 30 July 1915 confirmed the prohibition on the import of South West African stones and the export of rough diamonds except under licence, granted after a certificate of approval by the diamond export committee. A similar committee consisting of dealers trusted by Mosely was set up in Holland to monitor the trade from that end through the British consulate in Amsterdam.[20]

This effective stranglehold on an already centralized market was welcomed by the London diamond syndicate which had been unable to come to terms with the German *Diamanten Regie* for a regular share of South West exports and had to buy them in competition with Antwerp. Similarly, the syndicate had no contract with the Premier (Transvaal) Diamond Mining Company in which the Union government had a 60 per cent interest and which preferred to market separately through its own office in London. There was now a possibility that both sources could be brought into the system of contracts which operated for the De Beers and New Jagersfontein companies which supplied most of the world's rough gemstones.

At the outbreak of the war, moreover, there had been a glut on the market. An accumulation of some £3 million in small diamonds was divided between the Regie, an Antwerp syndicate and the London syndicate. With this accumulation frozen or restricted, a dangerous competition ended for the moment; and the syndicate readily accepted a prohibition on the sale of South West diamonds, provided this applied to the Union government as well. In February 1916, Bonar Law, as Secretary of State for Colonies, reminded the South Africans through the governor-general that no such sales could be made, so long as stocks in London were locked up.[21] News of German smuggling through Scandinavia for export to the United States and clandestine exports by members of the Defence Force in South West Africa reinforced the unwillingness of the War Trade Department to tolerate a market for South West goods which could not be distinguished from German pre-war stocks.

To explain this message in detail, Mosely toured South Africa in May 1916 warning against separate deals through Antwerp, but recommending acceptance of tenders by the London syndicate for restricted monthly deliveries of South West production to keep the mines operating. On his return, Mosely was sent to Holland to arrange for the cutting of these stones by trusted firms. And from these manufacturers, advised the Colonial Office, cut stones were to be returned to London for sale in North and South America by brokers approved by the diamond committee.[22]

After sample parcels were sent to Mosely at the end of the year, the Union government and the administrator had no choice but to accept this outlet, while pressing for a ceiling of 50,000 carats a month. On 3 March 1917, the government through the mines department reluctantly concluded its first agreement with the London diamond syndicate to deliver all monthly production from South West Africa up to 330,000 carats a year only, at a basic price of 46s 6d per carat with profit-sharing on sales. As an earnest of this contract for sales through a monopoly channel, the syndicate demanded the captured 'Seitz' diamonds as well.

A second reason for the dearth of diamond income was that the new administration did not understand the working of the Imperial Diamond Taxation Ordinance of 1912 which required a provisional and final assessment of the amount to be paid by companies at the rate of 60 per cent on sales with a return of 70 per cent of working costs. No such assessments were made for 1915 and 1916. The first assessment for tax was not made till the second half of 1917; and it was not paid over until the fiscal year 1919/20, while the companies waited on their income from sales abroad and disputed the administration's calculations.

Consequently, the administration of the captured colony made very little from its major source of income for the rest of the war. Apart from the delay in recovering taxes, there was a muddle over methods of evaluation applied in Luderitzbucht and in London which divided the South African Treasury from the Department of Mines. The department refused, moreover, to hand over the Seitz stones and reserved a right (contrary to the contract) to sell excess production elsewhere. The minister, F.S. Malan, and the South West producers considered the syndicate's commission of 10 per cent on re-sales too high. Suspicion of profiteering from rising diamond prices fed a departmental prejudice against the syndicate and strengthened the view that the Premier mine and South West companies would be sacrificed for the sake of sales of high-quality gem roughs from De Beers and New Jagersfontein in which there was a dominant share ownership by London merchants. From 1915, departmental officials led by the Government Mining Engineer, R.N. Kotze, looked approvingly at the German system of marketing through a 'control board' and seriously considered full or partial nationalization of the diamond industry in the captured territory and in the Union.[23]

II

Such forward planning raised long-term questions about the eventual fate of German assets in the colonies and elsewhere. The possibility of retaining the captured territories, voiced by Holmes at Rabaul as early as December 1914, and implicit in much of the Union's departmental minutes on South West Africa from 1916, was taken up at much higher levels, when Sir Lewis Harcourt presented a memorandum to Cabinet in March 1915 titled 'The Spoils'. For the Colonial Secretary it was 'out of the question to part with any of the territories now in the occupation of New Zealand and Australia'. South West Africa, as yet only half occupied, was also to be retained 'as part of the British Empire', unless used as a pawn to obtain Portuguese East Africa – the 'missing link' between the Cape and Cairo.[24]

Andrew Fisher, in his last year of office as Labour Prime Minister, and Hughes, who was about to replace him, would have shared this view, to keep out Japanese from the islands as much as the Germans. Fisher willingly accepted the Colonial Office ruling that the equator divided Japanese and Australian spheres of occupation in German Melanesia and Micronesia, encouraged by the sympathetic attitude of the governor-general, Munro-Ferguson, towards sub-imperial aspirations. And the governor-general, in turn, was influenced by the arguments presented by James Burns for acquisition of the plantations and a monopoly supply of bulk cargo for carriers in the Pacific – a point repeated and emphasized by the trade commission of 1916.[25]

But Hughes and the Australian attorney-general, Garran, like their counterparts, Smuts and J. de V. Roos in South Africa, were well aware that such speculation depended on the terms of the peace treaty. In the meantime, Australia enforced its advantages through war regulations to monopolize New Guinea's transit trade. And Hughes, in co-operation with Lucas who became his personal adviser on island affairs, extended mercantile contracts with German firms for a further six months from April 1918, refusing all requests from the Japanese and the Dutch to take up cargo Burns Philp could not carry. For, with an armistice in sight, there was a risk that the Germans might turn once again to other carriers operating from the Far East, before a peace treaty decided their fate.

While the Prime Minister kept rivals at bay, Lucas prepared a plan in June 1919 for a commission to take stock of German assets and run them, as soon as Australia was given this authority.[26]

At the same time, quite a different scheme for buying out the Germans through an 'Anglo-Australian company' for about £2.5 million was prepared by Burns with the support of the acting Prime Minister, W.A. Watt, at the end of 1918. An even more ambitious project to float a 'British Australian Pacific Estates Company' for £5 million under the direction of Lord Inchcape, Lord Leverhulme and Burns with total control of New Guinea's copra exports, depots and shipping was forwarded to the governor-general and Lord Milner.[27]

It was, moreover, assumed that there would be a total expropriation, when Lucas and Atlee Hunt, secretary of the Home and Territories Department, wrote a majority opinion opposing amalgamation with Papua for a royal commission report at the end of 1919. This investigation into the future of New Guinea which they carried out with Lieutenant-Governor J.H.P. Murray was decisive on a number of issues. It was agreed German properties should be sold on preferential terms to Australian servicemen; and they agreed on the need for protective tariffs and subsidized shipping to safeguard Australia's carrying trade with the two territories. But Murray's argument for amalgamation was rejected, because Papua's laws and labour costs might prevail over the harsher and cheaper system continued under military rule – 'influenced by and imbued with German principles'. Any possibility of assimilation to a 'British tradition' was firmly set aside by Brigadier-General Johnston, as military administrator, in his unpublished submissions to the commissioners which emphasized the need for high head taxes and government-assisted recruitment to maintain the production and value of the plantations.[28]

The majority report confirmed the strongly-held opinions of Hughes who had argued Australia's case at the Imperial War Cabinet in December 1918 and accepted the mandate compromise in Paris in January 1919, with the full intention of applying the Australian Navigation Act of 1913 in all its restrictive clauses to New Guinea. When Hughes returned to Australia, the government decided to set up a board to manage the estates on the lines suggested by Lucas. The Peace Treaty Act passed by the Commonwealth Parliament did not come into effect, however, till 10 January 1920. Atlee Hunt urged action. Rules for liquidation were framed in March 1920; and an expropriation ordinance vested German properties in a public trustee from 1 September 1920, under the 'economic clauses' of Articles 121, 122 and 297 of the treaty. As chairman of the new expropriation board, Lucas was already busy at Rabaul impounding records and closing stores.

German civilians were repatriated. And as the board took over in the last months of 1920, the secretary to the prime minister's department, Percy Deane, doubled as custodian of expropriated properties. Thus, Hughes was able to keep a close watch on the territory's plunder, assisted by Lucas at Melbourne and the board's business manager, ex-consul F.R. Jolley at Rabaul. In accordance with Hughes's wartime promises, returned soldiers swelled the ranks of clerks, overseers, store managers and assistants hired to bring order into the confusion left by the departing Germans. To keep plantations up to strength, major recruiting drives had to be undertaken. The five German trading companies which had funded the planters had to be supported by advances through the board from the public trustee and the Commonwealth Bank for the period of the board's operations, 1920–27. After seven years of public management separate from the civil administration, the German properties were valued at £3 million and were judged ready for sale by tender. With rising copra prices and keen competition for bulking facilities, the 470 plantations, trade stations and undeveloped blocks of land fetched £3.4 million advanced by the banks and mercantile companies on behalf of themselves and 343 soldier-settlers whose tied mortgages burdened the local economy through the 1930s.

In South Africa a very different policy prevailed over the intimations of state intervention from within the mines department. Expropriation was not seriously considered, and the fate of German assets was closely bound up with the location and seizure of German-owned shares in the Union and abroad, invested in British mining companies and in German-registered companies.

From 1917, the British advisory committee on trading with the enemy took the line that capital invested by Germans in British companies in the Union or South West Africa would have to be vested in the public trustee, if located in England, or in the Union's custodian of enemy property. Any scheme to purchase enemy shares cheaply was rejected as 'premature'. But the Board of Trade conceded to Edmund Davis, the Australian-born mining engineer and chairman of the South West Africa Company, that enemy shareholders might be bought out through the *Discontogesellschaft* 'in some neutral town'.[29] The Colonial Office disapproved of this clandestine dealing, but Davis's company acted as 'manager' for the German copper mines, and the example set a precedent for other deals with mining companies as the war came to an end.

German properties seized within the Union fell under the custodian, W.H. Fowle, who reported in June 1917 on assets worth £12.2 million, including about 100 business properties, which were wound up or in the course of liquidation. As in Australia, there was considerable discretion about who was interned. Of 649 German entrepreneurs, 335 went into detention, compared with 5,400 in the Commonwealth.[30] The custodians in both dominions also took over shares and share dividends paid by German companies or by British companies to Germans. But none of this touched the status of German companies in South West Africa. And apart from the overtures made by Davis, there were no moves on their share capital, until the first relaxation of the wartime prohibition against dealing in ex-enemy shares early in 1919 in the United Kingdom.

Significantly, this was led by the purchase for Consolidated Mines

Selection of all enemy shares held by the public trustee which were offered at cost to other shareholders.[31] Consolidated Mines had been formed by Dunkelsbuhler and Co. who included the Oppenheimers and W.L. Honnold of Anglo American for the management of gold interests on Far East Rand properties. Indeed, participatory rights in Consolidated's leases had led to the formation of Anglo in 1917, as a way of finding sources of American capital for the enormous investments required for deep-level mining. In July 1919, the British Treasury formally permitted sales of ex-enemy shares by British subjects overseas which opened the way for other deals.

Unfortunately, the course of capital acquisitions in South West Africa is less easy to chart, because of the timing of negotiations with German proprietors and the decent interval allowed by the South African government, before approving the take-over of the diamond mining companies. Although a case has been made by Ernest Oppenheimer's biographers for his initiative in investing through Anglo in South West diamonds, it is more likely that the idea of outright purchase of German assets originated with his partner and ex-politician, Henry Hull, and the Cape businessman, Sir David de Villiers Graaff, who organized a trust to raise money and approached the German managers at Luderitzbucht. Oppenheimer was in Europe early in 1919 and accompanied Smuts to the Versailles conference as an observer, and he did not return to South Africa until the initial overtures had been made by Hull. He was aware, however, that both Smuts and Botha approved of the application of American capital to the problem of German assets which had not been taken over by the custodian.[32] Possibly all three – Hull, Graaff and Oppenheimer – left hurriedly for Europe together with Dr Erich Lubbert, W. Bradow and A. Stauch for the managers (only the movements of Hull are verifiable from passenger lists), arriving in early September to negotiate with German representatives in the Hague. There, the details of company titles were obtained and options were arranged for the sale of the mines for shares and cash, at the current rate of the devalued mark, without reference to any custodian and before formal acceptance of the terms of the Peace Treaty Ratification Bill and the Mandate Bill which were introduced to the Cape Assembly from 8 September.

Notice of the success of this coup reached the financial press on 6 September, when it was announced that a new 'South West Diamond Company' registered at the Cape had acquired the property rights of one of the German companies in the Luderitz area, but nothing more was said, while the Peace Treaty was being debated.[33] On 27 September, the government announced its method of disposing of enemy assets in the Union, where property of resident Germans was to be returned, the claims of allied nationals were to be paid and the balance – some £9 million – was not finally decided till 1920. None of this included South West property.

Such property was clearly not to be expropriated, while finance was being arranged for its purchase. The governor-general, Lord Buxton, toured South West Africa in 1919 and reassured German managers and workers on this point.[34] In August, South West's diamond mines were automatically included in plans for a revival of the 1914 quota agreement between the Union mines and the Germans, as part of the negotiations with the diamond syndicate, under the auspices of the minister of mines. The first full announcement of the takeover reached the press in London and South Africa on 1 November with the statement that Anglo had control of all the South West diamond companies. Reuters reported that H.C. Hull had completed the purchase at the Hague for £3.5 million paid by Anglo and other 'financial groups' for 'transference from Berlin to the Union' of the diamond fields. In the middle of the month there was a hitch over company titles to land owned by the *Deutsche Kolonial Gesellschaft* and Messrs Bredow, Lubbert, Scholz and Stauch were recalled to South Africa to fix the selling price of shares to be paid to smaller shareholders.[35]

Later evidence suggests that the deal was concluded in early September, but the formal agreement was dated 23 November for the sale of eleven German companies already held by the Hull-Graaff trust for a nominal sum of £3.5 million in shares and cash on behalf of Consolidated Diamond Mines of South West Africa Ltd., registered at the Cape later on 9 February 1920. The real price was much less (£2.8 million) because of the depreciation of the mark in 1919. By a second agreement, 24 November 1919, the obligation of the *Deutsche Kolonial Gesellschaft* to pay royalties to older proprietors which had also been acquired by the trust was transferred to the new company, and the South West Finance Corporation was set up separately from Consolidated Diamond Mines, on 13 April 1920, to administer these rights. The directors of Consolidated and the Corporation were identical and included Hull, Graaff, Bredow, Lubbert and Stauch.[36]

The whole transfer was made more mysterious than necessary by the government's evident desire to keep enemy assets in the captured colony a separate issue from its treatment of similar assets in the Union. The timing of announcements was, therefore, important. The documents released in the form of a parliamentary paper confirm that purchases were made before the formation of Consolidated Mines, but no dates of purchase were stated in Oppenheimer's letter to Malan, 31 October 1919. The purpose of the letter, in any case, was not to clarify the affair but to seek a formal assurance from the government that all titles would be recognized (though the German land registers were closed and they could not be confirmed). Permission was sought to make a cash payment to German owners overseas who had already received down payments for options from the trust. A formal letter from Administrator Gorges stated the titles were sound, although the *Kolonial Gesellschaft* concession on which all others rested was under investigation. The mines department, though not the minister, gave the deal a formal blessing in a letter from a junior official, adding for general consumption that the mines were to be worked in the interests of the Protectorate and the Union.[37]

Everything points, then, to a hasty conclusion to the transfer, before the terms of the Treaty or the Mandate had been ratified by the South African Assembly and before the method of handling ex-enemy assets through a custodian of enemy property had been formally decided. For the purpose of capitalization of Consolidated Diamonds and the amalgamation of the properties, German assets were regarded as transferred from 1 October 1919, while the capital for the venture was still being arranged through J.P. Morgan and Company on behalf of Anglo. A hurried proclamation (No. 59 of 1919) brought the territory under Union mining laws and cancelled German company concessions held from the *Kolonial Gesellschaft*, following a report in September 1919 by a 'minerals concession commission' which accepted the validity of the original land titles, though it continued to investigate the complex relations between the concessionary company and the colonial state which the government of the Mandate inherited. News of the successful flotation of Consolidated Diamonds was conveyed to government departments immediately in October, while the more formal exchange of notes between Oppenheimer and Malan on the proposed amalgamation of the German companies was safely delayed till the end of the month for release to Parliament. The essential position, as noted by Gorges in his letter of 3 November to Malan, was that although 'power is given in the Peace Treaty to eliminate German interests by expropriation and the transfer of proceeds to the Allied Reparation Commission . . . the Union Government have decided not to avail themselves of these powers in respect of property in South-West Africa'.[38]

The transfer meant that the principal prize was owned by a South African company approved by the government and the administrator, before the question of the fate of other enemy assets had to be resolved. There were considerable difficulties in the way of handling this complex spread of investments liable for seizure and accounting against reparations under Article 297 of the Peace Treaty. The British Treasury thought the dominions might 'pool' such assets, but the Colonial Office took the line that they would have to sort this out for themselves. The Union was entitled, in any case, to hand back £1,250,000 to Germans resident in South Africa at the outbreak of war and to pay claims amounting to £1 million which counted against reparations. In the Union, Smuts laid down that none of the subsequent discussion of assets would touch the titles to diamond properties 'the validity of which was recognized by the German Government'. The custodian of enemy property, W.H. Fowle, stood out against any scheme for transferring shares of companies registered in the United Kingdom and suggested that the balance of £9 millions in his hands should be held for 30 years as a forced loan, in return for government stock. In this way, Germans in South Africa and abroad whose assets had been confiscated would receive 'far more favourable treatment than Germans in any other part of the Allied world'.[39]

This plan commended itself to Smuts, who took sweeping powers under a proclamation of 27 August 1920 to call in all enemy assets in the form of shares held in South Africa or overseas which conflicted with the Board of Trade's policy of treating 'English assets' as the property of its own public trustee. The gesture did not result in any swapping of enemy shares with the dominion; and Rand mining companies were reluctant to assist in the arduous business of tracing ownership of bearer shares. But Smuts was able to announce to the Assembly in August 1920 the comprehensive search for share assets and the much milder treatment of property in the Union as a forced loan paying four per cent. In South West Africa, private property was left untouched, except for £700,000 which had accumulated in dividends from the mining companies, and these were treated in the same way as assets in the Union.[40] There were doubts in the Reparations Commission whether Article 297 could be interpreted in this way. For the Union had not treated enemy property as a South African asset acquired by war, but as a debt of the Union to its German owners: 'It would be anomalous to reckon a liability of an Allied Power to German nationals as being something to which that Power has to give credit to Germany'. But no enquiry was held, as requested by the British delegation's legal service.[41] And although 6,347 military, officials and police, plus a number of 'undesirables' were repatriated, 5,918 Germans remained in South West Africa and grew to 7,855 by immigration at the date of the 1921 census.

III

What began, then, as an imperial exercise in capturing strategic communications ended in the acquisition by expropriation or sale of the productive assets of two colonial economies. There was more to the war in Melanesia or the Namib desert than extension of territory for defence. South Africa had no need of a buffer zone. There was no threat from the Portuguese, and no claims were laid by the dominion to Tanganyika, after the East African campaign. The only danger presented by South West Africa lay in the subversion of Afrikaner loyalties within the Union among those who saw the British as traditional enemies.

In Australia's case there was an argument for regarding New Guinea and its archipelago as a frontier zone, but only if the exclusive immigration and mercantilist policies of the Commonwealth were extended north to keep out Asians as well as Germans. With an identity of interest between Australia's major Pacific carrier and a government dedicated to reviving and extending the 1913 Navigation Act there was little difficulty in formulating a chauvinistic policy to accompany Hughes' onslaught on German mineral interests in the Commonwealth and his populist promises of rewards for servicemen.

In both territories, moreover, there were strategic commodities which fell under the regulations of the British War Trade Department which aimed at cutting off German supplies of raw materials, stopping contraband through neutrals and capturing the marketing and manufacturing base for German industry which by 1916 was thought to be closely linked with German possession of colonies. Copra as a source of vegetable oil was important for the transfer of the oil-seed crushing industry into British hands, but it was not essential to Australia. War Trade Department regulations ensured that the Australian supply was not exported to the United States until 1919, in return for a less than strict interpretation of legislation against trading with the enemy and lengthy trans-shipment through Australian ports. Diamonds, too, were recognized as strategically important for wartime industry, for the first time. Under the Order in Council of July 1915, the imperfect central channel organized by the London diamond syndicate by 1913 was perfected and the South African government was forced to concede to the merchants a contract for all production from South West companies and the Premier mine. Separate sales to Antwerp or Amsterdam were stopped; and there was no cutting industry in the United States to offer an alternative outlet. Under pressure from the South African Treasury the Department of Mines accepted this contractual bottleneck with bad grace, working to extend state control on the model of the German *Regie* and to establish a cutting industry in South Africa itself.

There was, then, collaboration in the alliance at the periphery, in the shadow of much greater events and heavier sacrifices on the battlefields of Europe. Within the military administrations of the two territories there was also co-operation from German civilians who ran the plantation and trading economy in New Guinea and revived the mining industry in South West Africa. At the level of daily operations, after the flags had been changed, there was, too, a measure of common interest between Europeans as ruling minorities in Melanesia and the Namib desert. Possibly, this condition was understood more quickly by South Africans in the Defence Force than by the incoming Australians (there were fewer anti-German incidents at Windhuk than at Rabaul). But the Australians soon learned to allow the German system to work to their advantage, refusing ultimately to change its authoritarian ways by amalgamation with Papua. Evidence was collected in both territories on German colonial 'atrocities', and there was a demand for confiscation of assets, following German seizure of credit balances in Belgian banks in February 1917. But none of this was pushed very far, and labour regulations were hardly changed, where they were most severe, in New Guinea. The official history of the Australian occupation written by Seaforth Mackenzie, the advocate-general, was a most unwarlike tome.[42]

Where the two territories differed most was in the manner and style of their treatment of German residents and their properties. The method used by Australia was expulsion and state expropriation, in common with New Zealand, Samoa and the British and French Cameroons. The plantations and trading companies were run for reparations with their titles vested ultimately in the custodian. Australian suspicions of overseas 'combines', whether British or German, and political pledges to the soldiers ensured that James Burns's scheme for buying out the Germans and establishing a grand mercantile and plantation monopoly stood no chance of acceptance. The South Africans were no less suspicious of monopolies directed from overseas. But Smuts welcomed capital investment through South African registered companies which allowed Anglo-American and Ernest Oppenheimer an opportunity to expand from gold back into diamonds. The technique of acquiring the German companies was locally inspired in the Cape Town trust set up by Hull and Graaff, though the financial backing and organisation of Consolidated Diamonds was essentially on the pattern of Anglo's entry into the Far East Rand.[43] The Germans were allowed to stay and many immigrated from 1919. The whole operation, moreover, was kept quite separate from the custodian's administration of German assets in the Union.

The question remains, then, whether the two dominions acted as 'ideal collaborators' (in Robinsonian terms), as a result of the wartime crisis acting on the imperial relationship. What the example reveals, perhaps, is that there were different levels of 'collaboration' between the imperial metropole and its allies, on the one hand, and within the captured colonies, on the other. There is an important typological distinction to be made between co-operation of newly-acquired subjects within a system of government, in order to keep it functioning with a minimum of social and economic disruption, after conquest; and, secondly, the patron and client relationship in international affairs which requires a measure of subordination to the senior partner to achieve common aims.

In its primary sense, a collaborative system was one of the oldest ploys in the imperial book, and the Germans fell into this role mainly at the level of production and services. A few senior officials were co-opted, but they were soon replaced at Rabaul and Windhuk, while civilians went about their business for the duration of the war. At the peace settlement, policies diverged: South Africa retained its German population (just as the Dutch had been retained after an earlier conquest); while the Australians turned to another imperial alternative – soldier settlement on the frontier, as a political reward and a reparation.

The dominions' relationship with the senior partner is another matter and cannot be considered as a system of imperial government, given the degree of autonomous evolution and the failure of imperial federation. The benefits arising from a degree of subordination in treaty-making or lack of extra-territorial jurisdiction lay principally in privileged access to sources of capital, the links of trade and transport within an imperial business network, and imperial defence. If the revised balance sheets of imperial funding are to be believed, the junior partners had done pretty well out of this alliance based on common laws and concepts of government, economic benefits and kinship.[44] When the chips were down and the alliance was under threat, they gave their manpower, accepting a large measure of imperial direction in three areas of wartime control: in the overall military operations which used dominions' forces in Europe and the Middle East; in Treasury restriction of dominions' borrowing to war funding rather than domestic infrastructure; and in reorganization of commodity markets to deny, as far as possible, raw materials to the enemy.

There were limits to co-operation. They would not accept conscription, for example. And by 1918 the experience of South African and Australian wartime governments in running the Union and the Commonwealth led to quite separate policies for dealing with captured German assets outside constraints set by the British Treasury and the Board of Trade. The war, in J.C. Beaglehole's phrase, was a 'constitutional forcing ground', as well as a training ground in international relations'.[45] But compared with the more obvious advance in status derived from the Peace Conference, the dominions' handling of reparations is a topic that requires further investigation which may well reveal a more subtle shift towards autonomous management of local corporate investment and commercial law. The conflicting policies of dominions' statesmen on reparations are better understood than the actual value and distribution of the capital stock and other assets they administered under the terms of the peace treaty.

'Collaboration', then, is only useful as a theory of imperial behaviour if the costs and benefits are spelled out at the level of government after conquest and the very different level of inter-state co-operation for perceived goals. Both systems imply a measure of deference which came more easily from surrendered colonists than dominion governments.

At the time, neither example of sub-imperial expansion produced much in the way of imperial theorizing, compared with the voluminous materials on imperial participation in the Versailles Conference. The Australians followed their instincts and the recommendation 'to get rid of Germany' both as a source of mining investment in Australia and competition in the Pacific, set out by Hughes in September 1916 as a foreword to C. Brunsdon Fletcher's *The New Pacific* which stated the moral and commercial reasons for retaining German colonies.[46] However much he was opposed to the policy of a 'vengeful peace' and large indemnities, Smuts was equally resolved to hold on to what had been won and treat the territory as an integral part of the Union.[47] On the whole it was a pragmatic and businesslike imperialism derived from locally-perceived interests. New Guinea and South West Africa were not lost 'on the fields of Liège and in the blackened ruins of Louvain', but in the corridors of Melbourne and Pretoria and the boardrooms of Anglo-American and Burns Philp.[48]

NOTES

1. See Neville Meaney, *A History of Australian Defence and Foreign Policy, 1901–23 Vol. 1, The Search for Security in the Pacific, 1901–14* (Sydney University Press, 1976), Ch. 1. For the notion of 'collaboration' adumbrated in an influential essay, see R.E. Robinson, 'Non-European foundations of European imperialism; sketch for a theory

of collaboration', in Roger Owen and Bob Sutcliffe (eds.), *Studies in the Theory of Imperialism* (London, 1972), 117–42; and for other references to collaboration in opposition to nationalism in South Africa, see R.E. Robinson, 'The Partition of Africa', in F.H. Hinsley (ed.), *The New Cambridge Modern History. Material Progress and World-Wide Problems, 1870–1898* (Cambridge, 1962), 635, 638–9. I am indebted to Mr Bernard Attard, St. Antony's College, Oxford, for comments on the Australian sections.
2. Meaney, 12.
3. Board of Trade to Colonial Office, 17 May 1917, CO 551/100.
4. Minutes and final agreement, 1914, Central Archives Depot (Pretoria), MNW 488; Gladstone to Harcourt, 7 May 1914, FO 368/1178.
5. 'Operations in British Dominions and Colonies August 1914, Secret'; 'Operations in the Union of South Africa and German South West Africa'; 'Operations against the German Possessions in New Guinea, Secret', Bodleian Library, MS Harcourt dep. 508.
6. 'Operations', 31 October 1914, ff. 210–12, MS Harcourt dep. 508.
7. W. Holmes, 'Diary of Events', 1 Nov. 1914, Mitchell Library (Sydney), W. Holmes MSS 15/1.
8. Gail-Maryse Cockram, *South West African Mandate* (Cape Town, 1976), Ch. 1.
9. South West Africa, killed and wounded: 385; rebellion, killed and wounded: 414; rebel losses: 190 killed and up to 350 wounded. 'Operations', f. 69, MS Harcourt dep. 508, Cf. *Cambridge History of the British Empire, vol. 8, South Africa, Rhodesia and the High Commission Territories* (Cambridge, 1963), 750, for different totals.
10. Department of Overseas Trade, *Report on the Conditions and Prospects of Trade in the Protectorate of South-West Africa* Cmd. 842 (London, 1920).
11. Stewart Firth, *New Guinea under the Germans* (Melbourne, 1982).
12. Choiseul Plantations files; Tetere land file, Burns, Philp and Company archives (Sydney); K. Buckley and K. Klugman, *The History of Burns Philp: The Australian Company in the South Pacific* (Sydney, 1981), 263–4.
13. 'Reports and memorandums', Burns to Lucas, 29 September 1914, Burns, Philp and Company archives; Forsayth to Hughes, 23 December 1915; Defence, minute, 17 Aug. 1916, CRS A4, Australian Archives (Canberra); FO to CO, 25 April 1915 and minutes, CO 418/14.
14. Atlee Hunt papers, memorandum, 19 Jan. 1915, National Library (Canberra).
15. S.S. Mackenzie, *The Australians at Rabaul. The Capture and Administration of the German Possessions in the Southern Pacific* (Sydney, 1927), Ch. 15.
16. Comptroller-general, memorandum, 29 March 1916; Pearce to Munro-Ferguson, 24 May 1916, Australian Archives, A. 3934 SC 30; Commonwealth Parliamentary Papers 1917–18 No. 66, *British and Australian Trade in the South Pacific*.
17. Munro-Ferguson to Harcourt, 10 March 1915, MS Harcourt dep. 479.
18. United States Consul, Zurich, 9 Sept. 1915; National Bank of South Africa to Finance, 18 Sept. 1915, Central Archives Depot TES 866 F5/951; Colonial Office Confidential Print African (South) No. 1054, 23; Cockram, *South West African Mandate*, 13–25.
19. Mosely to Board of Trade, 4 and 8 June 1915, BT 11/9 C, 18875. Alfred Mosely (1855–1917) had been a miner on the Kimberley diamond fields, a diamond dealer, a tariff reformer and member of government commissions after his return to the United Kingdom. The *Annual Register* makes no reference to his wartime function of co-ordinator of diamond policy for the Board of Trade. At his death, the export committee was run by Norman Melland, L. Breitmeyer, L. Abrahams and F.W. Green.
20. Memorandum, 'The Diamond Trade' [July 1915], BT 11/9 C. 18875; C. 26760; Mosely to British Consul, Amsterdam, 2 Sept. 1915, C. 30171/15. The Dutch committee consisted of A. Assher, H.H. Rozelaar and J. Rozelaar.
21. Bonar Law to Buxton, 9 Feb. 1916, Central Archives Depot, TES 886 F5/951.
22. Bonar Law to Buxton, 6 Sept. 1916, Central Archives Depot, MNW 432 MM 2455/18.
23. Minutes and memoranda by Sheridan, Kotze and the Mining Surveyor, A.C.

Sutherland, 1915; Kotze to Malan, 8 March 1915, Central Archives Depot, TES 863 F5/90.
24. Memorandum, 'The Spoils', 25 March 1915 CAB 37/126/27.
25. 'Most Secret Japan-Australia', and Harcourt to Munro-Ferguson, 23 February, 19 March 1915, MS Harcourt dep. 495.
26. Lucas to Hunt, 5 June, 4 July 1919, National Library, 52/1625, 52/1623.
27. Burns to Munro-Ferguson, 25 Nov. 1918, National Library, 696/7032–7151.
28. Commonwealth Parliamentary Papers, 1920, *Interim and Final Reports of the Royal Commission on Late German New Guinea*, 42–3; Johnston to Ferrands, 20 Oct. 1919, National Library, 696/6664–6685.
29. BT to CO, 17 May, 19 Dec. 1917, CO 551/100.
30. *The African World*, 9 June 1917; *Cambridge History of the British Empire, vol. 7, part 1, Australia* (Cambridge, 1933), 570.
31. CO 687/82; *The African World*, 18 January 1919.
32. Cf. Anthony Hocking, *Oppenheimer and Son* (Johannesburg, 1973), 80–81, 87. No dates or sources are supplied. Hull arrived in Europe on the *Cap Polonio*, 4 Sept. 1919. Hocking is wrong in stating the mines were taken over by the Custodian of Enemy Property. The whole point of the sale was to avoid this.
33. *The African World*, 6 Sept. 1919.
34. Colonial Office Confidential Print Africa (South), 'Visit of the Governor-General to the South West Territory in October, 1919', (1920), 21.
35. *The African World*, 1 and 15 Nov. 1919; and for a later investigation of the purchase, J.H. Munnik, 'South West African Diamonds', 1927, Central Archives Depot, MNW 890 MM 1687/27.
36. Consolidated Diamond Mines, *Report of the Directors*, 1920.
37. A. 1–20, *Correspondence relating to the transfer of certain interests and concessions in the South West African Protectorate to the South West Africa Consolidated Diamond Company Limited*. And for documents omitted, Central Archives Depot, MNW 488 MM 2741/19. Receipt of this print by the Colonial Office was the first indication that such a deal had been concluded. It occasioned little comment and was not passed on to the Board of Trade. CO 551/127.
38. Gorges to Malan, 3 Nov. 1919, Central Archives Depot, MNW 488 MM 2741/19.
39. Fowle, memorandum, 29 April 1920, CO 551/126; Smuts, minute No. 371, 22 April 1920, CO 551/125.
40. *The Times*, 19 Aug. 1920; Treasury to CO, 5 Oct. 1920, CO 551/135.
41. Report by John Bradbury, 21 Sept. 1920, encl. in Treasury to CO, 5 Oct. 1920, CO 551/135.
42. Mackenzie, *The Australians at Rabaul*.
43. Cf. Duncan Innes, *Anglo American and the Rise of Modern South Africa*, (Johannesburg, 1984), 98–9; Hocking, *Oppenheimer and Son*, 87–8.
44. Lance E. Davis and Robert A. Huttenback, *Mammon and the Pursuit of Empire. The Political Economy of British Imperialism, 1860–1912* (Cambridge, New York, 1986), esp. Ch. 6 on subsidies.
45. J.C. Beaglehole, 'The British Commonwealth of Nations' in David Thomson (ed.), *The New Cambridge Modern History, vol. xii, The Era of Violence* (Cambridge, 1964), 536.
46. C. Brunsdon Fletcher, *The New Pacific, British Policy and German Aims* (London, 1917).
47. W.K. Hancock, *Smuts. The Sanguine Years, 1870–1919* (Cambridge, 1963), Ch. 19 esp. 429, 498.
48. Cited in Wm. Roger Louis, *Great Britain and Germany's Lost Colonies 1914–1919* (Oxford, 1967), 9.

Imperial Collaboration and Great Depression: Britain, Canada and the World Wheat Crisis, 1929-35

by

Robert Holland

In recent years some historians have cast a good deal of new light on the economic relations between the United Kingdom and the self-governing Dominions between 1918 and 1939. These fresh treatments have largely taken the form of 'pure' economic history; the most celebrated among them, however, – those by the Canadian historian, Ian Drummond – are only loosely connected with the broad sweep of imperial historiography.[1] It may, therefore, prove worthwhile to approach at least a fragment of this aspect of Anglo-Dominion history from the standpoint of Ronald Robinson's concept of collaborative bargain-making as the true stuff of empire; and in particular his classic remark that it was the white colonist who was '. . . the ideal, pre-fabricated collaborator . . . [with the result that in] white colonies . . . collaboration proved both stable and effective'.[2]

Of course, in sketching his theoretical model, Robinson was essentially concerned with the period between 1870 and 1914. Even for this heyday of British imperial leverage, indeed, at least one commentator has expressed strong, if preliminary, reservations as to how 'ideal' the white colonist was as a commercial partner.[3] There is considerable mileage left in this debate. But when Robinson adumbrates collaboration as the motor of imperial relationships he does not envisage 1914 as a cut-off date; in his view – and that of Jack Gallagher – the essence of later decolonizations lay in the bankruptcy of hitherto copper-bottomed bargains. By extension, this process of unravelling was also likely to assume a streamlined, classical shape in the case of the white colonies because it, too, could be mediated through the smooth and efficient operations of an open market. As it turned out, however, the open market was anything but smooth after the Great War, and from the later 1920s was characterized by an acute deflation. As a consequence, commercial frictions and related shifts in political sentiment, usually so elusive and evanescent to observers, became stark; established alliances throughout the international system were turned upside down. It is with the course and texture of British imperial collaboration in mind that this article seeks to elucidate (chiefly from a macro-economic and inter-governmental perspective) one aspect of these commodity dilemmas: the violent downswing in world wheat values after 1928 as they cut across the interlocking interests of the two greatest Dominions within the British Commonwealth, the United Kingdom and Canada.

I

At the outset of the Great Depression, Canada was easily the world's greatest exporter of wheat; in 1928 it accounted for approximately 20 per cent of international trade in that prime commodity. The vast bulk of this surplus Canadian grain issued from the western prairie provinces of Manitoba, Saskatchewan and Alberta. The emergence of the prairie wheat economy as one of the great agricultural regions of the world had happened very late in the day; the classic phase of accelerated settlement had occurred between 1900 and 1914. Of all the possible 'ideal-types' of Robinson's prefabricated white-colonial collaborator, it is arguable that none could fit the profile better than the western Canadian grain-growing homesteader of the Edwardian age, a high percentage of them British or British-Canadian in culture and stock, profoundly 'loyalist' in political instinct and grounded in the habit of measuring individual worth and aspirations by the shifting values on the Liverpool corn exchange. He was not, however, a passive creature; and it is in the implication of passiveness ('prefabricated') that perhaps the Robinsonian armour has a chink. Certainly in the years before 1914 the prairie grain-grower locked horns with a marketing system which, in his eyes, deprived the producer of a fair return. Significant victories had been won with the Manitoba Grain Act of 1900, procedural reforms within the Winnipeg Grain Exchange and the first moves towards the co-operative principle with the establishment of the United Grain Growers' Company in 1907. This is a story which has often been told and need not be repeated here.[4] But in emerging as a deeply political animal, the prairie producer located his enemies between the local elevator point where he initially took his grain for consignment and the ocean-shipping terminal at Montreal, Buffalo or Vancouver; in other words, the villain lay at one of the many intricate stages within the Canadian marketing network (the elevator agent, the private grain trader, the railway cartel with its assorted scoundrels, the government grade inspector), not on the other side of the Atlantic in Liverpool or London.[5] British import values, precisely because they constituted the 'refined truth' of a genuinely world market, were taken as authentic and unquestioned; the prairie growers were fundamentalists in economics as well as religion. It was within the limits set by this relatively modest demonology that the growers' reformist energies were contained in the years before 1914.

The Great War was a lucky break for the Canadian prairies. The settlement boom had flagged in 1913, and although prices had recuperated it seemed that values had entered a phase of more subdued advance. The war, however, brought bonanza to North American agriculture: it knocked out grain production in much of western and eastern Europe, dislocated (by revolution) the great wheat-exporting apparatus of southern Russia and stimulated vast Allied orders for foodstuffs, backed by British credit. Nowhere was this inflationary cycle more beneficially experienced than in the hamlets and homesteads of the Canadian prairies. The grain-growers snapped up new mortgages and loans to extend their acreage and, since labour was short, to mechanize their production. It was this prolonged adjustment of a dynamic settlement region to wartime levels of export prices and credit that underlay the peace-time trauma ahead.

In retrospect it might seem incredible that the prairie farmers thus loaded themselves with debt when the future course of prices remained so uncertain. This, however, leaves out of account that 'pioneer psychology' which the war did so much to reinvigorate – perhaps the last great wave of imperial economic expansion in the classical sense. Furthermore, between 1914 and 1919 there were persuasive reasons for believing that investment in enhanced production was entirely rational. The scale of the disaster in Europe gave force to the assumption that the shift in the centre of gravity in the world wheat economy from the Old World to the New was irreversible. More concretely, during 1917 the Canadian government had set up a federal Wheat Board to take control of all marketing at guaranteed prices. Producers were encouraged to expand their operations on the expectation that effective protection would be provided (courtesy of the federal Treasury) against future deflation. In 1920, however, faced with a massive fall in wheat prices, the Union government of Robert Borden dismantled the Wheat Board and left the prairie farmers to face a now hostile market-place. Many were ruined; those who kept their homesteads only did so through a dose of austerity that would have inflamed Jarrow or Ebbw Vale to instant revolution. It was as a reaction to this 'adjustment process' that the great Canadian Wheat Pools emerged in the middle 1920s.

The theory of the producers' pool is simple enough: farmers 'pooled' their grain, receiving an initial payment, plus a deferred certificate entitling them to further payments depending on the final price obtained by the pools' managers.[6] The concept had been developed in the hothouse world of American agrarian radicalism; and one of the chief architects of the prairie wheat pools in these early years was the organizing genius of farm protest from across the border, Aaron Sapiro. From their inception in western Canada, the pools were in sharp competition with the private grain trade for the patronage of the growers. The pools offered initial payment and the prospect of more; the grain companies offered an immediate return, cash on the barrel. The resulting rivalry underpinned a doctrinal debate within the pool managements: there were 'moderates' who contended that the pools could only gradually displace the private traders by obtaining 'efficiency savings' and passing them on to their members, and 'radicals' who saw much greater scope for driving up the pool-price by 'orderly marketing'.[7] The impassioned logic of 'orderly marketing' soon brought a new opponent within the range of pool tacticians: the European (especially British) importers. It was at this point that the fabric of imperial collaboration between Liverpool and Medicine Hat, apparently seamless for so long, became liable to wear.

This incipient instability arising from pool radicalism would almost certainly have remained suppressed if the renewed prairie prosperity after 1925 had been consolidated. Prices rose as European (not least British) demand recovered; heightened confidence led to new investment; and prairie municipalities assumed fresh tranches of bonded debt to establish telephone systems, drainage facilities and basic health care. But this prairie modernization was built on extremely insecure foundations. Higher wheat prices had also resuscitated the traditional export surplus of the Danube Basin (principally in Hungary and Roumania) and encouraged the revival of agrarian protectionism in western and southern Europe.[8] For a brief span it was possible for these various developments to run in harmony with (rather than obstructing) each other. But in 1928, combined with extended acreage in many producer regions, average yields were boosted by exceptionally fine weather. All the New World exporters (including Canada) registered record production, and although the cumulative European figure was not greatly above that of the previous year, the crop quality was extraordinarily fine. By the end of 1928 supply had outstripped demand in the world market by an estimated 100 million bushels (mbs). This formed the original core of a wheat carry-over, or glut, which was to lie at the centre of international agricultural depression for most of the 1930s, and whose imagined shapes and proportions must have been the stuff of uncountable nightmares on the part of destitute farmers.

II

Faced with the problem of handling the 1928–9 prairie wheat surplus as prices sagged, the Canadian Pools resorted to a rigorous form of 'orderly marketing', feeding the market in small packets, but keeping huge accumulations in storage. This partial 'sellers' strike' by the world's greatest exporter arose primarily from a habitual sense of market superiority. There was an *a priori* belief that 'premium' hard Canadian wheat was indispensable to the quality-loaf so beloved by the brand-conscious British housewife. But not only were the competing Argentine and Australian products inferior in Canadian eyes: the lack of modern storage facilities in those countries also meant that the grain had to be shipped immediately or be left to rot. By holding off the market, Australian and Argentine shippers could be left to satiate themselves on low prices, while the Canadian Pools looked forward eagerly to enforcing bonus returns for themselves once the 'natural' supply-demand relationship had been re-asserted.[9] The Americans, of course, had their own surplus and modern silos to go with it. But American farmers were even choosier about prices than their prairie counterparts, and had more political muscle. As long as the US Federal Farm Board was financed by Washington to keep the mid-western grower from painful recourse to rapacious European buyers, the Canadian pools could look forward to beating the world price upwards in due course.

It was obvious as 1929 ran its course that the tussle between the pools and the Anglo-European importers was not going to be easily resolved. News was pouring into the trading houses of Liverpool, Amsterdam and Hamburg that European farmers, needing cash as consumer prices rose, were rushing their produce to market with an alacrity not seen since the war.[10] By late summer prices prevailing on the Chicago and Winnipeg grain exchanges appeared to harden at a 'band' altogether higher than that operating in Liverpool and other European centres: two hostile price-zones, in effect, faced each other across the Atlantic.[11] In playing for these large stakes the Canadian pools – who, unlike the Americans, could not permanently forsake European markets – were risking a good deal. But their commercial nerve was stiffened by the political consideration that the imminent Federal election in Canada put the Liberal government under much pressure to provide whatever financial resources were required to 'see the thing through'. They were not, in the first instance, disappointed, since in February 1930 the Federal authorities extended qualified approval to the provincial cabinets and banks who were underpinning the pools' accumulating deficits. Nor was it far from the minds of the pool managements that an Imperial Conference in London was scheduled for October 1930, at which the British government might be manoeuvred into some settlement favourable to the prairie grain-grower. The 'loyalist' card had many uses.

The pools' resistance to what (viewed from Liverpool) seemed the iron law of market trends, however, must also be ascribed to a crucial shift of ideas and alignments. To illustrate this we can turn for convenience to a book published in 1930 by two Canadian agricultural economists, W.W. Swanson and P.C. Armstrong, which outlined the pools' case.[12] In sketching the background to their subject, they emphasized that since the Great War the prairie west had come to occupy a pivotal position within Canadian Federal politics, such that it was no longer possible for a government in Ottawa to distance itself from the anxieties of western producers. The prairie provinces, for their part, held the maintenance of farm incomes to be the touchstone of this enhanced political status; and the means of that maintenance lay in the pool organizations. 'It is the insistence of a whole community,' the authors perorated, 'that what has been won from the wilderness is to be held.'[13] The threat to the status quo, however, did not come from producers elsewhere in the world: Swanson and Armstrong were convinced that the Australians were too committed to high standards of living, the Soviets too stretched to meet even domestic demand and the scope for agricultural development in Western Europe too constrained to blunt Canadian bargaining power. Rather, the writers focused on the nature of the British import marts. These had always operated in such a way as to deprive overseas producers of a fair return. The sellers' power was inherently dispersed, with the varied harvesting cycles from the Southern Russian plains to the pampas of the Argentine, from the Danubian granary to the Canadian prairies ensuring an even flow of produce to the European centres at all seasons. In contrast, the buyers' power was physically concentrated in Europe and equipped with modern communications to co-ordinate commercial strategies; and its heart was the Liverpool-London nexus. It was the instinctive tendencies of these latter exchange centres which was crucial:

> Chicago and Winnipeg, Montreal and New York, are traders in wheat. They can make a profit out of a rising market or a falling one. London and Liverpool are not averse to earning a penny per bushel out of a rise in the market, but their fundamental aim is to buy wheat, and to buy wheat cheaply. It is almost a matter of patriotism . . . In this, the greatest of all markets for wheat, there is but one desirable course for prices to take, and that is downwards.[14]

According to Swanson and Armstrong, the British importers, driven by the political and market logic of cheap food, were feverishly at work exploiting the 'incipient' deflation of 1929–30 to cut producers' returns to a minimum. Farmers the world over would be 'weighed . . . and gauged' to see which group would be contented with least[15]; and in these circumstances the highly geared system in western Canada would have to fight for its very life. The emergence and radicalization of the Canadian pools, however, was the first serious attempt in *world* markets (as opposed to the hermetically-sealed conditions in the United States) to break into this deflationary cycle. Swanson and Armstrong anticipated that once the Australians and Argentines recognized the Canadian pools' ability to resist the pressures emanating from Liverpool and London, they too would equip themselves with the infrastructures and – as important – the mentality to secure stable and equitable returns. In this way the Canadians would have pioneered a triumph, not only for themselves, but for farmers everywhere. Somewhere along the line of this evolution towards a 'farmers' front' (and not too far either) the subtle links of imperial commercial collaboration would be well and truly eroded.

The British grain traders and their Continental allies were in no doubt as to the significance of the challenge posed by the Canadian pools. But providing the politicians did not interfere (a matter on which they felt some disquiet) the importers were confident of coming out on top. This confidence was essentially grounded in the belief that throughout the New World it was possible for improved technology to sustain production at lower price-levels than currently prevailed. Farmers and politicians overseas would naturally resist this process, but ultimately the facts would tell.[16] Sooner rather than later even the American taxpayer would baulk at subsidizing artificial cereal prices, and US growers would be forced into accepting whatever cash was going on the world market. Even before this breaking-point of the US Federal Farm Board was reached, however, it was reckoned likely that the Canadians would move in the same direction, since the failure actually to ship wheat was already causing spectacular congestion throughout 1929 in Montreal and back along the inland water route to Fort William.[17] Quite apart from generating horrendous storage costs, this had a paralysing effect across much of Canadian commerce by disrupting its normal level of cash-flows. If a collapse of American farm policies did not send the Canadian pools rushing off to the St Lawrence docks, then the catastrophic effects of current policies on the local banking system would. At the heart of such second-guessing among the Anglo-European importers lay the conviction that the prairie provinces would not be able to whistle up Federal support on the scale required to circumvent market forces.

The British commercial determination to break the nascent agrarian cartel of the North American plains, however, had a particular edge. Few United Kingdom industries were more conservative during the 1920s than the milling trades. Amalgamation had been fiercely resisted. But after May 1929 these interests were assailed not only by falling profits but by the possibility that the new Labour government would nationalize the bread-making business. Bringing the mills under public ownership had long been a key left-wing plank within Labour ranks, and had featured prominently in the 1929 General Election.[18] The argument here was alluring: since wheat prices had fallen sharply since 1914, and bread prices had not, it was transparent that milling capital had pocketed all the gains of technical and distributive improvements.[19] With the threat of 'socialization' overhanging them, the great milling houses began to run the gauntlet of rationalization and combination under the trustifying aegis of James V. Rank. But exposed to close public scrutiny, and with unemployment rising through the recession, Rank and his associates had to prove beyond doubt their commitment to the historic function of the national milling community: to provide even the poorest British breakfast table with the cheapest and best loaf going, come hell or – in this case – Canadian price-fixers. Hence it was not surprising that the bread combines launched a bitter publicity drive against the 'monopolistic' pools, strove to substitute cheap foreign wheats for Canadian varieties and even, it was alleged, instigated the use of retail posters proudly announcing 'We Do Use North American Flour'.[20] It is a curious novelty that this little transatlantic contest was shortly decided by the intervention of Joseph Stalin.

'A trade prepared for "corners" and not unaccustomed to "bear raids" ', *The Economist* reported in September 1930, 'has been none the less startled and disconcerted by the Russian Government's appearance on the wheat market as a considerable seller for September and October delivery'.[21] The motivations and course of the great Soviet wheat dump of 1930–31 cannot detain us here. All sorts of news filtering out of the Soviet Union, such as the lengthening bread-queues in the cities, was taken to foreshadow a termination of Russian exports;[22] but in the event the grain kept flowing through the Crimean ports. The Canadians were therefore faced with the question of whether, having yielded their markets to the

Argentines in 1929–30, they were now prepared to do the same for the Russians in 1930–31. There could only be one answer. The Federal authorities in Ottawa refused to guarantee current pool prices for the 1930 prairie crop, forcing them into the hands of their bankers.[23] When the banks insisted on assuming prices which meant producers would often only average 25 cents per bushel, the pool-memberships began to desert for the open market in droves.[24] The pool directors tried to bludgeon the prairie provincial governments into helping them out, but when this forlorn hope evaporated they were left with the one recourse they dreaded most of all – a 'reconciliation' with the overseas buyers. The final prop was knocked from under their position when the Anglo-Canadian economic dialogue carried on beneath the umbrella of the 1930 Imperial Conference led nowhere,[25] while it became plain that the Argentines would match Soviet price-cutting rouble for rouble. Through prairie spectacles, British capitalists – with the connivance of a Labour government – had sought an unholy alliance in Moscow and Buenos Aires to smash the price-level on which their community aspirations were based. Indeed *The Economist*, quoting 'authoritative opinion', had throughout espoused the view that the small prairie producer would have to accept an East European standard of living to survive. As the prospect of this bleak future bore down on many small Canadian farmers, British traders could not resist crowing at their victory. 'The new policy,' the *Corn Trade News* remarked with reference to the pools' turnaround on sales, 'has been received with satisfaction on all markets', adding rather ominously, however, that the Canadians nevertheless could not expect that years of sinister business methods would be forgotten 'at the stroke of the pen'.[26]

After the Great War, therefore, social and economic development in the prairie provinces of Canada had come to hinge more than ever on the 'premium' status of its outstanding staple. That status was itself acutely dependent on British milling practice, with the privileges it accorded the 'hard' wheat strains of Manitoba. This delicate balance between distant communities of producers and consumers, however, was swiftly upset when a prolonged phase of price instability took shape. A polarity emerged between, on the one hand, the range of 'adjustment' and 'flexibility' within prairie social arrangements, and, on the other hand, the historic British commitment to 'cheap food' as the leitmotif of national political economy. In the event the British milling interests were able to bend the Canadian pools to the old Peelite yoke. As we shall see, however, the effect of this was ultimately not to refurbish the imperial collaborative model of sturdy but pliable homesteaders mediated through metropolitan agency, but to set the scene for an alternative interventionism based on state, not pool, power: Federalism displaced Imperialism. It is with this tendency in mind that we may turn to the next phase in Anglo-Canadian exchanges, culminating in the Imperial Economic Conference at Ottawa during the summer of 1932.

III

The prairie pool organizations had been unlucky that their own finances had brought about the collapse of their selling policies just as the British authorities were becoming susceptible to the concept of 'imperial accords' in which the cheap food cry might at least be muted. At the Imperial Conference of autumn 1930 the Chancellor of the Exchequer, Philip Snowden, had, admittedly, been able to shape UK responses in the image of his own orthodoxy and fend off Dominion, principally Canadian, pressures for market-rigging agreements which would guarantee their stake in the British market. But this bid fair to be Custer's last stand. As the UK's employment and external payments position deteriorated sharply in the last quarter of 1930, a protectionist consensus (cutting across party and ideological lines) began to emerge and Snowden's influence was curtailed. British industry began to toy with slogans of 'imperial development' which held out the prospect of heightened preferences for their products in Dominion markets. But if the UK hoped to extract industrial concessions from the other Dominions, then something substantial had to be offered in return on the agricultural front. The lobbying of Canada's newly-elected Conservative premier, R.B. Bennett, in London had not gone entirely unrequited.

There is a more general dimension, however, which underlies the shift in British economic perspectives at this stage. As late as July 1930 the UK government's chief Treasury adviser, Sir Frederick Leith-Ross, argued that however severe the current commodity deflation might become, the maximum British concession should be to advocate some easing of Central Bank credit: fundamentally overseas farmers had to adjust themselves to new circumstances.[27] By the turn of 1931–32 this *sang froid* was badly shaken. The possibility arose that some of the agricultural exporting nations, bereft of so much income, might actually default; and since some of the potential defaulters (Australia was the main case in point) were sterling countries, the British pound might not prove strong enough to avoid being sucked into the morass. It was not least, therefore, the prospect of a chain of defaults triggered in the first instance by primary producers overseas which for the first time seized the British of the need to shore up artificially the agricultural incomes of its closest partners. Impelled by these anxieties, the Labour government – having already had to give up nationalization of the milling industry as beyond its financial resources – turned to the idea of an 'Empire Wheat Quota' which had previously been urged upon it by Bennett.

The Labour government was still considering the quota option when it was overwhelmed by the financial crisis of May 1931. But one of the Labour ministers who subsequently took office under Ramsay MacDonald was J.H. Thomas, who had recently been converted to 'empire trade' (for want of anything better) as an anti-recession device. Once he was appointed Secretary of State for the Dominions, his advocacy of a quota was reinforced by the support of his departmental officials who grasped at some means of patching up the Anglo-Canadian rift. That rift threatened to widen with the devaluation of sterling in September 1931; since the Canadian dollar (unlike the Australian and Argentine currencies) was not similarly devalued, prairie farmers had had depreciated pounds foisted on them, without any off-setting increase in commodity prices.[28] R.B. Bennett had to find some means of compensating Canadian grain-growers for this further erosion of their sectional position; and the British – such were the knock-on effects within imperial relations – had to find some means of compensating Bennett. If an Empire Wheat Quota had held attractions for the Labour government in Britain, its National successor briefly fell in love with the idea as a means of making the forthcoming Imperial Economic Conference a success.

The argument surrounding the (ultimately abortive) proposal for a Dominion Wheat Quota is significant not least because it marked a critical passage in the struggle waged from early 1930 between the stalwarts and foes of 'cheap food' as the lynch-pin of British political economy. The British Cabinet sub-committee authorized to negotiate a wheat quota with the home lobbies knew that they faced resolute opposition. The scheme they came up with had two main safeguards against manipulation. The price to be fixed for empire quota wheat was to be 'reasonably equivalent' to world levels, and the machinery would be suspended if at any time United Kingdom millers found that the supply of Dominion cereals at such reasonably equivalent prices had mysteriously dried up. In other words, Dominion wheat-growers were not to be allowed to rifle the British housewife's purse so outrageously as to become self-evident. The millers and brokers were not reassured: they had, it seemed, defeated the Canadian grain hold-up of 1929–30 only for the British government to legislate away the interests of the domestic consumer and (what concerned them most) their own commercial freedom of manoeuvre. They had no faith in the strength of British ministers to resist Dominion pressures to fudge the 'reasonable equivalent' rule. 'We do not know what "reasonably equivalent" might mean', they remonstrated in a deputation confronting Thomas, and with the Imperial Conference only a month away 'We do not know if it is a shilling, or two shillings [higher than non-Empire wheat] or what it might be, and yet men trading months ahead have this all the time over their heads as to what "reasonable equivalent" might be decided on by the minister. It would be impossible for anybody to go on trading months ahead with any certainty'.[29] The threat in this was clear enough: if the National Government disregarded them, the traders would go on strike, and a bread shortage would ensue – with consequences for the fragile new ministry which were wholly predictable. Thomas was aggrieved. 'It is no good to come here and tell me that you are a lot of philanthropists,' he said, 'who want to buy every day . . . you are lying idle now if it does not suit you to buy.' But without the co-operation of the British trade, and without the credible threat of nationalization to bring this about, the quota plan was stone dead. Subsequently a millers' delegation, led by James V. Rank himself, went to 'mind' the British negotiators at the Imperial Conference in Ottawa lest, in a weak moment of imperial enthusiasm, the latter caved in to the imprecations of Bennett.[30]

Without a wheat quota, then, what did the British ministers take with them to Ottawa which might ameliorate Bennett's mounting problems in the prairies? After all, in Manitoba, Saskatchewan and Alberta many farmers were now dependent on public relief and a political backlash against the established party system was becoming manifest. The Canadian Prime Minister could not emerge from the Imperial Conference having secured opportunities in the UK market for dairy-farmers in Ontario, say, and nothing for western grain-growers. With Rank's reluctant consent, Neville Chamberlain and Jim Thomas had two bargaining chips at their disposal: an empire wheat preference in the British tariff and some limitation on Russian commodity imports. Both of these were practically worthless. As for the preference, any Argentine or Russian supplies thereby displaced in the UK market would only spill over into third markets and pull down the general price level a further notch; and since Canada's export surplus easily outstripped total British import demand the resultant loss would outweigh any gains.[31] But quite apart from such reasoning, the Argentines had made it plain that they were not prepared to quit the British market, and would undercut any conceivable preference the Canadians could wangle out of Whitehall. As for any specific limitation on Russian grain shipments to Britain, this too was a hollow gift since the Soviet Union had at last slipped into that disastrous famine which experts had been predicting for many months.[32] Whatever other Canadian producers may have benefited from Bennett's boisterous style of negotiation at Ottawa, the grain producers got precious little. The 2/- per quarter preference accorded by the UK on Canadian wheat, for example, was excoriated by rural representatives in the Dominion Parliament as a gross irrelevence;[33] and not all Bennett's 'hyping' of the Western provincial press could conceal the truth of this. Viewed from the prairie homesteads the long-heralded imperial gathering had regarded their shabby and intensifying destitution with a cold silence. The profound effects of this on the psychological and cultural assumptions of prairie society can only be surmised; but it is easy to imagine many bitter-sad conversations at meagre family breakfasts in which the British connection – once such an emblem of security and improvement – was scarcely lionized.

By mid-1932 western Canadian producers had become the fall-guys of North American depression. Within their national confederation they were exposed to the most violent blast of world deflation, and yet left least protected against it. The industrial populations of the eastern sections were increasingly sheltered by the blanket subsidy of protection; the western grain-growers were simply reminded – as they were by the 1931 Stamp Commission on Futures Trading in Wheat – how healthy the open market was for them. Critics of the prairies were not slow to point out that the westerners had only themselves to blame for sticking too long to a primitive, earth-scratching mono-culture; it was up to them to effect a shift into mixed farming where producer incomes were more resilient – a transition well under way in rural Ontario. But whatever the economic rights and wrongs, by mid-1932 the sectional disparities were threatening to inflict permanent damage on the Dominion. Bennett's British-imperial card had kept the game going for a while, but the Ottawa Conference had revealed its low scoring potential. Already the farmers' lobby was calling for a generalized inflation which might erode debts 'at a stroke' and give a hike to nominal incomes – leaving the future to look after itself, and regardless of its effects on other parts of the imperial system. These demands intensified with the election of Franklin D. Roosevelt to the United States Presidency on a price-raising ticket. After that, getting a slice of the New Deal's inflationary action was the touchstone of much Canadian politics. But 'working in' with the Americans involved a degree of subordination on matters of general policy, and in particular cleaving to the United States line in international economic negotiations. Hence when the World Economic Conference (WEC) convened in London during June 1933 the texture of Anglo-Canadian relations was rather different from what it had been (for all the vexations on that occasion) in Ottawa nine months before. In fact the WEC was to be characterized by a conference-within-a-conference, for although its main plenary sessions were concerned with the great (but wholly intractable) monetary issues, the focus of attention gradually shifted towards parallel talks concerned with the wheat situation. Ironically, it was the latter confabulations which produced the only significant achievement in what *The Times* described as 'economic disarmament applied to one of the great primary commodities of the world'.[34]

For the British, the WEC held out the danger that their old balancing act between overseas primary producers and industrialized Europe would finally fall apart. Certainly in London (not least because of French commitment to gold 'parity) the prospects of a monetary agreement were always regarded as minimal. It was to navigate around this difficulty that British officials became enamoured (as the Chancellor of the Exchequer, Neville Chamberlain, had been from the Ottawa Conference onwards) with the concept of 'regulated production' as a counterpoint to inflationary demands emanating from the North American wheatlands. 'Regulated production' naturally entailed 'regulated prices'. But even the UK Treasury now recognized the need to slide some floor beneath the collapsing incomes of the primary producing countries, and to do something for Roosevelt. Naturally, too, there would have to be safeguards for importers against being fixed into a price-ring. 'In such cases [of price control]', the Treasury nevertheless argued, 'the evident disadvantages of anything in the way of a cartel, e.g. the evident disadvantages of inefficient producers and the discouragement of enterprise, may, on balance, be less than the disadvantages of a continued alternation between prosperity and ruin to very large numbers of people'.[35] This sense of priorities had long prevailed in Moose Jaw, Alberta; it took the roller-coaster of a great depression to impress its merits – as they affected overseas commodity producers – on Treasury Chambers in Great George Street. Indeed, in the context of British economic history, here was an important staging-post in that transition by which stability, not growth, became the instinctive preference at the heart of the metropolitan bureauracy, and so reflected the burgeoning consensualism of party politics soon to be consummated by another world war.

The WEC spun out very much as Whitehall anticipated. From the start a West European bloc formed against an internationally-concerted inflation. Ramsay MacDonald, who chaired proceedings as host premier, refused to be budged by combined Canadian and Australian threats to depreciate their currencies against the British pound *pari passu* with the falling American dollar.[36] But he was deeply concerned to see that the conference 'came down steadily and smoothly like a regulated aeroplane and not in a nose-dive'.[37] In particular, some consensus on commodity control could break the momentum of dollar depreciation. 'The higher the price [of wheat] was raised [by regulation]', MacDonald explained, 'the less need there would be for inflation'.[38] It was around this approach that an Anglo-American compromise was constructed: the thrust of the argument was that the overseas exporters of wheat would restrict their production within certain limits on the proviso that the European importers would set about diluting their systems of agricultural protection. The Canadians, however, were not at all happy about a regulatory regime which put on them the onus to limit their export growth, and this reluctance was accentuated as news of the rising anger thus generated among prairie opinion filtered through to London.[39] But they were caught in a vice pressed irresistibly from both the American and the British ends. It was the threat by the United States – often made before, but more plausible when wielded by Roosevelt's radical commercial nationalism – to dump its massive grain stocks which finally herded recalcitrants, be they aggressive New World exporters such as the Canadians or stubborn European protectionists, into co-operation. By the time the WEC formally adjourned on 20 July the exporting and importing nations had at last begun detailed negotiation, and the final Wheat Agreement was drawn up – essentially under American auspices – at a separate meeting in London on 25 August.[40] Out of a meagre anticipated world import demand of 560 mbs, the Canadians were allotted 200 mbs, a figure which allowed no margin for actually disposing of their huge carry-over. To open up scope for such liquidation, in the 1934–35 season the exporters agreed to restrict their exports by 15 per cent below the 1931–35 average. In return, the European importers contracted (subject to suspiciously ambiguous qualifications) to begin reducing their grain tariffs once prices reached a 'trigger' price of 12 gold francs per quintal.

Here, arguably, was a rational approach to restructuring international agricultural markets, in which American economic and political power was harnessed (with British help) to the goal of correcting deformations which had their origins in the Great War. But from the first vested interests and national psychologies were pitted against the Agreement's success; prices fell on its announcement as a mark of traders' pessimism. It was less likely than ever, for example, that the larger European powers would scale down their bloated agricultures, the strategic significance of which were increasing, not decreasing, almost by the day. Equally, it was not at all clear that the great non-European exporter-governments would face up to disciplining their own producers. In Canada, hard though Bennett strove to portray the Agreement as virtually a personal triumph over evil European protectionism, prairie opinion apprehended that their aspirations for the future had been capped. It was William Dafoe, the renowned editor of the *Manitoba Free Press*, who caught this sentiment most dramatically. 'Canada's agricultural development,' he wrote, 'has been suspended by official enactment; Canadian agriculture is in retreat. That, and not a few extra cents on the price, is the fact which is striking the country in the face like a granite brick.'[41]

IV

If the events surrounding the WEC and the Wheat Agreement had represented a crisis in relationships between Europe and North America, and therefore between the UK and Canada, it also marked an important shift in the Canadian federal government's approach to the internal dilemmas posed by deflated grain prices. This internal dimension, because of its interaction with imperial themes, requires a brief digression.[42] In November 1930, when the pools' finances had reached breaking point, the Canadian government had reluctantly moved in to guarantee the sale of that season's crop. Ottawa's price for this intervention had been the appointment of John I. McFarland to be the general manager of the pools' Central Selling Agency. McFarland's remit was to return the pools' sales to orthodox channels (closing down, for example, the London office which had been established to cut out exchange brokers) and dispose of the obstacles to a genuinely 'market-clearing' price. Almost immediately, however, the return on one of the prime grades – No. 1 Northern – threatened to fall through the 50 cents per bushel barrier. McFarland was authorized by the federal authority to step in and shore up the market by buying futures, a tactic which obviated the physical storage of wheat and permitted secrecy. As the Central Selling Agency accumulated futures in the following months, however, it proved necessary to switch from near-by to more distant contract dates as delivery points for 'real' wheat loomed. It was in this *ad hoc* fashion that Bennett attempted to 'hold' the domestic wheat position whilst he went off in search of imperial, and ultimately international, solutions to the problems of the prairie economy. But as such solutions proved elusive, the more McFarland's covert domestic price-support operation had to be extended across a broader front, until it amounted to *de facto* stabilization. With each twist of the stabilization ratchet, the federal government's financial commitment became so huge that – if the futures bluff was ever called – national insolvency would beckon. The fact that McFarland's operations had never (by their very nature) been other than obliquely debated in Parliament meant that Bennett was terribly vulnerable. When, on December 16 1932, wheat prices for immediate delivery in Winnipeg fell below 40 cents per bushel Bennett's political career, the federal finances and prairie society were each edged closer to a precipice.

In these circumstances the speculative 'bubble' associated with Roosevelt's New Deal appeared from early 1933 as the fragile last hope of Canadian recovery.[43] McFarland, in particular, saw an opportunity, if Rooseveltian inflation could be reinforced by starving the market of Canadian supplies, to transform the wheat position. Ironically, he was drawn into that 'orderly marketing' which previously under the aegis of the pools he had severely criticized. The inflationary hype preceding and surrounding the WEC in late June and early July 1933 led McFarland to believe that this time the Canadian leverage (if only because it had American support) would tell. Bennett was less sanguine. He did not expect the speculation to be sustained, and wanted the euphoria of the WEC to be used as a cover for the Canadian wheat stocks (and with it the Federal commitments) to be floated off. From London he insisted that McFarland 'open the silos'. When McFarland refused, and threatened to resign if pushed, Bennett asked him why. 'Well', McFarland shouted down the wire from Winnipeg, 'those people over there have been skinning us alive for three years; now the shoe is on the other foot and we are going to make the —— pay.'[44]

But Liverpool did not pay, or, as a leading British trade journal smugly asserted, political orders from across the Atlantic could not impose values on Europe.[45] After 'violent wobbling' wheat prices collapsed; on 22 July, the day of the WEC's adjournment, the Chicago level hit 15 cents per bushel. Whether or not McFarland had indeed missed an opportunity to smuggle away the Canadian carryover under the temporary cover of Roosevelt's inflationary rhetoric, the Dominion was now locked into the financial stranglehold exerted by the surplus. If the International Wheat Agreement (IWA) did not 'clear the markets', then the federal government would have to face up to some expensive local solution (that is, a new Wheat Board) to fend off a political smash at home. Certainly it was from this point that McFarland's own emotions towards privately-led markets (through which imperial connections and sentiments had long been mediated) turned sour and impelled him towards the advocacy of federal intervention.

In fact the IWA was swiftly doomed. In late 1933 both France and Germany were emerging as net wheat *exporters*; this was hardly an inducement for North Americans to fulfil their acreage reduction commitments.[46] As prices dropped, the Agreement's administering body, the Wheat Advisory Council, quickly floated an emergency 'minimum price pact' to govern internationally-traded wheat. This gained lots of support, for the unsurprising but fatal reason that by this stage there was only one important country actually buying the commodity across the exchanges and who would thereby subsidize the minimum price: the United Kingdom. Indeed, some British officials were prepared to advocate such a sacrifice to facilitate the adjustment of agricultural systems in overseas nations.[47] But they were in a decided minority. By the end of 1933 a domestic British recovery was under way, powered internally by a building-cum-cheap-money boom, and externally by cheap food and raw materials. Rarely had United Kingdom opinion been less disposed to underwrite other people's salvations. When the WAC convened in Rome two executives from the London Corn Trade Association accompanied the Board of Trade official to stiffen his resistance against the minimum price or any similar device others might seek to fix upon him.[48] In the event the British never had to kill off the IWA because the Argentines did it for them. With a record crop, and confident of undercutting their competitors, the authorities in Buenos Aires shipped wheat out of the River Plate during the first half of 1934 without restraint. The Americans, Canadians and Australians appealed to the United Kingdom as the only power able to call the Argentine to heel.[49] Even if this had been possible, by mid-1934 the British had hardened their heart against international co-operation in which they were always supposed to fork out the money, especially when such pleas emanated from North America.[50] By June of that year the IWA continued to exist on paper, but to all intents and purposes its letter as well as its spirit was dead.

It was against the background of this Argentine *coup de grâce* to the IWA that McFarland finally signified to Bennett his conversion to the policy of a monopoly of Canadian grain marketing under a statutory Board.[51] This decision was coloured by the fact that all imperially or internationally negotiated restraints on deflation had run into the ground, making an extension of internal controls the only available option. There were other factors at work, however, of which the most compelling was the likelihood of an imminent General Election in which western protest would clearly be a feature: Mackenzie King's Liberals and such 'rogue' elements as Reverend William Aberhart's Social Credit Party in Alberta would press to evict the Conservatives from any lodgement in the prairies.[52] As the great North American drought fixed itself on the plains of western Canada (the 'dustbowl') from the summer of 1934 onwards, Bennett's first decision was to spin out his tenure of office into 1935, and his second was to begin the laborious process of legislating for a grain marketing board. In the parliamentary fracas which ensued the board's character became voluntary, not compulsory, and it was to cover wheat rather than all grains; the Canadian Wheat Board Act finally passed into the statute book in July 1935, and with it the financial stake built up by McFarland's stabilization exercise was assumed by the Federal power.

Fortuitously – though it hardly helped the fly-blown wheat-growers – the dangers of this extension of Federal responsibility was concurrently reduced by the drought which wiped out the Canadian surplus; when the post-1931 stabilization account was finally unwound it actually showed a profit.[53] By then, however, Bennett had suffered a humiliating defeat at the October 1935 election and soon retired to the British countryside. But in 'federalizing' the prairie wheat problem he had initiated a revolution which his successor, Mackenzie King, could not reverse even when the trading environment changed for the better; henceforth the grain-grower sold to the private trade when prices were high, and unloaded on to the Wheat Board (that is, other Canadian taxpayers) when prices were low. They had, in fact, succeeded in attaining the dream of the old western pools which had been so rudely shattered in 1929–30: disciplining the market-place. It was, contemporary observers would have been surprised to learn, the pinched, malnourished prairie farmers who faced a golden future, and Liverpool (that emporium of free world markets in grain) that soon slid into a long-drawn-out eclipse.

V

The general significance of Canadian wheat supplies to Britain's food position did not diminish after 1935: in fact, it increased during successive phases of stockpiling, war and reconstruction. But these latter sequences were characterized by inter-governmental bulk purchases. The market linkage between prairie farmers and British commercial interests, that classical apparatus of informalized collaboration, was fractured beyond repair, and producers measured their welfare by Wheat Board announcements at home, not by 'commercial sentiment' in Liverpool or London. This process, with its considerable political overtones, was scarcely inaugurated and completed within the short time-span covered by this article, but the changes involved were crucially shaped and accelerated by the secular movements of the Great Depression.

How, then, can we summarize this transformation? By playing 'core' to Western Canada's 'periphery', the British breakfast-table had underpinned a new social world in the distant prairies. But this bilateral, colonial relationship was splayed into the more complex webbing of the world market. It thrived as long as world prices continued to make production profitable, and as long as the Canadian West retained the social and psychological flexibility of a pioneering community to ride the parabolic motions of the market. This largely changed in the 1920s. Much prairie political debate began to turn on a natural desire to hammer protective elements into the regional economic structure. These tendencies were soon squashed by a market downturn seemingly egged on by exploitative British private interests. Instinctively, prairie growers looked to the old 'home government' in London to cushion them against the suddenly harsh environment. Yet in Britain, despite fierce political controversy after 1929–30 in which imperial rhetoric multiplied and concessions were shovelled out to domestic farmers, the cheap food principle was reinforced by depression;[54] and a strong awareness subsequently prevailed that the United Kingdom was peculiarly advantaged by the way that other people's surpluses (be they Canadian, Australian, Argentine or Russian) were crowded into British ports as other outlets were closed down. The National government after the summer of 1931 was buoyed along by real increases in living-standards raked-off at the expense of Canadian grain-growers, Australian fruit-farmers and Brazilian coffee-producers. Prairie society found that its salvation was more graspable through Federal politicking at home, where the necessities of national integration afforded new possibilities for western leverage, than through an imperial economy whose relevance had been so sharply curtailed. Henceforth regional orientations within a federal system, and its varied pickings, not the Dominion's place within an imperial system, was to be the touchstone of Canadian affairs. The divorce between Liverpool and Medicine Hat which lies at the heart of this article is thus only an aspect of these broader shifts in contemporary economic roles and alliances.

Our final remarks, however, must bring us back to Ronald Robinson's concern with the white colonist as '. . . the ideal, prefabricated collaborator . . . [with the result that in] white colonies . . . collaboration proved both stable and effective'. Certainly before the 1920s Liverpool and London prices set the guidelines around which an immensely complex Canadian production and marketing system was constructed; so that if all the other elements were subject to periodic agitation and reform, the latter were canonically accepted as a true and immutable reflection of the 'world position'. But the very scale and sophistication of this system, which made it such a smooth collaborative affair in a pioneering boom, was bound to cause problems in a more mature phase, when expectations, habits and social cultures required a certain price level to maintain equilibrium. In these latter circumstances a natural determination manifested itself to make the price (that is, Liverpool) fit the productive and social realities of Western Canada, rather than vice versa. This relegation of British agencies within the hierarchy of Canadian wheat marketing is what happened, with many ups and downs and at some fiscal cost to the Dominion, during the 1930s. The same story (in its theoretical outline) could be replicated with regard to other commodities and other Dominions, as the latter were equipped with the internal apparatus of state marketing agencies, storage infrastructures, Central Banks and independent credit policies.[55] In Canada, Australia, South Africa and even in gentle New Zealand the 1930s were characterized by moves to unscramble all those neat little imperial 'packages' which for decades had been an essential foundation of 'national development'; they were rebound in ways that were internally more secreted and only loosely meshed into imperial networks, however relatively important the British remained as conventional trading partners. Here, therefore, it is possible to discern an ideal, prefabricated decolonization, one essentially mediated through the commercial rather than the political market-place. It is surprising, given the scale of the historical professions in what were once the self-governing Dominions, that these intriguing themes have been left largely unexplored. Should government funding ever allow this interpretative neglect to be corrected, the researchers of the future would be well advised to take as one of their *points d'appui* those shrewd, pliable and characteristically crisp reconstructions of the British imperial process which made Ronald Robinson's tenure of the Beit Chair at Oxford one of the most distinguished intellectual episodes in modern British historiography.

NOTES

1. See I.M. Drummond, *British Economic Policy and the Empire, 1919–1939* (London, 1972) and *Imperial Economic Policy, 1917–1939* (London, 1974).
2. R.E. Robinson, 'Non-European foundations of European imperialism: sketch for a theory of collaboration', in R. Owen and B. Sutcliffe (eds.), *Studies in the Theory of Imperialism* (London, 1972), 125.
3. Andrew Porter, 'Britain, the Cape Colony and Natal, 1870–1914: Capital, Shipping and the Imperial Connection', *Economic History Review*, 4 (November 1981).
4. The best summary is in Vernon C. Fowke, *The National Policy and the Wheat Economy* (Toronto, 1957). A classic near-contemporary text is Louis Aubrey Wood, *A History of Farmers' Movements in Canada* (Toronto, 1924), especially 159–299.
5. Fowke, *National Policy*, 127–52.
6. For the theory of commodity pools see H.C. Filley, *Cooperation in Agriculture* (New York, 1927). Its practice in the Canadian setting is described in H.S. Patton, *Grain Growers' Cooperation in Western Canada* (Cambridge, MA, 1928) and Walter P. Davison, *Pooling Wheat in Canada* (Ottawa, 1927).
7. This cleavage can be followed in Fowke, *National Policy*, 219–42 and H.A. Innis, *The Diary of Alexander James McPhail* (Toronto, 1940).
8. The growth of European agricultural protectionism is crucial to the background of this article. For a brief overview, and for the argument that 1925 marked a critical stage on the way to world deflation, see the League of Nations publication *Considerations on the Present Evolution of Agricultural Protectionism* (Geneva, 1935).
9. *Corn Trade News*, 1 Oct. 1928. I am grateful to the National Association of British and Irish Millers (NABIM) for granting access to their holdings of both the *Corn Trade News* and *Milling*.
10. *Corn Trade News*, 13 Aug. 1929.
11. Ibid.
12. W.W. Swanson and P.C. Armstrong, *Wheat* (Toronto, 1930).
13. Ibid., 37.
14. Ibid., 79.
15. Ibid., 164.
16. *Corn Trade News*, 11 Dec. 1928.
17. *Corn Trade News*, 7 May 1929.
18. This was part of the 'Living Wage' campaign. For some background see David Marquand, *Ramsay MacDonald* (London, 1977), 450–65.
19. The ILP rationale is set out in A.H. Hirst, *The Bread of Britain* (Oxford, 1930).
20. This allegation first surfaced in the American trade journal *The Southwestern Miller*, and was soon taken up by the Canadian prairie press. The acrimony of this dispute between the various transatlantic interests is reflected in the various reports and articles in *Milling* during the first quarter of 1930.
21. *The Economist*, 27 Sept. 1930.
22. Ibid.
23. *The Economist*, 20 Sept. 1930.

24. *Corn Trade News*, 1 Dec. 1930.
25. See Drummond, *Imperial Economic Policy*, 145–169 and R.F. Holland, *Britain and the Commonwealth Alliance, 1918–39* (London, 1981), 115–26.
26. *Corn Trade News*, 16 Dec. 1930.
27. Memorandum by Sir Frederick Leith Ross, 'The Fall of World Prices', 28 July 1930, PRO 30/69/257, Ramsay MacDonald papers, Public Record Office (henceforth PRO).
28. For a full analysis of these currency issues see I.M. Drummond, *The Floating Pound and the Sterling Area, 1931–1939* (Cambridge, 1981).
29. 'Note of a Meeting between the Secretary of State for the Dominions, the Minister of Agriculture and the Representatives of the Millers, Corn Trades and Cooperative Societies', Ministry of Agriculture and Fisheries (hereafter MAF), 1 June 1932, MAF 40/24, PRO.
30. See the report of the Liverpool Corn Trade representatives on the Ottawa Conference in *Milling*, 27 Sept. 1932.
31. It should be noted, however, that at least one expert commentator did subsequently contend that a British wheat preference was of substantial value to Canadian producers. For the rather abstruse, and hence not altogether convincing, argument see D.A. MacGibbon, *The Canadian Grain Trade, 1931–51* (Toronto, 1952), 22–5.
32. See Robert Conquest, *Harvest of Sorrow* (London, 1986).
33. J. LeRoutegel to J.H. Thomas, 10 Nov. 1932, MAF 40/25, PRO.'
34. *The Times*, 6 June 1933.
35. Treasury Memorandum, 'Policy on the World Conference', Dec. 1931, T172/1814 (Treasury Papers), PRO.
36. 'Note of Inter-Imperial Conversations', 30 June 1933, T172/1814, PRO.
37. 'Note of Meeting between the President and Vice-Presidents of the World Conference', 3 July 1933, T172/1811, PRO.
38. 'Minutes of the 18th Meeting of the U.K. Delegates to the World Conference', 5 July 1933, T172/1810A, PRO.
39. 'Report on the International Wheat Conference held at Canada House, London', 21 July–6 August, FO 371/17329 W10047 (Foreign Office Papers), PRO.
40. For a full treatment of the International Wheat Agreement see C.F. Wilson, *A Century of Canadian Grain: Government Policy to 1951* (Saskatoon, 1978), 364–88. This is an indispensable account for any student of wheat economies in the period, written by a distinguished Canadian public servant close to the events in question.
41. *Manitoba Free Press*, 1 Sept. 1933.
42. See Wilson, *Canadian Grain*, 416–93.
43. For the New Deal and Canada see R.F. Holland, 'The End of an Imperial Economy: Anglo-Canadian Disengagement in the 1930s', *Journal of Imperial and Commonwealth History*, XI, 2 (January 1983), 159–74.
44. R.K. Finlayson, 'That Man R.B. Bennett', (unpublished manuscript quoted in Wilson, *A Century of Canadian Grain*, 437).
45. *Milling*, 12 Aug. 1933.
46. The Bracken ministry in Manitoba went some way down the restrictionist path, but soon retreated. For the experience of a leading prairie premier in the Depression see John Kendle, *John Bracken: A Political Biography* (Toronto, 1979).
47. 'Minutes of Inter-Departmental Meeting', 7 March 1934, MAF 40/148, PRO.
48. British grain interests at this juncture were extremely nervous that the National Government would be manoeuvred into an international agreement which further constrained their own freedom of trade. For the private pressure that was brought to bear in Whitehall see the record of the London Corn Trade deputation to the Ministry of Agriculture in MAF 40/144. The records of the London Corn Trade Association, although sparse, are also occasionally suggestive on this theme; the papers are held by the Grain and Feed Trades Association in St Mary Axe, London. The author is grateful for the grant of access to them. Future researchers, however, are advised to don anti-rodent wear.
49. 'Argentina and the Wheat Agreement: Extract from a note by Dr Ezekiel and Mr MacDougall', 8 May 1934, MAF 40/144, PRO.

50. 1934 marked a significant decline in the quality of Anglo-American relations. See R.F. Holland, *Britain and the Commonwealth Alliance*, 169.
51. MacFarland to Bennett, 2 June 1934, quoted in Wilson, *A Century of Canadian Grain*, 460.
52. The classic sociological treatment of the Depression-hit prairies is S.M. Lipset, *Agrarian Socialism: The Cooperative Commonwealth Federation in Saskatchewan: A Study in Political Sociology* (New York, 1950).
53. Wilson, *A Century of Canadian Grain*, 481–93.
54. For the aggression with which British trade negotiators exerted their heightened leverage on traditional commercial partners, especially those in Europe, during this period see T.J. Rooth, 'British Commercial Policy in the 1930s, with special reference to overseas primary producers', thesis submitted for the Degree of Doctor of Philosophy, University of Hull, 1984.
55. The argument at this point clearly bears a resemblance to the guiding themes in A.G. Hopkins, *An Economic History of West Africa* (London, 1973).

Sir Alan Cunningham and the End of British Rule in Palestine

by

Wm. Roger Louis

'[I]s the last soldier to see the last locomotive into the engine shed, lock the door and keep the key?'[1] The question posed by the last High Commissioner and Commander-in-Chief, Sir Alan Cunningham, went to the heart of the British dilemma in the closing months of the Palestine mandate. To state the problem in the terminology of Robinson and Gallagher, how did the proconsul respond when faced with the breakdown of the collaborative mechanism? To whom should the assets and authority of the Palestine government be transferred? There were further questions that perplexed Cunningham. Was it possible, or desirable, simply to withdraw without tilting the advantage to either the Jews or the Arabs? What should be the attitude towards the United Nations representatives who would arrive to supervise the partition of the territory? On a fundamental point in Ronald Robinson's general enquiry, to what extent did the initiative in answering those questions come from the Palestine administration? What was the influence of the High Commissioner in the actual decisions? In any British dependency during a time of crisis the part played by the colonial governor, or in this case the High Commissioner, could be decisive, or at any rate critical. Was Cunningham's? Might things have turned out slightly differently had he pursued a bolder line, or proved to be more accommodating to either side? Those questions will provide a focus to examine the British response to the civil war between the Arabs and the Jews from the time of the United Nations partition resolution on 29 November 1947 to the end of the mandate on 14–15 May 1948. The answers in turn will obliquely provide a commentary on the extent to which Robinson's theory of collaboration is useful in understanding the collapse of British influence in the Middle East.[2]

I

A contemporary Zionist account well catches the atmosphere of the last days of the Palestine administration as well as the popular impression of Cunningham's impenetrable personality. From the Jewish point of view he was a highly unsatisfactory High Commissioner:

> In their approaches to the High Commissioner the Jewish leaders

expressed their anxiety that the parting from Britain, in spite of the recent past, might be without bitterness, and in such conditions as might preface a cordial future. Would he allow the preparation of personnel, would he suffer a shadow re-organisation of departments, would he raise the strength of the Jewish supernumerary police and give them adequate weapons? Whatever may have been Sir Alan Cunningham's personal sentiments, he had his orders.

There was to be no co-operation in the setting up of a Jewish State. How, in any case, could a Jewish State survive the cancer of terrorism? Let Jews and Arabs come to terms. How, on what basis, through what mediation? Of this no hint. It was words which did not mask utter bankruptcy. The railways ceased to run, the post ceased gradually to function. The files were burnt in bonfires outside the offices.[3]

From the Zionist perspective, Cunningham thus presided over the wilful destruction of the Palestine administration.

From the Arab point of view his outlook was also perturbing. When Arab irregular troops crossed the frontiers into Palestine in mid-March 1948, they looked to the High Commissioner for tacit if not tangible support. They were rebuffed. They demonstrated, in Cunningham's phrase, 'extreme surprise'. He telegraphed to the Colonial Secretary: 'They have no idea what an embarrassment they are to this Government'. They had actually hoped to greet the High Commissioner with a guard of honour. Instead they were informed that they would be treated 'just as much as illegal immigrants as the Jews whom [they] . . . have constantly clamoured for us to stop'.[4] Here was a High Commissioner who perhaps had not succeeded in making clear the British goal of neutrality between Arab and Jew, but who intended as far as possible to remain even-handed.

Cunningham's private papers make clear that behind the mask of neutrality he was a Zionist, or at least that he believed that partition was the sole, practical solution. He had assumed his duties in Palestine in November 1945. He had not been there long, he reflected much later, when he began 'leaning to the opinion that partition was the only answer'. He seldom elaborated on his political outlook. Unfortunately for the historian, he had a soldier's reticence towards expressing his innermost thoughts. Usually he did not attempt to influence high policy. He respected Ernest Bevin, the Foreign Secretary who dominated British Palestine policy. 'I had the deepest admiration for him', Cunningham wrote later, even though he believed Bevin to be misguided in the belief that the Jews and Arabs could be reconciled. By mid-1947, when even Bevin recognized that partition had become inevitable, it was then, in Cunningham's judgement, too late for a peaceful settlement. 'Both Jews and Arabs were spoiling to get at each other's throat', he wrote, 'and we decided to leave'.[5] The decision to evacuate was taken by the British Cabinet on 20 September 1947 after a majority report by a committee of the United Nations (UNSCOP) had recommended partition.[6] In the subsequent period up to the time of the actual liquidation in May of the next year, Cunningham saw his job principally as holding the ring while the civil administration closed down and British troops evacuated.

During the war Cunningham had become famous as the military commander who had led the drive against Italian troops in East Africa. In his attack on Ethiopia, with widely acknowledged courage and boldness, he had covered 1,700 miles in less than two months, occupied 360,000 square miles of territory, and captured 50,000 prisoners. The surrender of Addis Ababa on 6 April 1941 marked the pinnacle of his military career. He then commanded the British Eighth Army in Egypt in the offensive against Rommel's *Afrika Corps* in November. At a critical stage of the campaign Cunningham judged that British troops should disengage. He was relieved of his command by General Sir Claude Auchinleck, who believed that Cunningham had begun 'to think defensively'.[7] '[H]e lost his nerve', Auchinleck commented later.[8] In Palestine the indictment of losing his nerve could never remotely be levelled against Cunningham. Indeed, the cloud over his military reputation probably made him even more determined to be remembered in history as a resolute High Commissioner. Nevertheless, the charge that he thought 'defensively' had relevance to his tenure of office in Palestine. Circumstances allowed him little other than a defensive stance.

Cunningham's harshest critic was the Chief of the Imperial General Staff, Field-Marshal Montgomery. 'He was always trying to persuade the British Government', Cunningham wrote later, 'that I was preventing the soldiers from doing their job'.[9] Montgomery denounced Cunningham and the Colonial Office for pursuing a policy of 'appeasement' towards the Jews. The CIGS believed in a military solution to the problem of Zionist terrorism. He wished to break the Hagana and the Irgun by the imposition of martial law that would be ruthlessly enforced. In response to this challenge Cunningham persistently held that repression of the Jews would lead to all-out urban guerrilla warfare, and that in any case the aim of the British should be to leave Palestine on as good as terms as possible with the Jews as well as with the Arabs. Cunningham's was essentially a political outlook. But from his own military background he keenly resented Montgomery's slur that he had tied the hands of the soldiers – 'a most base insinuation', in his phrase.[10] Both Cunningham and the General Officer Commanding British troops in Palestine, Sir Gordon MacMillan, believed that the principal duty of the army should be to provide security, not to administer a police state. In this contest between civil and military authority, Cunningham won out. This was the one area where he perhaps exerted a critical influence. He was not merely a civilian High Commissioner. He was also an old army man, still formally addressed as 'General Sir Alan Cunningham'. If he had been so inclined, he could probably have thrown his weight in the other direction and ended the British era with a military regime.

Cunningham wished to avert the 'bloodshed and chaos' that he felt would inevitably accompany a quick departure. He wanted to avoid the humiliation of anything that might resemble a scuttle. He still held out hope of securing the collaboration of Jewish and Arab municipal and other local authorities to keep the essential public services running and to minimize the disruption of British withdrawal. Above all he urged repeatedly that Jerusalem should not be abandoned 'to anarchy and bloodshed'.[11] After the termination of the mandate, Jerusalem should still be held by a small British force, perhaps civilian police, in concert with the United Nations. It would be to the obvious interest of both sides, in his judgement, to preserve order and to protect the Holy Places. Apart from Jerusalem, Cunningham established as strategic priorities the control of the airfield at Lydda and the port at Haifa. He believed that the civil administration should close down slightly in advance of the military withdrawal, but that the actual date for the termination of British rule should be determined by military considerations. 'It is . . . clear that the controlling factors in respect of time required for withdrawal', Cunningham telegraphed to the Colonial Office, 'will be military and not civil'.[12] Perhaps because of his own military background as well as the nature of the situation, Cunningham tended to concede the initiative to the military. In London, the Colonial Secretary, Arthur Creech Jones, feared the wrath of Montgomery. The military influence was thus a basic ingredient in the decisions about the pace and timing of withdrawal.

Cunningham's telegrams and correspondence reveal that he genuinely wished to see an orderly transfer of authority to 'a UNO Commission with teeth'.[13] In early November 1947 no one knew for certain whether the Zionists would succeed in mobilizing the two-thirds majority necessary for a resolution favouring partition in the General Assembly of the United Nations. Whichever way the vote might go, Cunningham assumed that the British would accept the outcome and co-operate with the United Nations. 'To walk out leaving chaos must surely be a last resort', he telegraphed to the Colonial Office on 5 November.[14] This was a persistent theme in the High Commissioner's telegrams: 'we are anxious to avoid the chaos and worse that would arise in a vacuum'.[15] Cunningham actually used the phrase 'transfer of power' with all the implications of an orderly and decisive transfer of authority to successor states on the model of India and Pakistan.

Yet the situation in Palestine was radically different. Cunningham had no answer to the question of how to obtain Arab acquiescence in the partition, still less to the problem of which Arab state or states might be the successor. '[T]here is as yet no cohesive organisation of the Arabs which could control any but local outbreaks', Cunningham telegraphed on the eve of the partition vote in New York.[16] If the Arabs could not preserve order, how could they provide the rudiments of an administration? The more he studied the problem the more Cunningham gloomily forecast that all the British might do to help the Arabs would be to maintain the civil administration as long as possible as a safeguard against Zionist encroachment: 'If we wish to go out of this country with the maximum of Arab goodwill it is surely essential that we should remain until we have been able to take sufficient steps to see that their civil interests are safeguarded in the future.'[17] Here, too, further study cast a cloud over the hopes for co-operation with the United Nations. If a United Nations commission arrived in Palestine to implement partition, the Arabs would unquestionably resist. Cunningham's mind was beginning to move in the same direction as those who were studying the problem in London. The risks of the British associating themselves with the United Nations might be too great. In any event Cunningham was now convinced that there could be no sharing of responsibility: 'a quite impossible situation would be created here if a UNO Commission were given any powers to enforce partition in Palestine while our Administration was still in existence. . . .'.[18]

Four days before the partition vote at the United Nations, an inter-departmental committee in Whitehall completed the 'Plan of Withdrawal'. The military timetable was as follows:

Phase I. – Gaza civil district: By 29 February.
Phase II. – Jerusalem, Lydda and part of Samaria: By 31 May.
Phase III. – Remainder of Samaria and Galilee: By 30 June.
Phase IV. – The remaining enclave round Haifa: By 31 July.[19]

With the exception of the Gaza district, the civil administration would continue until the termination of the mandate. The maintenance of civil authority was a condition imposed by Montgomery, who had said at a meeting earlier in the month: 'The civil administration and the troops would have to be withdrawn more or less concurrently, since it would be out of the question for the Army to take over the civil administration'.[20] The Palestine government would thus persevere, but the circumstances of its survival, and eventual liquidation, could not be foretold. If the United Nations resolution favouring partition were defeated, then the administration would probably face a renewal of Jewish terrorism. If it passed, then there would be the probability of full-scale Arab resistance. There was a further complication for which the British had to brace themselves. The United Nations might send, or attempt to send, a commission with executive authority. What then should be the attitude of the British? A failure to co-operate would bring charges of attempting to sabotage not only the Jewish state but also the United Nations itself. On the other hand collaboration with the Jews and the United Nations would destroy the goodwill between Britain and the Arab world.

Until late November 1947 the British could not give definite solutions to those hypothetical situations. Then came the historic United Nations vote in favour of partition on the 29th. Five days later Bevin, Creech Jones, and the Chiefs of Staff placed before the Cabinet the final version of the plan for withdrawal. The military evacuation in May would be based on the principle of 'clear cut backward moves' into an enclave around Haifa. In the meantime, according to Bevin and Creech Jones, the British administration should 'in no circumstances' become involved in enforcing the decision to partition. Such emphatic language gave Cunningham virtually no room for manoeuvre. Nor would he be allowed to take a flexible attitude towards an international solution. Since the sharing of authority with a United Nations commission would be 'intolerable', according to Bevin (and his compliant partner, Creech Jones), the British would do everything they could to thwart its arrival until the last two weeks or so before their own departure.[21] Cunningham's hopes for a 'UNO Commission with teeth', and supported by the British, were thus dashed. These plans were endorsed by the Cabinet on 4 December and announced in the House of Commons on the 11th. Though the military evacuation would not be complete until the summer of 1948, the termination of the civil administration was now set for 15 May.

II

Immediately after the UN resolution, Cunningham told a representative of the Arab Higher Committee (the body representing the political leadership of the Palestinian Arabs) that the British would now aim at making 'a clean withdrawal'.[22] Only now, Cunningham believed, were the Arabs fully beginning to comprehend the significance of the British departure. Much of the Arab response would be determined by the Mufti, Haj Amin al Husseini, the leader of the anti-British and extreme anti-Zionist faction of the Palestinian Arabs. Cunningham had written a year earlier about Arab impulses:

> In regard to the Arabs in Palestine, the leadership . . . is at present vested in men who have repeated the same parrot cry for so long that they are completely incapable of seeing any other point of view but their own or of appreciating any changing influences which time brings. Without the Mufti their power for harm appears at present to be confined to the urban areas. The villages are enjoying a period of comparative prosperity never before known to them and the bulk of them remember too well the hardships of the Arab rebellion to show much inclination to undergo similar trials once more.[23]

The UN resolution had now roused the Arabs in the villages as well as in the urban areas. There was now the danger that the Mufti might mobilize them against the Jews and the United Nations mission, thus forcing the British to intervene in a disastrous chain of events. In any event, Cunningham telegraphed Creech Jones on 6 December, there could be no doubt that, as soon as the British departed, 'the Arabs will attack the Jews'.[24]

Like most British officials, Cunningham believed that ultimately the Arabs would prevail in holding the Jews in a small and compact state along the coast. He did not begin to modify his view until early 1948. He thought that in their own self-interest the Jews would recognize that, the smaller the Jewish state, the more likely the Arabs would be to acquiesce.

Cunningham's view epitomized the rational, optimistic British outlook. He had written earlier about the prospects of partition:

> The argument against partition providing a final solution arises mainly from the fear that it would merely be a step towards further Jewish expansion in the future. I feel this fear is apt to be exaggerated. Should they get their State, the Jews will surely require a period of peace in which to develop it, and the bulk of them are responsible enough to realize that a small Jewish State with expansionist ideas in the middle of the Arab States could only result in keeping the Palestine problem in the condition of a running sore.[25]

As with the Arabs, the UN partition resolution now caused Cunningham to be more pessimistic about a reasonable compromise with the Jews. Extreme emotions were now stirred up on both sides. He wrote how difficult it was for the British to steer their way through 'the Scylla and Charibidis [sic] of Arab and Jewish passions'. Of the two, however, Cunningham did not doubt that the Jews now represented the greater danger. The UN resolution had instilled a sense of confidence and purpose in the Yishuv that was palpably more aggressive than previously. He telegraphed to the Colonial Office: 'The Jews in their present state of mixed hysteria and braggadocio are of the two more liable to provoke trouble during the period immediately facing us'.[26]

Cunningham was appalled by the Jewish 'brutality' against Arab demonstrators in early December 1947. The UN partition resolution had triggered off protests. 'The initial Arab outbreaks', he telegraphed about disturbances in Jerusalem, Haifa, and Jaffa-Tel Aviv, 'were spontaneous and unorganised . . . the weapons initially employed were sticks and stones. . . .' But the Jews had responded with firearms. The demonstrations became confrontations. 'The Hagana's policy,' Cunningham continued, 'was initially of defence and restraint, which quickly gave place to counter-operations involving destruction of Arab property. . .'.[27] He had no doubt that the Arabs had provoked the Jews, but the Jews themselves, in his judgement, had responded without restraint:

> The truth is that Jewish attacks on Arabs and Arab property have been scarely less numerous and serious than attacks by Arabs on Jews and Jewish property. The tendency of [the] Jewish press to picture [the] Yishuv as strictly on the defensive cannot stand enquiry; even the *Palestine Post* has been unable to put gloss on the bombing of a station of Arab buses in Haifa on 12th December in which four Arabs were killed.[28]

Cunningham was explicit in stating that the 'Jews have inflicted many more casualties on the Arabs than the reverse.' 'Practically all attacks', he telegraphed, 'have been against buses or in civilian centres.' Cunningham believed that it was 'unmitigated folly' for the Jews to pursue such a course of action that would permanently embitter the Arabs, and he condemned it in strong language as 'an offence to civilisation'.[29]

By mid-December Cunningham had to report that the control over clashes between Jews and Arabs was 'outstripping the resources of the police'.[30] The only hope of preventing the escalation of violence on the Arab side would be, in his judgement, through the leadership of the Arab Higher Committee and perhaps through the influence of the Mufti himself. Haj Amin al Husseini might appear to have been an unlikely recruit on the side of moderation. To most British officials he was little more than a renegade who had cast his lot with the Nazis during the war and was blinded by his anti-Zionist and anti-British fanaticism. If his own rhetoric were to be believed, he aimed to destroy the Jews and to create an Arab state in all of Palestine. Realistically he might have accepted less, at least as a temporary measure. Cunningham believed that there were military as well as political reasons why the Mufti might wish to co-operate with the British in keeping Palestine as peaceful as possible. The Arabs needed time to prepare for the showdown. 'Certainly the present frittering away of their resources in attacks which lead nowhere,' Cunningham telegraphed, 'cannot suit their book, whatever they intend to do in the future.'[31] If the Arabs could be persuaded to restrain themselves, the British at least would have a better chance for peaceful evacuation. Cunningham therefore made the following request: 'to bring pressure on the Mufti through the Arab League to get him to dissuade local Arabs from further violence. . .'[32] The High Commissioner thought this was a reasonable demand because he knew that one of the Mufti's closest associates, Hassan Salameh, was actually in Palestine. Cunningham described him as one of the key 'gang leaders'. As a link between the Mufti and the local Arabs, he might be used to British advantage.

Cunningham's proposal was dealt with in the Colonial Office by John Martin and the Permanent Under-Secretary, Sir Thomas Lloyd. 'I do not think that any approach to the Mufti on this matter would be politic or effective', Martin wrote. Lloyd concurred. So also did the Foreign Office. Those in control of the grand strategy of Britain's Palestine policy were wary of aligning themselves in any way with the Mufti, for reasons that were later well described in a Foreign Office minute during the war of 1948. Haj Amin would create an Arab state that would have disastrous anti-British consequences:

> The disadvantages of a separate Arab state under the Mufti are too obvious to need elaboration. It would be a hotbed of ineffectual Arab fanaticism and after causing maximum disturbance to our relations with the Arabs would very likely fall in the end under Jewish influence and be finally absorbed in the Jewish state, thereby increasing the area of possible Russian influence and excluding the possibility of our obtaining strategic requirements in any part of Palestine.[33]

Cunningham was rebuffed. The British made no approach to the Mufti. The incident demonstrated yet again that high policy would be determined in London, not Jerusalem, and that initiatives by the High Commissioner would not be encouraged.

Cunningham nevertheless remained essentially optimistic. He thought that the Zionist leaders could be reasoned with to modify the strategy of 'aggressive defence', if only because they would surely be persuaded that unrestrained attacks against the Arabs would jeopardize the long-term future of the Jewish state. He further believed that the situation could be kept localized because of the inability of the Arab states, with the possible exception of Jordan, to sustain offensive operations. Cunningham was glad to have confirmed from British posts in the Arab capitals that, with the exception of Jordan and possibly Iraq, the prevailing judgement was: 'The Arab Armies will not march on Palestine and . . . the problem can be localised mainly in Palestine itself'. Here was Cunningham's own assessment: 'I have always myself held the opinion that when it came to the point this would be the case, if only for the military reason that these armies have neither the training, the equipment nor the reserves of ammunition etc. to maintain an army in the field far from their bases for any length of time, if at all.'[34] For his part, Cunningham would step up efforts to keep the frontiers as secure as possible to prevent Arab arms-running, and with the Jews he would continue to persuade them 'to abandon what they call aggressive defence'.

In early 1948 Cunningham began to grow more pessimistic. '[I]f the Jews continue in their policy of blowing up innocent Arabs,' he warned, '. . . it seems probable that the position will worsen.' One particular incident he regarded as a grave omen. On 5 January the Hagana blew up part of the Semiramis Hotel in Jerusalem. There was a miscalculation about the wings of the building. The explosion killed 14 civilians including the Spanish Consul. Cunningham was again appalled. He repeated the phrase 'an offence to civilisation'. He reported his conversation the following day with David Ben-Gurion:

> I impressed on him the utter futility of such acts and told him if the Hagana continued this policy they would find themselves increasingly engaged in action with British troops. I asked him how they expected to defend themselves against world opinion for the crime of blowing up innocent people by [Jewish] Agency controlled forces.
>
> Mr Ben Gurion was clearly upset by this event. He assured me that it had been carried out without central direction. I am inclined to believe this and that the Agency are not able to control the local Haganah commanders.[35]

Cunningham was entirely willing to believe that Ben-Gurion himself bore no blame, but the lack of control over the Hagana made the situation all the more alarming.

The High Commissioner drew exactly the same conclusion from the

Arab handling of local dissidents. The Arab Higher Committee had lost control. So also to some extent had the British administration. Despite renewed efforts to patrol the borders, bands of Arab irregulars continued to cross the frontier from Syria. Cunningham was certain that the Arabs themselves were responsible for initiating conflicts with the Jews, but the Jews then retaliated with devastating effect. '[The] violence was started by the Arabs,' Cunningham telegraphed about a frontier incident in which 25 Arabs were killed, 'and Syria and Syrians are playing their part in keeping it alive.' The hope that the situation could be localized was proving to be vain. '[T]he local Arab leaders . . .,' the High Commissioner concluded, 'are unable to control these gangs from abroad.'[36]

The grand strategy to keep the situation stable was to allow King Abdullah to take over most of Arab Palestine. This was a delicate matter, as Cunningham fully recognized. Transjordan was a British client state. Abdullah was a British puppet. The Arab Legion, the most effective fighting unit in the Middle East, was commanded by a British officer, Brigadier Sir John Glubb. If Abdullah occupied the area designated as Arab by the United Nations, but then desisted, he would be accused of self-aggrandizement throughout the Arab world. Both he and the British would be denounced for collusion with the Zionists. On the other hand if he attempted to move into Jewish areas he, and of course the British as well, would be denounced for attempting to subvert the United Nations solution. Cunningham played only a marginal part in these calculations. He knew that Bevin and the Foreign Office 'saw some advantage in intervention by Abdullah'.[37] The High Commissioner was also well aware that if Abdullah acted precipitately, or indiscreetly, he would embroil the British not only with the other Arab countries but also with the United States. The Americans regarded the Arab Legion as a British force in all but name. It might determine the fate of Palestine. Yet the High Commissioner had little influence.

Cunningham now presided over an administration whose purpose had become the facilitation of military evacuation rather than government:

> I do not suppose ever before has a Civil Government had to carry on under conditions such as exist at present in Palestine, and, paradoxically . . . the decision to keep the Civil Government in being till May 15th was taken solely on account of military considerations. In fact in one sense the Civil Government is in support of the Military instead of the customary reverse situation.[38]

As of mid-January 1948, the civil courts had been unable to sit for a month, the General Post Office had been closed for the same period of time, and some 30 departments of the government opened only sporadically because Arab and Jewish officials refused to work in 'hostile' quarters of particular towns and cities. The Haifa oil installations had closed down. There would be severe fuel shortages. 'Civil Government can only limp along from now on,' Cunningham wrote, and, he continued, 'I cannot either refrain from mentioning the steady toll of lives in the Police and the Army quite apart from daily murderous attacks of one community against the other.' The High Commissioner therefore believed that it might be desirable to terminate the mandate earlier than had been planned. According to General MacMillan, the evacuation of stores could be completed by late March. Cunningham proposed the date of 1 April to end the mandate. He wished it to be understood, however, that the civil administration would continue to function as long as necessary. 'There is no question of the Civil Government running out and leaving the Army in the lurch just because there are some extra bombs and bullets.'[39] Cunningham thus made it emphatically clear that the civil administration would close down early only because the authority of the Palestine government had severely diminished and because the military reason for prolonging it no longer existed – not because of loss of nerve. Cunningham had good reason to urge the early termination of the mandate, but in this and other cases he seemed to justify the charge that he wobbled. 'Windy' was the damning word used by Montgomery to describe the inconclusive suggestions put forward by the High Commissioner.[40]

Cunningham was a public servant who wished to fulfil his assignment to the letter. He sought, perhaps excessively, to accommodate the military as well as the Colonial Office and the Foreign Office, without losing sight of the larger international dimension of the problem, and without being unfair to either Arab or Jew. In short he was placed in an almost impossible position. He did not regard himself as a formulator of policy as much as an executor, and his problem arose perhaps from his military background of expecting definite orders. He would have preferred clear-cut instructions on how to respond, for example, to the plans for the United Nations Commission to take over from the British. But Ernest Bevin did not wish this transfer of power to take place until late in the day. There were no plans. The British did not take the initiative in the UN debates. They merely responded to discussions that Cunningham regarded as 'so unrealistic as to be almost unbelievable'. While the delegates at Lake Success debated whether or not the two sides should be disarmed, and discussed the method and time when the British police should hand over arms and equipment to the international force, Cunningham observed that for the Arabs 'the killing of Jews now transcends all other considerations'.[41] The arrival of a UN Commission, Cunningham warned, would constitute a 'D day' for the Arabs.[42] Yet by February 1948 he still did not know when or even if the commission would arrive.

The UN Commission had been set up on 30 December 1947. It consisted of representatives of five countries (Czechoslovakia, Bolivia, Denmark, Panama, and the Philippines). At a distance Cunningham observed its proceedings with considerable exasperation. The members of the commission appeared to be mainly interested, in his judgement, with 'questions dealing with Jewish immigration' and seemed to have no conception of the 'utmost and catastrophic urgency' to ensure an orderly transfer of authority.[43] Unlike many of his colleagues in London, the High Commissioner sincerely wished to co-operate with the United Nations. 'I have always been anxious,' he wrote, '. . . in the interests of Palestine, [that] we should hand over to the Commission with as little dislocation as possible, and furthermore that we should avoid being placed in the position . . . of being accused of obstruction.'[44] He suggested three areas of collaboration with the United Nations:

(a) the prevention or limiting of violence between Arab & Jew.
(b) the preservation of the economic structure of the country to the greatest extent possible.
(c) the safeguarding of JERUSALEM.[45]

Cunningham eventually began to despair of concerted action to prevent conflict, and, as the weeks progressed, he became pessimistic about maintaining utilities and public services essential to the economic life of the country; but he continued to hold out hope that Jerusalem might be neutralized.

The High Commissioner held that it was a matter of common sense that the British should do all they could to preserve the peace in Jerusalem. 'It is unthinkable that Jerusalem should just be left to become a cockpit of internecine strife and that the Holy City should lapse into a pitched battlefield. It is for this reason that I would again stress the paramount importance of immediate planning and action to prevent such a catastrophe.'[46]

He believed that at the time of the termination of the mandate the Jews would be too busy defending themselves in the coastal plain to be able to attack the Arabs in Jerusalem, nor in any case would the Jews wish to come into conflict with a UN peace-keeping force. The Arabs would also be preoccupied in the struggle in the west. Thus the neutralization of Jerusalem seemed to be possible. By late February, however, Cunningham had begun to lose heart:

> Poor Jerusalem! Is there no way of at the least detaching her from the conflict? If there was any way of setting up the Jerusalem State outside the UNO Commission it might have a chance, but I recognise it would not be an economic proposition. The alternative is to find an International Force for Jerusalem only, with the object of keeping the city as much out of the conflict as possible.[47]

By mid-March it was still not clear whether even an advance guard of staff members of the UN Commission would arrive before the termination of the mandate. Cunningham telegraphed to Creech Jones: 'It cannot be in our interests to allow Palestine to fall into complete chaos or Jerusalem to become a cockpit'.[48] Yet the drift was now clearly in that direction.

Cunningham's estimates about the United Nations as an effective peacekeeping force were proving to be misguided, as were his assessments of Arab and Jewish fighting units. In late February 1948 he finally began to change his mind about the Arabs ultimately winning.

'There seems to be little signs of any Arab State other than Trans-Jordan intending at any time to exert their full military strength,' he wrote to John Martin in the Colonial Office, '. . . and apart from the blowings-up, the Arab operations have been lamentable from a military point of view.' Cunningham explained the reasons for his new outlook:

> . . . I am much less certain now of the final outcome, purely due to the apparent military ineptitude of the Arabs. They should be able to paralyse the Jews who depend entirely on open communications. But have they the military sense to see this? At the moment they can only think of 'killing the Yehudis' and the Jews are winning at that game, as more Arabs are being killed than Jews.[49]

Nevertheless Cunningham remained curiously optimistic about the Arabs, as if he were unable to liberate himself from the traditional British view that in any sustained conflict the Arabs would prove themselves militarily superior to the Jews. Indeed the outcome of relatively balanced forces might not be entirely unsatisfactory from a British point of view:

> On the whole I am inclined to think now that the Arabs will be unable to prevent partition of some sort, even though it looks as if no international force will be forthcoming . . . the Jews should be able to hold the coastal plain, so it might well all end in a partition more on the lines of what we would consider fair.[50]

Even with a slightly more fatalistic attitude there was still one question that plagued Cunningham. If the UN Commission failed to arrive, to whom should the British transfer authority? To whom would they give the key to the locomotive shed?

III

By the spring of 1948 Britain had become only one of several contending powers in Palestine. Cunningham believed that the members of the Arab League aimed to divide the country into 'spheres of influence', Syria controlling eastern Galilee, Egypt the Negev, and Transjordan the areas of Samaria and Hebron. Jerusalem would be a test of strength between Abdullah and the Mufti. The most significant development, in the High Commissioner's view, was the entry into Palestine by the leader of the Arab Army of Liberation, Fawzi al-Qawukji, on 5 March 1948. He had been preceded on 24 February by between 500 and 1000 Lebanese, Syrian, Egyptian, and Transjordanian irregular forces invading Samaria and Galilee.[51] The British estimated the irregulars in Palestine and the neighbouring countries at 6,000 to 7,000. Cunningham and his colleagues did not have a high military esteem for these 'gangs', or for their leader. Sir Alec Kirkbride, the British Ambassador in Jordan, referred to Qawukji as 'little short of a menace to his own side'.[52] Nevertheless, the Arab mobilization was under way. So also was the Zionist. By mid-March, according to Cunningham's intelligence reports, 70,000 Jews were under arms.[53] On the Arab civilian side, the salient and problematical feature was deficient leadership: 'there are no influential Palestine Arabs in Palestine', Cunningham reported on 17 March. On the Jewish side Cunningham was struck by the growing confidence of David Ben-Gurion. 'I found him arrogant, self satisfied and bombastic', the High Commissioner reported after a conversation with him. Cunningham had listened with disbelief when Ben-Gurion had described the attitude of the Palestinian Arabs: 'He said he knew none of the Palestine Arabs wanted to fight and that if it were not for outside influences they would not do so. On this point he is clearly in a fool's paradise'.[54]

The rapidly developing events in March to early May 1948 caused Cunningham to see clearly what he had vaguely feared over the past months: 'The Jewish military star is now in the ascendant'.[55] The consequent Arab demoralization was far greater than he had anticipated. 'Wherever the Arabs are in contact with the Jews [in military encounter],' he wrote, 'their morale has practically collapsed and we are finding increasing difficulty in bolstering them up.'[56] The High Commissioner attributed the plummeting Arab morale to the flight of responsible leaders at all levels, military as well as civil, especially at the municipal rank:

> [T]he collapsing Arab morale in Palestine is in some measure due to the increasing tendency of those who should be leading them to leave the country. For instance in Jaffa the Mayor went on 4 days leave 12 days ago and has not returned, and half the National Committee has left.
>
> In Haifa the Arab members of the municipality left some time ago; the two leaders of the Arab Liberation Army left actually during the recent battle. Now the Chief Arab Magistrate has left. In all parts of the country the effendi class has been evacuating in large numbers over a considerable period and the tempo is increasing.[57]

Cunningham himself was puzzled about the precipitate Arab evacuation, all the more so when he received word from Haifa that the Arab high command appeared to be encouraging the exodus. He telegraphed to London: 'British authorities at Haifa have formed the impression that total evacuation is being urged on the Haifa Arabs from higher Arab quarters and that the townsfolk themselves are against it'.[58]

Even before the fall of Haifa, the General Officer Commanding British troops in Palestine had urged an earlier evacuation from Jerusalem. MacMillan did not believe he could indefinitely hold open the line of retreat. 'Our resources in Jerusalem are so stretched,' Cunningham telegraphed after consultation with him, 'that any further attacks against our positions or against our routes for withdrawal via Hebron and Ramallah would be difficult to counter.'[59] The British feared further Zionist terrorist attacks. If subsequent events followed the pattern in Haifa, then the collapsing Arab position would place the British in an increasingly dangerous position. The Arabs would feel betrayed and would eventually turn on them. By late April the Jewish attacks had led to a crisis with ominous and intolerable implications for the British:

> Recent Jewish military successes (if indeed operations based on the mortaring of terrified women and children can be classed as such) have aroused extravagant reactions in the Jewish press . . . Jewish broadcasts, both in content and in manner of delivery, are remarkably like those of Nazi Germany . . . on the roads, Hagana armoured cars are increasingly impudent and intrusive. . . .
>
> The Arabs of the large towns, who have borne the brunt of recent Jewish offensive action are . . . bitter against the British. . . . They must pin the blame on someone, and who [are] more deserving than the British?[60]

Cunningham now feared more than anything else the repetition in Jerusalem of the events in Haifa. He was therefore impressed with the argument that the British should evacuate Jerusalem before they were ignominiously pushed out.

On 21 April, in the midst of the Haifa crisis, Cunningham had telegraphed that he might have to choose between the two evils of leaving Jerusalem early or being forced to leave. Unless Jerusalem were evacuated, Haifa might also be lost. But he warned that he could not leave Jerusalem without terminating the mandate. 'It is unthinkable,' he advised, 'that a so-called Government should be in Haifa with Jerusalem a battlefield behind it.'[61] Cunningham rather unimaginatively assumed that the military withdrawal would relentlessly continue, thereby forcing British troops into a precarious position. He was following the lead of General MacMillan rather than putting forward a constructive proposal of his own, though he felt strongly about Jerusalem. When the Prime Minister and other members of the Cabinet dealt with the matter on 27 April, they saw immediately that Jerusalem would have to be held until 15 May:

> [W]e should be regarded throughout the world as having suffered a humiliating reverse, if we were unable to adhere to our plans on account of Arab and Jewish military pressure.
>
> It should therefore be made plain to the Commanders-in-Chief, Middle East, that Jerusalem must be held until 15th May by the employment of all necessary military, naval and air force resources; to the extent required, reinforcements should be sent to Palestine from elsewhere.[62]

Creech Jones, who was presiding over Britain's Palestine business at the United Nations, telegraphed to Cunningham' 'an earlier termination of the mandate would bring general dismay, a very serious loss of reputation here with intensification of malicious criticism. . . .'.[63] Like his colleagues in London, the Colonial Secretary believed that Jerusalem should be held until the end.

It was definitely a failure of imagination on Cunningham's part not to recognize that political considerations should prevail over the military plans for withdrawal, or to request additional troops. 'No mention was made of the possibility of reinforcement from outside', he weakly rejoined, '[so] I assumed it was impossible.' On the other hand the High Commissioner's motives were unimpeachable. 'It is the lives of soldiers and police I have in mind rather than the danger to the administration', he explained.[64] From beginning to end Cunningham personified the soldierly virtues of loyalty and courage, and, consistent with his own character, he tended to believe the best of his subordinates. The officers of the civil administration, he affirmed, had 'stuck it out with infinite patience and courage'.[65]

During the last two weeks Cunningham worked tirelessly for a cease-fire and truce in Jerusalem. This was one of the causes he sincerely and passionately supported for altruistic reasons, but he had sound military motives as well. 'Unless there is a truce,' he telegraphed towards the end of the first week in May, 'this [evacuation] is going to be an extremely tricky operation as both Arabs and Jews want to get control of the route the troops must take.'[66] The High Commissioner was able to achieve the cease-fire because it was advantageous, at that time, to both the Jews and Arabs. In Jerusalem both sides were precariously balanced. Nevertheless the cease-fire held. The High Commissioner and his party left Jerusalem on 14 May without disturbances.

IV

The British Consul in Jerusalem, R.A. Beaumont, provided a memorable account of Cunningham's departure from Jerusalem:

> [A]t about ten minutes past eight o'clock local time on 14th May, Sir Alan Cunningham, His Majesty's High Commissioner for Palestine, passed the gate of this building on his way out of Jerusalem. A colour-party of the Suffolk Regiment bearing flags of the New Zealand War and the First World War inscribed with the regimental battle honours gave the salute as he passed.
>
> A few bedraggled Arabs who happened to have gathered near the Damascus Gate, raised a feeble cheer. It is difficult to assess their motive, gratitude to the last representative of the British mandate or relief at his departure. As a sentimentalist, I incline to believe the former. It was a pathetic epilogue to nigh thirty years of toil and sacrifice.[67]

Cunningham nevertheless had presided over a well-organized and carefully planned withdrawal that took place entirely according to plan.

And the key to the locomotive shed? Part of the answer is in the diary of Henry Gurney, the Chief Secretary of the Palestine administration:

> The Police locked up their stores (worth over £1m) and brought the keys to the United Nations, who refused to receive them. I had to

point out that the United Nations would be responsible for the administration of Palestine in a few hours' time (in accordance with the November Resolution) and that we should leave the keys on their doorstep whether they accepted them or not; which we did.[68]

And the success in evacuating stores? According to a British military historian, 'the amount of stores evacuated exceeded the estimate, and it would have been larger but for some heavy stealing, for which Jews and Arabs could not claim full responsibility'.[69] There is virtually no evidence in Cunningham's papers that he was aware of the seamier side of the British evacuation. There is indeed no reason not to take his recapitulation as views that he passionately and consistently held:

> For three years or more we had been ruling in Palestine without a policy, amid turbulence, vilification, assassination and kidnapping. That the British should have been able to stand the strain for so long, without a goal to aim at, was due to the superlative quality of the civil service, whose integrity, impartiality and courage were beyond praise, and to the tolerance and patience of the soldiers and the police, the standard of which could have been reached by no other nation.[70]

Cunningham's words reflect his own achievement. He enabled the British to depart from Palestine with a modest amount of dignity and, in their own eyes, self-respect, which at least is a contrast with the end of the story of British imperialism in Egypt in 1956.

Here then is a proconsul just as remarkable as the soldiers, statesmen, and buccaneers whose pen portraits made the themes of *Africa and the Victorians* so resplendent. As an exponent of British imperialism in the Middle East, Cunningham tried, but failed absolutely, to hold the balance between Arab and Jew. He discovered that the attempt to collaborate with two irreconcilable antagonists leads ultimately to a dead end, as British statecraft might have anticipated, but did not, in 1917. In Palestine the theory of the fabulous artificer of collaboration illuminates a variation of the solution found in India, but with a less felicitous outcome: informally dividing, formally quitting, without the Commonwealth as a consolation prize.

NOTES

* A much expanded version of this essay is being published in Hebrew under the auspices of the Davis Institute of the Hebrew University.

1. Cunningham to Arthur Creech Jones (Secretary of State for the Colonies), 'Top Secret & Personal' telegram, 25 Nov. 1947, Cunningham Papers II/3/111, St. Antony's College, Oxford. The telegrams between the High Commissioner and the Colonial Secretary in the Cunningham Papers form the most complete record of the last months of the mandate. There is a less complete set in the Creech Jones Papers, Rhodes House, Oxford. Many of the key Colonial Office files have been withheld, but a substantial

number of Cunningham's telegrams and letters may be found in Foreign Office files. All references to CAB[inet], C[olonial] O[ffice], F[oreign] O[ffice], and PREM[ier] records are to documents at the Public Record Office, London. In this essay I have greatly benefited from the essays published in Wm. Roger Louis and Robert W. Stookey (eds.), *The End of the Palestine Mandate* (University of Texas Press, 1984).
2. Ronald Robinson, 'Non-European Foundations of European Imperialism', in Roger Owen and Bob Sutcliffe (eds.), *Studies in the Theory of Imperialism* (London, 1972), reprinted in W.R. Louis, *Imperialism: the Robinson and Gallagher Controversy* (New York, 1976).
3. Harry Sacher, *Israel: The Establishment of a State* (London, 1952), 112.
4. Cunningham to Creech Jones, 'Top Secret' telegram, 15 March 1948, Cunningham Papers III/2/25.
5. 'Note' by Cunningham, no date, Cunningham Papers IV/2/11. In this tantalizingly brief assessment of his own Palestine career, Cunningham lamented the inability of the United Nations to sponsor an effective 'international police force'. He added, obviously much later, 'And after this the Congo!' His published memoir is: Sir Alan Cunningham, 'Palestine – The Last Days of the Mandate', *International Affairs* (October, 1948).
6. For an analysis from the British perspective, see Wm. Roger Louis, *The British Empire in the Middle East 1945–1951* (Oxford, 1984), part IV, Chapter 5; and Michael J. Cohen, *Palestine and the Great Powers 1945–1948* (Princeton, 1982), Chapters 10–11. Two works by Amikam Nachmani are also especially useful: 'Generals at Bay in Post-War Palestine', *Journal of Strategic Studies*, 6, 4 (December 1983), and *Great Power discord in Palestine: The Anglo-American Committee of Inquiry into the Problems of European Jewry and Palestine 1945–1946* (London, 1986).
7. Winston S. Churchill, *The Grand Alliance* (Boston, 1951), 569.
8. Philip Warner, *Auchinleck: The Lonely Soldier* (London, 1981), 110.
9. Cunningham's 'Note', cited note 5.
10. Cunningham to Creech Jones, 'Top Secret & Personal' telegram, 26 Feb. 1948, Cunningham Papers III/I/118.
11. See e.g. Cunningham to Creech Jones, 'Top Secret' telegram, 8 Oct. 1947, Cunningham Papers II/2/127.
12. Ibid.
13. Cunningham to John Martin (Colonial Office), 'Top Secret & Personal' telegram, 5 Nov. 1947, Cunningham Papers II/3/23.
14. Ibid.
15. Cunningham to Creech Jones, 'Top Secret & Personal' telegram, 12 Nov. 1947, Cunningham Papers II/3/45.
16. Cunningham to Creech Jones, 'Top Secret & Personal' telegram, 23 Nov. 1947, Cunningham Papers II/3/95.
17. Ibid.
18. Cunningham to Creech Jones, 'Top Secret & Personal' telegram, 19 Nov. 1947, Cunningham Papers II/3/74.
19. Memorandum by the Official Committee on Palestine, 'Palestine – Plan of Withdrawal', D.O. (47) 91, 25 Nov. 1947.
20. D.O. (47) 23rd Meeting, 7 Nov. 1947.
21. Memorandum by Bevin and Creech Jones, C.P. (47) 320, 3 Dec. 1947, CAB 129/22; Annex B is the plan by the Chiefs of Staff.
22. Cunningham to Creech Jones, 'Top Secret & Personal' telegram, 1 Dec. 1947, Cunningham Papers II/3/122.
23. Cunningham to Hall, 'Top Secret and Personal', 20 Sept. 1946, FO 371/52562; quoted in Louis, *British Empire in the Middle East*, 449.
24. Cunningham to Creech Jones, 'Top Secret and Personal' telegram, 6 Dec. 1947, Cunningham Papers II/3/132.
25. Cunningham to Hall, 20 Sept. 1946, FO 371/52562; quoted in Louis, *British Empire in the Middle East*, 450.
26. Cunningham to Creech Jones, 'Top Secret & Personal' telegram, 9 Dec. 1948, Cunningham Papers II/3/136.

27. Cunningham to Creech Jones, 'Top Secret' telegram, 13 Dec. 1947, CO 537/2363.
28. Ibid.
29. Cunningham to Creech Jones, 'Top Secret and Personal' telegram, 15 Dec. 1947, CO 537/2363.
30. Cunningham to Creech Jones, 'Top Secret', 13 Dec. 1947, CO 537/2363.
31. Cunningham to Creech Jones, 'Top Secret and Personal' telegram, 15 Dec. 1947, CO 537/2363.
32. Ibid.
33. Minute by Bernard Burrows, 17 Aug. 1948, FO 371/68822.
34. Cunningham to Creech Jones, 'Top Secret & Personal' telegram, 28 Dec. 1947, Cunningham Papers II/3/161.
35. Cunningham to Creech Jones, 'Secret and Personal' telegram, 7 Jan. 1948, Cunningham Papers III/1/9.
36. Cunningham to Creech Jones, 'Top Secret & Personal' telegram, 12 Jan. 1948, Cunningham Papers III/1/20.
37. Cunningham to Martin, 'Top Secret and Personal', 27 Jan. 1948, Cunningham Papers III/1/54.
38. Cunningham to Creech Jones, 'Top Secret & Personal' telegram, 26 Feb. 1948, Cunningham Papers III/1/118.
39. Extracts from a letter by Cunningham circulated to the Palestine Committee, 13 Jan. 1948, FO 371/68612.
40. *The Memoirs of Field-Marshal the Viscount Montgomery of Alamein, K.G.* (Cleveland, 1958), 424.
41. Cunningham to Creech Jones, 'Top Secret & Personal telegram, 19 Jan. 1948, Cunningham Papers III/1/29.
42. Cunningham to Creech Jones, 'Top Secret & Personal' telegram, 4 Feb. 1948, Cunningham Papers III/1/75.
43. Cunningham to Creech Jones, 'Top Secret & Personal' telegram, 19 Jan. 1948, Cunningham Papers III/1/29.
44. Cunningham to Creech Jones, 'Top Secret & Personal' telegram, 4 Feb. 1948, Cunningham Papers III/1/75.
45. Cunningham to Creech Jones, 'Top Secret & Personal' telegram, 13 March 1948, Cunningham Papers III/2/29.
46. Cunningham to Sir Thomas Lloyd, 'Top Secret & Personal', 15 January 1948, FO 371/68531.
47. Cunningham to Martin, 24 February 1948, FO 371/68537.
48. Cunningham to Creech Jones, 'Top Secret & Personal' telegram, 13 March 1948, Cunningham Papers III/2/29.
49. Cunningham to Martin, 24 Feb. 1948, FO 371/68537.
50. Ibid.
51. Cunningham to Creech Jones, 11 March 1948, Cunningham Papers III/2/20.
52. Cohen, *Palestine and the Great Powers*, 338.
53. Cunningham to Creech Jones, 'Top Secret & Personal' telegram, 17 March 1948, Cunningham Papers, III/2/38.
54. Cunningham to Creech Jones, 'Top Secret and Personal', 9 March 1948, Cunningham Papers III/2/11.
55. Cunningham to Creech Jones, 'Top Secret' telegram, 23 April 1948, Cunningham Papers III/4/16.
56. Cunningham to Creech Jones, 'Top Secret' telegram, 1 May 1948, Cunningham Papers III/5/25.
57. Cunningham to Creech Jones, 'Top Secret' telegram, 26 April 1948, Cunningham Papers III/4/71.
58. Cunningham to Creech Jones, 'Secret' telegram, 25 April 1948, Cunningham Papers III/4/52.
59. Cunningham to Creech Jones, 'Top Secret & Personal' telegram, 27 April 1948, Cunningham Papers III/4/87.
60. Cunningham to Creech Jones, 'Top Secret' telegram, 30 April 1948, Cunningham Papers III/4/152.

61. Cunningham to Creech Jones, 'Top Secret & Personal' telegram, 21 April 1948, Cunningham Papers III/3/119.
62. Meeting of Ministers, 27 April 1948, PREM 8/860.
63. Creech Jones to Cunningham, 'Top Secret' telegram, 29 April 1948, FO 371/68546.
64. Cunningham to Creech Jones, 'Personal' telegram, 5 May 1948, Cunningham Papers III/5/24.
65. Cunningham to Creech Jones, 'Top Secret & Personal' telegram, 18 April 1948, Cunningham Papers III/3/98.
66. Cunningham to Creech Jones, 'Top Secret' telegram, 5 May 1948, Cunningham Papers III/5/91.
67. Beaumont to Bevin, 29 May 1948, FO 371/68621.
68. Gurney Diary, 13 May 1948, Middle East Centre, St Antony's College, Oxford; Walid Khalidi, 'The Arab Perspective', in Louis and Stookey, *End of the Palestine Mandate*, 132.
69. Blaxland, *The Regiments Depart*, 59.
70. Cunningham, 'Palestine – The Last Days of the Mandate', 490.

Africa and the Labour Government, 1945–1951

by

Ronald Hyam

> With Creech Jones and Cohen the African empire came deliberately to the end of the beginning and the beginning of the end where the rise toppled over into decline and fall.

> Had British planners decided that nationalism was the continuation of imperialism by other and more efficient means? Perhaps.

> A metropolitan 'new deal' in local collaboration for purposes of developing the colonies economically was translated into terms of political independence.

> We thought we weren't giving away an empire, we were creating a great, practical, cultural Commonwealth. . . . If you look at the arguments put forth for the transfer of power, half the argument was that this will prolong the Empire. The other half was that it will lead to constructive rebuilding.

As these quotations indicate, no-one has done more than Ronald Robinson to penetrate the inwardness of Britain's post-war African policy, and to try to relate it to 'a general theory of imperialism'. After a lifetime's thinking about Africa and applying his Colonial Office experience to its history, none knows better than he the truth of the moral philosopher's words: 'We carry within us the wonders we seek without us: There is all Africa and her prodigies in us' (Sir Thomas Browne, *Religio Medici*).

Two quintessential themes dominated the work of the Labour government between 1945 and 1951: economic recovery and Russian expansion. Both problems pointed to an increased interest in the empire in general and in Africa in particular. 'My mind turns more and more', wrote Chancellor of the Exchequer Hugh Dalton in 1947, 'towards a consolidation in Africa'.[1] In October 1949 the Minister of Defence, A.V. Alexander ('King Albert Victorious'), defined the government's three main policy objectives as: (i) securing 'our people against aggression', (ii) sustaining a foreign policy dominated by 'resistance to the onrush of Communist influence' everywhere, from Greece to Hong Kong, and (iii) achieving 'the most rapid development practicable of our overseas possessions, since without such Colonial development there can be no major improvement in the standard of living of our own people at home'.[2] (An astonishing admission! – where now is Lord Lugard? where Lord Hailey?) As far as Foreign Secretary Ernest Bevin was concerned, from the moment that that neo-Palmerstonian took office he saw 'the utmost importance' from political, economic and defence points of view of developing Africa and making its resources 'available to all'. Stepping up the flow of strategic raw materials out of Africa would help to free Britain from financial dependence on America. Bevin's pet projects were to sell manganese ore from Sierra Leone to the United States, and coal from Wankie to Argentina in return for beef. Always dreaming cosmoplastic dreams, he also talked about a new triangular oceanic trade between eastern Africa, India and Australia. But more than this: Bevin feared the Russians would sooner or later 'make a major drive against our position in Africa'.[3] In Attlee's world-picture too, Africa presented the same duality of concern: economically it was immoral not to develop its 'great estates', while politically the Cold War pointed to the necessity of an increasing reliance on African manpower, as well as coming to terms with African nationalism. On the one hand he wanted to increase European settlement in under-populated areas of east-central Africa, but on the other, recognised that in Gold Coast and Nigeria 'an attempt to maintain the old colonialism would, I am sure, have immensely aided Communism'.[4]

Several Labour ministers believed they were called 'to bring the modern state to Africa'.[5] John Strachey – of all people – as Minister of Food foisted the mechanized groundnuts project on Tanganyika to improve the British margarine ration, arguing that only by such enterprises could African possessions be rapidly developed, and 'become an asset and not a liability as they largely now are'. Even Sir Stafford Cripps wanted to 'force the pace' of African economic development in order to close the dollar gap.[6] At the same time, if Britain was to remain a world power, they realized they had to control rising nationalist tension in Africa because, as James Griffiths (the able latter-day Secretary of State for the Colonies) put it in 1950, 'we had to face an ideological battle in the world, especially in the Colonies', and the next ten years would be crucial.[7] 'A glance at Asia', Herbert Morrison declared, was enough to show the kind of troubles which 'could break loose' in Africa if they did not adjust their policies to promote political and economic change as a matter of 'two-way teamwork' between the metropolis and Africans.[8] Beyond that, and for Attlee especially, it was a challenge to statesmanship to meet the susceptibilities of Afro-Asian peoples while maintaining and expanding the Commonwealth. The Prime Minister believed Britain was its 'material and spiritual head', and that it could be a multi-racial international bridge, as well as an effective global barrier against Communist aggression. One of Attlee's principal long-term preoccupations was to prevent newly-independent states seceding from the Commonwealth, since this would be exploited by Russia as a failure and would automatically diminish British influence throughout the world.[9]

The four great axes of Labour's engagement with Africa were political, strategic, economic and racial. Not in any one of these spheres was a simple, straightforward policy possible.

By 1946 the Colonial Office planners were acutely aware of the need for a clear policy based on the political advancement of Africans. There were perhaps five main reasons for this. First, African political consciousness had been stimulated by the war, and the white man's prestige destroyed as an instrument of government, particularly in the eyes (it was thought) of returning black ex-servicemen. Secondly, to carry out the new social welfare and economic development programmes, a new political instrument was required, namely African participation. Thirdly, Colonial Service attitudes had to be reconstructed: morale was bad, the nostrums of Lugard and Cameron were moribund, and officers felt frustrated by newly-emerging African criticisms of them. The men on the spot needed a new sense of 'mission', a fresh constructive goal to work to. A redefinition of policy was thus obviously overdue. Fourthly, it seemed Britain had to retain a positive initiative in the formulation of African policy, otherwise control would pass to 'settler' regimes (South African, Rhodesian and Portuguese), to whom it was a matter of life and death. This would imperil British trusteeship policies; indeed, after the adoption of apartheid in South Africa from 1948, an actual policy-conflict existed. Finally, and perhaps most important of all, international pressures from the United Nations, American and 'world opinion' were (as Secretary of State for the Colonies Arthur Creech Jones said) directing 'the play of a fierce searchlight' over Africa.[10] These outside influences were expected to stimulate the demand for self-government. 'Prejudiced, ignorant and hostile' criticism and interference from 'the anti-colonial bloc' (Communist and Latin American countries, together with India, and, most vocal adversary of all, the Philippines) would be grounded not in trying to reform imperial systems but in abolishing them entirely and instantly as anachronistic. Officials regarded this as a recipe for widespread post-imperial disintegration, as it took no account of fitness for self-government:

> We are just as concerned to see our colonial peoples achieve self-government, but in conditions in which they really can stand on their own, without the risk of subsequently falling under foreign political or economic domination, or under the control of an undemocratic minority seeking power for its own selfish ends.

Britain aimed at establishing stable, effective and representative political systems. This was a delicate operation in which they must not be dictated to by '58 back-seat drivers without responsibility'.[11]

These reasons, internal and international, 'demanded a new approach to policy in Africa' (Ivor Thomas, Parliamentary Under-Secretary at the Colonial Office). A unified, logical, coherent and convincing policy was essential.[12] The process of defining it centred on Andrew Cohen (*'alter ego* of Creech Jones'), head of the African department – he of the purple shirt and spikey handwriting, once a Cambridge Apostle, now 'Emperor of Africa'. Cohen insisted that what was wanted was not another set of platitudinous generalizations but an actual programme of practical policies. 'There will be no question of imposing a stereotyped blueprint. All we can do is to indicate the broad objective. . .'. The first fruit of Cohen's initiative (welcomed by Creech Jones) was a notable State Paper, the famous 'Local Government Despatch' of February 1947. It enjoined the promotion of efficient local government as a priority, and represented the victory of conciliar principles over the Indirect Rule tradition. This was the work of Cohen, G.B. Cartland and R.E. Robinson: Cohen called it 'a joint effort' by the three of them.[13] Robinson – he of the DFC and gravel-voice – was Cohen's special acolyte in the temple of African divination. His most significant job was to make the more conservative governors swallow the new directive, using his historical skills to demonstrate its logical development from previous policy. This most intellectual of Blues ever to think about the Blacks saw the aim of democratizing local government as providing 'some measure of political education'. He stressed the 'transition from local government through personalities to local government based on institutions'. It was no longer possible, Robinson argued, to preserve African societies against change, and British rulers must attempt to see the future. The economic bases of African societies left to themselves were in danger of collapse. Imperial indecision would be fatal: 'No policy of letting sleeping dogs lie is likely to succeed when the dogs are already barking'. (He learned early on that canine metaphors went down well in Great Smith Street.) But young Robinson was optimistic. Communism he thought 'outmoded' and unlikely to have any real future in Africa. Moreover, by constructing a political pyramid with a firm base in local government, there was a good chance that British rulers had 'dug out an adequate system of political irrigation channels before the rains of nationalism have burst into full flood upon them'.[14]

A conference of African governors in November 1947 chewed over the implications of the new local government strategy, not always amicably, together with most other aspects of African policy. A remarkable series of papers was prepared in the Colonial Office for this path-breaking conference. Creech Jones praised them as excellent. The crucial constitutional proposals about the stages of political evolution he did not specifically comment on. The strictly limited nature of this programme (as envisaged by Cohen and Sir Sydney Caine, Deputy Under-Secretary) needs to be stressed, in the light of the wilder misinterpretations which have been placed upon it. Even in the most advanced territory, the Gold Coast, Cohen wrote, 'internal self-government is unlikely to be achieved in much less than a generation'; elsewhere 'the process is likely to be considerably slower'. Accordingly, there must be a long-term plan, 'for 20 or 30 years or indeed longer', for ordered development under continuing British responsibility. Readiness for internal self-government (i.e. the stage attained by Southern Rhodesian whites in 1923) was still 'a long way off'; 'independence' (i.e. control of external affairs, with freedom to secede from the Commonwealth) was not even mentioned.* In his paper Caine assumed merely that 'perhaps within a generation many of the principal territories of the Colonial Empire will have attained or be within sight of the goal of full responsibility for *local affairs*' [my emphasis]. There would be a 'redistribution of power' and friendly association would have to replace 'benevolent domination', but he did not see this as involving the elimination of British power: it should continue to be possible to control the pace and 'influence the main line of policy and, provided the right new techniques are developed, the extent of that influence may remain very considerable'.[15]

Cohen was well aware of the probability that any constitutional programme would need to be radically rewritten from time to time. The crux of the problem was the risk that the demand for self-government ('stimulated by outside influences') might outpace the process of building up local government from below. Nevertheless, 'the rapid building up of local government through the process of devolution . . . is the most important of all the methods by which we must seek to foster political evolution in Africa'. Only thus could the 'evils of a class of professional politicians' be avoided. The Secretary of State agreed: the 'ignorant and gullable [sic] majority' must not be exploited by 'unrepresentative oligarchies'. Creech Jones was particularly interested in getting things started. The demand for a share in government responsibility was, he thought, certain to be made with increasing emphasis, and the demand must be satisfied. 'Time was knocking at the door and the art of government had to be learned.' Britain had thus to permit trial and error to Africans, reduce its spoonfeeding, and encourage a virile political self-reliance, without waiting for the educational qualifications it would like.[16]

The strategy of promoting political advancement on local government foundations was a policy to which Attlee was already totally committed. Indeed he noted the 'regrettable failure' in several colonies to develop municipal institutions as 'a first school of political and administrative training'. Politics could not be learned from a textbook. In his view also there was a most serious danger in assuming the Westminster Parliament to be the appropriate objective. Democracy could be fundamentally threatened by the concentration and centralisation of powers in the Westminster model. 'It would have been wiser in India to have followed the model of the United States constitution. . .'. This sort of mistake must not be repeated in Africa. (Has modern Britain ever had so prescient a Prime Minister?)[17]

---

* The distinction is fundamental. Some historians need to remember what Jim Hacker learned from Sir Humphrey Appleby: 'I *must* be clear on my African terminology, or else I could do irreparable damage' (J. Lynn and A. Jay, *The Complete 'Yes, Minister': The Diaries of a Cabinet Minister, by the Rt. Hon. James Hacker, MP* (London, 1984), 35).

So: *political advancement* of Africans – gradual, smooth and efficiently controlled – was the central purpose of policy. The goal was self-government, but self-government was not something to be hurried on. Demands for it seemed always to arise out of unrest, and invariably created awkward and unwelcome problems. Creech Jones urged the Cabinet to deal with economic and social discontents first, in order to lessen the immediate pressure for constitutional advance, thereby laying firmer foundations for 'liberal and efficient' self-government. Colonies – it was realized – could not be retained against their will, and any attempt to suppress national desires would be a disaster, but there would be no 'scuttling' out of Africa. Azikiwe would not intimidate them. Government must keep the initiative. Ceylon might be the model. Nor would there be any overall blueprint or prepared schedule. The timetable would be left vague. Fitness for political advancement in any individual colony would depend entirely on its own 'social and political viability and capability', and not on any 'extraneous considerations'.[18] Regional variations in Africa would be fully recognized. Cohen stated quite categorically: 'The conception of dealing with Africa as a whole in political questions is a wrong one'. (The Colonial Office accordingly scorned the notion of having a 'secretary of state for Africa'.)[19] The ultimate objective of Commonwealth association must be preserved. To this end, the early nineteenth-century theories of Macaulay and Fowell Buxton were dusted down. A Colonial Office paper on 'our main problems and policies' (1950) declared:

> We are engaged on a world-wide experiment in nation-building. Our aim is to create independence – independence within the Commonwealth – not to suppress it. No virtue is seen in permanent dependence. A vigorous, adult and willing partner is clearly more to be desired than one dependent, adolescent and unwilling. But there is no intention to abandon responsibilities prematurely. Self-government must be effective and democratic. . . .

Above all it must be within a Commonwealth framework, so as to ensure 'an ever-widening circle of democratic nations exerting a powerful stabilising influence in the world'. Premature withdrawal of British responsibility would only create a dangerous vacuum, within which nationalism would be usurped and 'perverted by extremists'. On the other hand, the imperial rulers must accustom themselves to the idea that 'the transfer of power is not a sign of weakness or of liquidation of the Empire, but is, in fact, a sign and source of strength'.[20] A Foreign Office paper on 'the problem of nationalism' (1952) concluded that it was possible to draw the constructive forces of nationalism to the British side and minimise the threatened erosion of British world power. It was a 'dynamic on the upsurge' which could not be stopped, but could be directed and encouraged into 'healthy and legitimate' channels. Destructive, extremist, xenophobic nationalism might be a potent instrument of Communist incitement, but a 'new and fruitful' relationship established with moderate nationalists through a policy of self-government could be the 'best prospect of resistance to Communism'. 'Greater maturity of thought in nationalist peoples and leaders' (without which any form of co-operation might prove temporary and illusory) might be induced by 'creating a class with a vested interest in co-operation', and involving it in social welfare and economic development projects. (The articulation of a 'collaborative bargains hypothesis' was thus well advanced by the time Labour left office.)[21]

All this theorizing was congenial to Cohen. He believed strongly in a continuing firm metropolitan grip on the situation, in being one jump ahead, in controlling and nurturing nationalist movements. This was, he believed, the only possible policy to secure the future stability and viability of territories. The sooner government acted, 'the more influence we were likely to have for a longer period'. In the best reformist traditions of the Colonial Office, he justified their policies as designed to 'strengthen not weaken the British connection'.[22]

In West Africa, the Colonial Office identified three 'political' categories: nationalists (the educated and part-educated), moderates (professional and business groups and the more enlightened chiefs), and rural populations (who were 'not politically-minded'). 'To be successful, policy must satisfy the second class while safeguarding the interests of the third, and going far enough to meet the aspirations of the first to secure some co-operation at any rate from all but the more extreme nationalists'. Accordingly, African representatives should play a major part in working out constitutional reforms. Executives should be re-modelled to give representatives a full share in the formulation and execution of policy. Legislatures should be extended and made 'fully representative of all parts of the country and not merely of the urban and more developed areas'.[23]

When in 1948 the Accra riots broke out in the Gold Coast, Creech Jones, canny and alert as ever, doubted the simplistic theory of 'Communist incitement' initially presented by the local administrators. In any case he was worried that this 'factor in the disturbances may be used so as to obscure or belittle . . . sincerely felt causes of dissatisfaction quite unconnected with Communism', or desires 'to accelerate constitutional development' – at however ill-considered a pace. Creech Jones believed the underlying causes were partly political and partly economic.[24] For him the Gold Coast held the key to future success in Britain's West African policy, and so he set up a commission of inquiry, and appointed Sir Charles Arden-Clarke, the very model of a modern colonial governor, to take over the administration. The new governor was a bit of a showman as well as a shrewd politician, with the reassuring appearance of a dog-lover advertising a good pipe-tobacco. Arden-Clarke's genius was to build on Moscow's known abandonment of Nkrumah as a useful contact, and to treat him as essentially a moderate, no longer 'our little local Hitler'; they were, he thought, in many ways lucky he had become so amenable. Nkrumah's position must be underwritten. The alternative was an inevitable further challenge to British authority, with increasing encouragement from Communist forces outside the country and later perhaps within it. Considerable African participation in the Gold Coast executive was therefore essential. The Cabinet was persuaded by the Coussey Report and Creech Jones's argument that without such progress 'moderate opinion will be alienated and the extremists given an opportunity of gaining further and weightier support and of making serious trouble'. They took a significant step forward, but of course it fell short of full self-government. Ministers refused to say when they would start discussing that.[25] Ideally, Cohen told them, in order to preserve efficient government there should be no further constitutional advance until 1954 or 1955, and it would not be in anyone's interest to have only a short transitional period to responsible government. But Nkrumah was in 1951 asking to take over from the governor the selection of ministers and to be given the title of prime minister.

> It must, of course, be recognised that we may not be able to adhere to an ideal timetable. We may be forced, if we are to keep on good terms with the more responsible political leaders such as Mr Nkrumah and his immediate colleagues and not to force the Gold Coast Government into the hands of extremists, to move more rapidly than ideally we should wish. . . . It would be fatal . . . to forfeit the goodwill of Mr Nkrumah and his colleagues by holding back excessively.

The imperatives of the collaborative mechanism had begun ineluctably to operate. Arden-Clarke diagnosed the salient feature of the situation: there was no alternative to a CPP government, and it could only be replaced by a similar one, or one of even more extreme nationalist tendencies. 'We have only one dog in our kennel. . . . All we can do is to build it up and feed it vitamins and cod liver oil. . . .'.[26]

Nigeria was launched almost automatically on a similar course as a result of Gold Coast developments. Cohen in 1948 quickly alerted Governor Sir John Macpherson to their relevance for neighbouring Nigeria. The principles of Nigerian political advancement were approved by the Cabinet in May 1950: greatly increased Nigerian participation in the executive, both at the centre and in the three regions; increased regional autonomy (within the unity of Nigeria, which was not negotiable); larger and more representative regional legislatures with increased powers. The Cabinet was especially concerned to ensure a smooth transfer of administrative responsibility by speeding up Africanization of the civil service on the lines that had worked well in India.[27] In 1952 Macpherson reflected that Nigeria had obtained a constitution 'in advance of its true capacity', but 'we could not put a ring-fence round Nigeria, and we had to take the initiative, and not wait to be overtaken by events, because of what was happening, and is continuing to happen, in the Gold Coast, the Sudan, Libya, etc, etc,'.[28]

Where had British planners got to in West Africa by 1951? The aim was self-government within the Commonwealth. But this, as Cohen saw it, meant something different for Nigeria and the Gold Coast, 'which can look forward to full responsibility for their own affairs', and for Sierra Leone and Gambia, which were not yet ready for African ministers, and must expect even in the long run to leave defence and foreign affairs to Britain. The Gold Coast was 'very far on towards internal self-government'; Nigeria was only a degree or two behind; but since there was little comparable nationalism in Sierra Leone and Gambia the two of them should be satisfied with a much more limited advance, and remain 'quite content' for 'a considerable time to come'. In all four, the government was trying to provide constitutions based on 'consent and consultation' – under the governor's ultimate authority. Maintaining confidence in British good faith was the essence of it, since this would slow down the pace. Simultaneously local government was being reformed and modernized, and Africanization was proceeding. The theory Cohen discerned behind all these changes was that full African participation provided 'the best defence against Communism', 'the only chance of friendly co-operation' with Britain, and the 'best chance' of persuading an African country voluntarily to remain in the Commonwealth. There could be no question of being deflected from political advancement and administrative devolution by the protests of France and South Africa.[29]

As far as East Africa was concerned, the final forms of government were 'less evident and less near' than in West Africa, but essentially the goal was the same. They would build up and improve the status and experience of Africans (through participation in local and central government) until disparities with Europeans and Indians were removed politically, economically and socially. They could then play a full part in a 'system in which all communities would participate on an equal basis' of genuine partnership. The problem of course was that the settlers objected to this, and indeed disapproved of the speed of African advance in West Africa. To force equality of representation upon the settlers would precipitate a major political crisis. Not that Creech Jones was unduly alarmed by such a prospect: 'whatever privilege they may have had in the past cannot be perpetuated much longer'. Many of the African grievances were, he thought, legitimate, but in such a vast area they ought not to demand exclusive rights, and 'a corrective to their irresponsible nationalism should be applied from time to time'.[30] Viscount Addison (the Cabinet's elder statesman, intermittently concerned with Commonwealth relations) argued the importance of reassuring settlers in order to avoid 'driving them into undesirable alliance with South Africa'. Griffiths, on the other hand, emphasised the necessity of reassuring Africans that ultimate British responsibility would be retained until they had 'narrowed the gap'. Out of these conflicting pressures came a parliamentary statement in December 1950, balancing irreconcilable interests in the well-worn fashion of the declarations of the inter-war years. The goal was 'true partnership' between races, but the immigrant communities had a part to play in the future of Kenya, and were not being asked to agree to 'their eventual eviction'. A certain *stasis* entered East African political advancement as a result. Resolution of the agonizing contradictions of Kenya was deferred, with Mau Mau as the consequence.[31]

North Africa was in many ways acting as the pace-maker for African political advancement. By concentrating on the Gold Coast for the 'beginnings of decolonization' historians have in fact been looking in the wrong place. Independence for Libya (1951) and Sudan (1956) pioneered the way, and arose out of fascinating international constraints. In the case of Libya, J.S. Bennett of the Colonial Office argued (in a series of papers in 1946–47, acknowledged by Cohen to be 'brilliant') that promoting independence would be a useful sop to international opinion and a promising bid for Arab friendship. Elsewhere in Africa, 'rapid political advancement towards independence is not yet in the realm of practical politics, and we are obliged to move more slowly at the price of increasing international criticism'. In Libya, by contrast, the 'prospect of early independence is not unreal'; it was an occupied ex-Italian colony and not a British possession, and thus provided the easiest way in which they could meet the obligations of the Atlantic Charter. A lot of paper about human rights was being generated by the UN: 'Here is a practical test-case, worth any amount of paper'. It was an ideal chance for once to forestall a nationalist protest, 'recognising the inevitable and cashing in on it in good time', instead of waiting to be forced into granting independence 'by local revolt and/or outside pressure'. Britain had some essential strategic requirements, at least in Cyrenaica, especially as a result of uncertainty over its Egyptian tenure, but promoting Libyan independence could be the best way of securing them.[32] Certainly in Sheikh Idris Britain had an 'ideal prefabricated collaborator'. Idris had indicated his willingness to grant bases and generally to allow the British considerable freedom of military action. At any rate the government concluded that the best solution, resolving a complex international tangle, was to back Idris and the Libyan claims for independence under UN auspices.[33]

In Sudan, too, Britain promoted independence. Validated in this case by Indian analogy, it was basically a means of countering the Egyptian claim to sovereignty (Farouk having been proclaimed 'King of the Sudan'). In part it was also a way of pre-empting a UN trust, with its risks of 'letting Russia into Africa'. But if independence would get the Sudan off its Egyptian hook, refusal to sell the Sudanese into Egyptian slavery dashed all Bevin's hopes of negotiating the crucially important new Canal Zone treaty with Egypt. ('I cannot do what I believe to be wrong and retrograde in order to get a quick treaty of alliance'.) This was because the Egyptians insisted on linking the two issues. As to the Suez base itself, Labour policy was to shift its defence on to Anglo-Egyptian co-operation and away from British occupation. Realising that effective use of the base was essentially dependent on Egyptian goodwill, and that ideal strategic requirements would have to be sacrificed in order to ensure it, Attlee in 1946 set the tone for treaty re-negotiation. In a masterly summing-up in Cabinet he declared that Britain could 'not remain forcibly on the ground':

> There was no more justification for this than for our claiming that our neighbours in the Continent of Europe should grant us bases for our defence. Our oil interests in the Middle East were indeed important, but our ability to defend them would only be impaired if we insisted on remaining in Egypt against the will of the Egyptian people and so worsened our relations with the remainder of the Arab world.

The Labour government continued to try to tempt Egypt into some sort of 'equal partnership' in a new Middle East defence scheme, but negotiations remained deadlocked. Attlee was unable to deliver Britain out of its Egyptian bondage.[34] Meanwhile he ruled out the use of force in dealing with the Iranian oil crisis of 1951. This was welcomed by officials as proof that the days were over of 'thinking in Edwardian terms of the use of military and economic power which we no longer possess'. Nationalism, all seemed to be agreed, must be met with diplomacy and publicity, not intervention and force.[35]

Strategically Attlee wanted to give up a 'hopeless' attempt to defend the Middle East oil-producing areas, and to work routinely round the Cape to the east and Australasia, instead of relying on an ever-more problematic Mediterranean route. In addition, he had always been anxious not to get drawn into UN trusteeships for 'deficit areas' in North Africa and the Horn. ('Somaliland has always been a dead loss and a nuisance to us.') His earliest and most iconoclastic initiative as Prime Minister was to demand a strategic reappraisal to take proper account of the atom bomb, the United Nations, and the impending loss of India. He was worried by the costs of continuing Mediterranean commitments he regarded as obsolescent. Nor did he like the idea of supporting the vested interests of a 'congeries of weak, backward and reactionary states' in the Middle East. With impressive 'Little Englander' pragmatism, remorselessly yet reasonably, and with occasional touches of irreverence, he pursued a confrontation with the Chiefs of Staff on these issues through endless committee meetings, and thoroughly rattled them. Attlee was supported by Dalton. This battle of the titans lasted almost 18 months. It ended with a victory for the traditionalist doctrines of the Chiefs of Staff (apparently threatening resignation), backed by Bevin and his formidable Foreign Office team. Their argument was that withdrawal from the Mediterranean route would leave a vacuum, into which Russia (even if not bent on world domination) would move, since 'the bear could not resist pushing its paw into soft places'. This would make a gift to Russia of Middle Eastern oil and manpower, and would dangerously signal to Russia, to America and the Commonwealth Britain's 'abdication as a world power'. Without a first line of defence in North Africa, the Russians would, they argued, rapidly be in the Congo and at the Victoria Falls. They rejected Attlee's concept of a disengagement from a 'neutral zone', putting 'a wide glacis of desert and Arabs between ourselves and the Russians'.[36]

However, despite this fundamental disagreement, there was common ground between Attlee, Bevin and the Chiefs of Staff about the desirability of a strategic base located in Kenya, which Attlee had seen as part of a more general shifting of military resources into less contentious and exposed regions. They all agreed that more use ought to be made of Africa as a manpower reserve, compensating for the loss of the Indian 'British barrack in the Oriental seas', and as a way of relieving the strain in Egypt. East Africa was expected to be more important in a future war, as a result of greater weapon ranges and the weakening of the British position in the Middle East. It would become a major training camp and storage depot. It would also defend 'our main support-area in South Africa'. Work began in September 1947 on the new base at Mackinnon Road, some sixty miles inland by rail from Mombasa.[37] All this tied in with new doctrines of colonial development. The new base in Kenya, Bevin argued, would 'modernise the whole character of our defence as well as our trade and bring into the British orbit economically and commercially a great area which is by no means fully developed yet'. Communications would need to be improved over a wide area. Bevin was keen to develop Mombasa as a major port, and link it to Lagos by a trans-African highway ('passing through the top of French Equatorial Africa', thus enabling Britain, if necessary, to protect the strategic deposits of the Belgian Congo). This scheme the experts pronounced impossible because of the administrative and maintenance costs of African 'all-weather' roads, to say nothing of the difficulty of co-operating with foreign powers. Bevin also campaigned to improve the outlets for Rhodesian strategic minerals to the sea. Railway links to the south were in consequence thoroughly investigated.[38]

A rail link between Rhodesia and Kenya from Ndola to Korogwe was the most favoured project. This would mean unifying the gauges (which ministers thought a strategically valuable exercise), by converting 3,520 miles of East African railways from metre to 3'6" – a five-year task. Tanganyikan authorities naively put their costs at £870,000, while Kenya (with more track and rolling stock) estimated their conversion at £16 million. The new 1,125 mile link itself might be built for £11 million. However, even a 3'6" railway could not carry oversize loads (such as big tanks) and would have to be duplicated by a much-improved road capable of carrying 70-ton weights. (Only a route able to carry heavy equipment would provide any appreciable saving over the shipping routes.) Cohen strongly favoured the 'great advantage of having an all-British railway link from the Cape to Kenya', possibly with a branchline to Kilwa or Mikindani to evacuate groundnuts. (See map.) The project lapsed, however, and for three reasons. There were doubts about the enormous costs and its economic profitability. (Creech Jones was decidedly sceptical – haunted, no doubt, by Labouchère's famous diatribe against

MAP 1   THE PROPOSED RAIL LINK BETWEEN RHODESIA AND KENYA

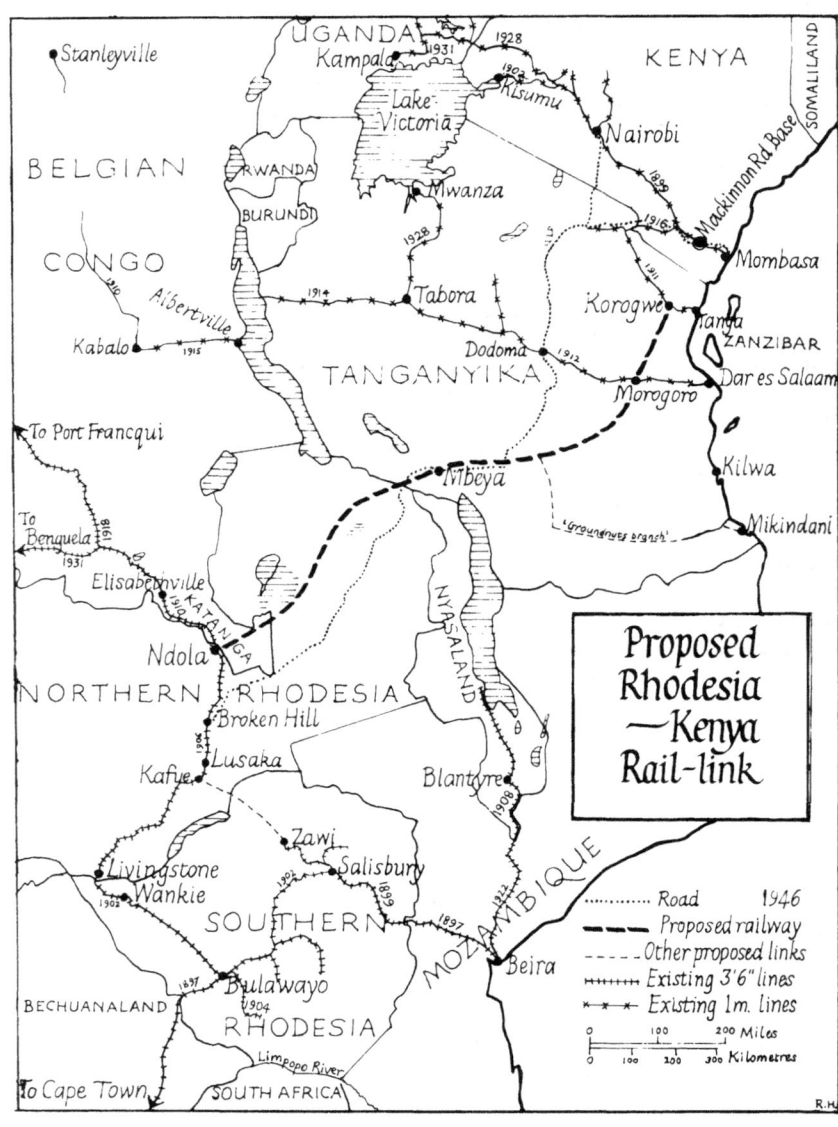

Source: CO 537/1231/102, COS(46)271, report on the development of African communications, 13 December 1946.

the Uganda railway: 'What it will carry there's none can define; . . . It clearly is naught but a lunatic line'.) Then there was the growing difficulty of being seen to co-operate with South Africa. Above all, the Chiefs of Staff decided they did not wish to develop Kenya as a major operational base: it was too far from the Middle East theatre, it had insufficient industrial back-up, and it was impracticable (for racial and political reasons) to import the quantities of white or Indian labour required. The Ndola rail link was accordingly down-graded to being 'strategically desirable but not essential', and at all events not sufficiently important to warrant a contribution from the UK defence vote. 'Cape-to-Cairo' was as far off as ever.[39]

The fate of the railway project was symptomatic of the sheer difficulty of developing Africa. Yet interest in the possible potential and the protean problems of Africa was sufficiently aroused for nine visits to be made by Colonial Office ministers in these years, four of them by secretaries of state. Field Marshal Montgomery (the Chief of the Imperial General Staff) also decided to make a tour of Africa at the end of 1947. ('It is terribly important to check up on Africa'.) He visited French Morocco, Gambia, Gold Coast, Nigeria, Belgian Congo, Union of South Africa, Southern Rhodesia, Kenya, Ethiopia, Sudan and Egypt. The result was an electric 76-page report, containing many a caustic phrase, though his most derisive strictures were reserved for Ethiopia (its 'pathetic Emperor', 'Gilbertian army', 'Addis in Wonderland', and elite of 'Hollywoodian ostentation'). His thesis was the 'immense possibilities' for African development, enabling Britain to 'maintain her standard of living', if not actually to survive, because 'these lands contain everything we need'. However, 'no real progress was being made', and the way was open for Communism. Government should 'think big'. There must be 'a grand design for African development as a whole, with a masterplan for each Colony or nation'. Invoking the spirit of Cecil Rhodes, and roundly condemning the settlers, the African ('a complete savage') and the Colonial Service alike, he demanded that those who said it could not be done should be 'ruthlessly eliminated'. Britain should 'import brains and "go-getters" '. 'Belly-aching will assume colossal proportions; it must be stamped on.' Administrative units should be boldly amalgamated; federations of Central Africa, East Africa and West Africa ought to be established. The High Commission Territories were an anomaly and should be 'abolished'. Eventually South Africa and Central Africa should be linked up. There should be much closer co-operation with other European powers too, and with the Americans.[40]

Despite the staccato tone of the presentation, with its arrogant amateurism presumptuously masquerading as geopolitical genius, senior ministers took this report seriously. Bevin called for its 'urgent study'. Attlee was 'much interested'. With remarkable speed Creech Jones came up with a comprehensive reply, in a 14-page memorandum dated 6 January 1948. (It is the central ministerial document on Labour's African policy, and its preparation must have ruined his Christmas and New

Year.) He agreed that quick and vigorous African development was essential on strategic, economic and political grounds to strengthen Britain and Western Europe; it was also needed to secure smooth African progress in social and political fields, and to help the world supply of food and raw materials. British departure from India and the reduction in its overseas investments generally had still further increased the economic importance of close links with Africa. But the imposition of a centralized 'grand design' drawn up in and directed from London 'would not be practical politics' (words which Attlee underlined in his copy). It would 'conflict with our declared policy of devolution in the progress of building up self-government' and ensuring that Africans attained it as 'part of the western world'. Central direction would not work. It was contrary to all British policy and historical experience. It would not secure the co-operation of local peoples, settler or African, without which effective development could not take place. Developing relationships between peoples over a period of years could not be dealt with on the analogy of a military operation. A blueprint could not be operated by orders in a chain of command, because colonies had powers and responsibilities which would progressively increase. They should be dealt with by devolution, which had worked successfully in India, Ceylon and Sudan. There was in fact no lack of planning. 'We have a clear and well-understood general policy for political and economic development in Africa.' All the territories had 10-year development plans. Montgomery had overestimated the material resources of Africa: 'Africa is not an undiscovered El Dorado. It is a poor continent which can only be developed at great expense in money and effort'. Vast areas were barely self-supporting in food, and could only be made so by a heavy capital expenditure on water, bush clearance, fertilizers and supervisory manpower. The crucial problem was not lack of brains or vigour, but lack of money and the 'pay your way' philosophy, which was now being rectified. African development might well be vital to the survival of Britain, but if so, it must have a much higher priority in supplies and technicians. The present bottleneck was the lack of capital equipment, especially an acute shortage of steel, and a deficiency of consumer goods to provide incentives.

Politically, too, Creech Jones continued, the right means of countering anti-British movements, the real answer to nationalism, 'does not lie in uniformity of policy, or in federation, or in any other imposed measure', but in 'the maintenance and development of our existing friendly relations with the African peoples'; in giving them 'a real part in the constructive work of government', and in building up responsible native institutions. Communists were *not* exploiting the lack of a uniform native policy; it would in fact be easier to exploit such a policy if it were imposed without regard to local conditions. But there *was* a broad overall uniformity, and regional co-ordination was certainly existing policy. Any link-up of African territories with South Africa was out of the question, and the High Commission Territories could not be handed over.[41]

Notwithstanding this drily devastating critique, the Montgomery

Report was a useful weapon in the fight to demand greater attention in Whitehall as a whole for African development needs. Ministers agreed they must urgently have a plan fully co-ordinated and integrated with British domestic economic policy. With some mild breast-beating, they admitted colonial economic development planning to have been defective, because they had not determined on broad lines what proportion of British resources should go overseas, or assessed the relative value of home and colonial projects. For example, there had been no agreed criterion for allocating priorities in agricultural machinery or steel between conflicting British and African demands. All this they would now try to put right. The new Chancellor of the Exchequer (Cripps) said the first thing was to inject a spirit of improvization, and improve the productivity of existing capital equipment, rather than initiating new, large-scale development schemes. The Economic Policy Committee agreed with Creech Jones that, however desirable, a more positive control of the African economic field was not possible, as it would be contrary to the fundamental policy of gradually transferring real power.[42]

Simultaneously with these discussions, Caine submitted a special report on colonial economic development to the Prime Minister. He too rejected the idea of a single centralized plan: they had to work within the Labour policy of 'political advancement'. He called for more liaison, more international collaboration, the allocation of priorities and the mobilization of all available agencies, including private enterprise. All this could be of inestimable value to colonial peoples and to Britain in a few years. They must prepare for the day American aid ran out. 'Prompt action now will mean that we shall by that time be enjoying the first fruits of this new form of colonial investment'. The essential problem was the removal of limitations to development. These were of three kinds: (i) virtually irremovable traditional social barriers (especially land tenure systems), (ii) basic conditions which were remediable in perhaps a generation (soil infertility, scarce labour and insufficient technicians), and (iii) limitations which could in theory be removed at any time by governmental decision (provision of finance, infrastructure and capital goods). Progress could only be gradual, however. Any revolutionary attack on agrarian problems would only cause serious political trouble. Government must therefore work within the limits set by the tolerable pace of social change. In dealing with soil infertility, too, they must be cautious, since they were not sure of the ecological effect of applying Western methods – they must not create a dustbowl even worse than in North America. And the provision of government help was bound to be restricted because of Britain's own needs for basic services and capital goods: iron, steel, machines and cement were all in short supply in Britain itself. A couple of months later Attlee received a report from Hilary Marquand, the Paymaster-General, on his seven weeks' tour of the eastern half of Africa, which reinforced many of these conclusions.[43]

Thus African economic development was faced with multiple

obstacles, clearly identified by the spring of 1948 in a cluster of memoranda. Africa was not amenable to the more euphoric hopes of exploiting it in the common good. Shakespeare and Pliny were equally confounded, as well as Strachey and Bevin: it was not filled with 'golden joys' and it was in fact not easy to conjure anything new out of Africa. The stunning recalcitrance of the environment even to mechanized assault was brought home by the groundnuts fiasco. Inadequate transport was perhaps at the heart of the overall problem. There was maddening difficulty in actually getting essential products out of Africa on an exiguous, congested, war-exhausted rail system; the export of uranium from the Congo, copper from Northern Rhodesia, coal and chrome from Southern Rhodesia, timber from the Gold Coast, and even groundnuts from Tanganyika, were all held up. There were seven different railway gauges in central Africa, yet the high cost of unifying even two of them surprised everyone. It was all very well for Bevin to demand that 'Africa should be as full as possible of transport', but the difficulties were immense. In this as in other sectors, British and African needs were competing. More generally, with the shortage of clothes and bicycles for export from Britain, the African worker could not be given all the incentives he needed. Nutritional problems and debilitating diseases also reduced his efficiency. (The iniquities of the tsetse fly, incidentally, generated more surviving Colonial Office paper than any other subject.) Finally, there was the obvious danger that too concerted a policy of demanding African action to meet Britain's domestic needs (a demand already pushed to the limit by the exigencies of the convertibility crisis of 1947) would be endlessly open to the damaging charge of exploitation, as Bevin was among the first to realize. (The Colonial Office thus sought to distance itself from the work of the new Colonial Development Corporation.) For this reason also international collaboration would remain limited: there must be no hint of 'ganging up' to turn Africa into a hinterland of Western Europe.[44]

Although much thought was given to the ways in which Africa might help to solve Britain's own strategic and economic problems, the empire would not stand or fall on the establishment of a base in Kenya, or poultry farms in Gambia, or the supply of bicycles to Blantyre, or even of peanuts and bananas to Battersea. More fundamental by far was the racial challenge of the stereotypes of Stellenbosch and the precepts of Pretoria.

The advent of the National Party regime in South Africa in 1948, dedicated to apartheid inside its borders and expansion outside them, had worrying implications for the whole of Britain's African policy. Griffiths spoke for all his colleagues when he described apartheid as 'totally repugnant'. South Africa itself, already angry over the perpetual withholding of the High Commission Territories, became alarmed at the Labour government's determination to press ahead with 'arming Africans' (raising troops for the defence of Africa and the Middle East). It was, moreover, outraged by the prospect of the Gold Coast's being turned into 'another Liberia'. Sir Evelyn Baring, the High Commissioner, warned that 'to despise or to ignore the strong and expanding force of South African nationalism in 1951 would be as unwise as it was to decry in March 1933 the power of Hitler to do harm'. Ministers took the point: if Afrikaner racial ideas spread north of the 'great grey-green, greasy Limpopo river' the whole of their African policy might be jeopardized. South Africa might even try to seduce the settlers in Kenya and Rhodesia from their British allegiance.[45] On the other hand, South Africa was deeply involved in, and had useful technical resources for dealing with, transport, soil erosion and disease problems (trypanosomiasis, rinderpest and locust-plague). Both sides wanted co-operation in these intractable matters, but it was clearly impossible for the British government to agree to extend discussion into the political arena or to be drawn into a local defence pact. Yet they did want South Africa to contribute to a Middle East defence system: this was 'an essential element we could not forgo' (according to P.C. Gordon Walker, Commonwealth Relations Secretary). In Whitehall there were generally held to be four reasons why the maintenance of good relations was important. First, strategically South Africa was a strong country in a pivotal geopolitical position. It had the basis for heavy industry, together with raw materials important in peace and vital in war (uranium, manganese, diamonds, chrome and coal); it was the only African country which could in war provide a large body of trained technicians. The Simonstown naval base was of the 'utmost importance' to Britain; the use of other ports was also required. South Africa would be needed as a transit area, an arsenal, and a troop-reserve for the Middle East. Second, economically Britain was 'in dire need of its gold' (Baring), since the stability of the Sterling Area depended on getting a substantial part of its gold output. It was also a valuable export market – indeed it headed the list of Britain's customers in 1947. Third, trusteeship ('the ethical code of the empire') meant protecting the vulnerable High Commission Territories. Departmentally this was seen as the critical reason for staying on the right side of South Africa, especially in the Seretse Khama case.[46] For many ministers, however, the determining factor was the fourth one: to preserve the Commonwealth. A quarrel with a 'founder member' would be highly embarrassing and 'immensely damaging to British world prestige'. A public dispute might 'break up the association overnight'. Philip Noel-Baker (Gordon Walker's predecessor at the Commonwealth Relations Office) even invoked some emotional (and inaccurate) 'inherited official historiography' about Campbell-Bannerman and Smuts – 1906 and all that.[47]

Unfortunately South Africa had put itself into the international dock by *de facto* incorporation in 1949 of the former mandated territory of South-West Africa, for which it was hauled before the International Court. Britain had at first tried to be friendly and helpful over this, but it was becoming harder all the time. How closely could it afford to side with South Africa at the UN over a case which might be thought weak if not bad? Civil servants were undecided. Some thought the British government was the only one which stood any chance of influencing the attitude of South Africa, but would lose what little influence it had if it 'joined the pack howling against them', so driving them out of the Commonwealth 'into an outer darkness of their own'. Others, while not wanting Britain to be 'tarred with the apartheid brush', thought it was hardly worth while imperilling a South African contribution to Middle East defence ('very nearly the biggest strategic interest of the UK') for the sake of making doubly sure British policy would not be confused with South Africa's. Some felt strategic requirements should be the over-riding consideration. *Per contra*, many officials argued that unless Britain rejected all visible compromise with the Union's native policy, Britain's own African policy would be endangered. (Sir Thomas Lloyd, Permanent Under-Secretary at the CO, complained of 'numerous and growing embarrassments' flowing from the failure to denounce its reactionary policies.) The South-West Africa dispute was formally analysed as requiring the pursuit of three conflicting objectives. Britain needed to preserve good relations with South Africa, but also 'to keep her reputation as a champion of liberal western civilisation', avoiding a conflict with Afro-Asian opinion. Above all, it had to defend its rights as a colonial power *vis-à-vis* the UN, which must not be allowed to establish the right of intervention in non-self-governing territories. If in South-West Africa the UN inserted the thin end of the wedge of a right to dictate policies and decide the future of all African peoples, it would 'bring British authority, peace and good government in Africa tumbling about our ears'.[48]

For the impending Cabinet debate on this difficult controversy, an inter-departmental paper was prepared, signed by Griffiths, Gordon Walker and Kenneth Younger (Minister of State at the Foreign Office). As drafting proceeded, over a period of five months, the recommendation to intervene at the International Court (in order to make British views known) was made stronger. (According to Galsworthy, some aspects of the dispute were 'supremely important' to the Colonial Office.) Griffiths insisted the main issue should be brought out unequivocally: the risk of being misrepresented as supporting South African native policies, as against the threat of the Court's making a decision adverse to British colonial interests. Attorney-General Sir Hartley Shawcross favoured intervention, though acknowledging that the arguments were 'very nicely balanced'; they would attract a great deal of opprobrium, but mostly from those 'who already have a pretty poor view of us in colonial matters'. Presenting the issue to the Cabinet, Griffiths declared himself on balance in favour of intervening, but at the same time he wanted it to be made clear that their appearance before the Court did not imply support for apartheid. Gordon Walker agreed, on 'strict grounds of British interest'. The Cabinet, however, rejected their recommendation. Most ministers felt that representation at or participation in the Court's proceedings would be bound to be misrepresented as implying support for South Africa, and would therefore 'incur political odium'. Indeed, it might actually invite the Court to pronounce on the colonial issues of concern to Britain, in a context most unfavourable to its case, which it could argue more convincingly in future if it had not been present.[49]

Following upon this hardening of opinion and unusual rejection of departmental advice, a Cabinet paper was prepared in the CRO to clarify the more general issues of Anglo-South African relations. Again, this was several months in preparation. It was finally presented by Gordon Walker at the end of September 1950. Indian hostility to South Africa was identified as a significant feature in the equation, since Britain was anxious to enlist India's 'great influence in Asia' to help in the solution of various far eastern problems. Moreover, 'any suspicion that the United Kingdom sympathised in any way with South Africa's native policies would so deeply disturb African and Indian public opinion in our African Colonies as to constitute a threat to their internal security'. On the other hand, it was important to continue to preserve good relations. The 'four reasons' for this were carefully rehearsed. The conclusion was drawn that Britain ought to show that it appreciated South Africa's difficulties, and not simply condemn and antagonise it. Unnecessary polemics should be avoided, and everything possible done 'to retain South Africa as a member of the Commonwealth, preferably as one owing direct allegiance to the Crown'.[50] Gordon Walker spoke to the paper in the Cabinet, emphasizing that strategically South Africa's goodwill was of special importance. Griffiths then examined the other side of the coin, expressing deep concern both about South Africa's expansionist ambitions and about the serious alarm South Africa's policies were arousing throughout black Africa. Aneurin Bevan drew this point out a little more sharply: the time might come when Britain would be forced to consider whether it lost more than it gained by its embarrassing association with South Africa. Other ministers countered this by underlining the strategic importance of securing South Africa's support in any struggle against Communism, and the 'great value' of the military support she now seemed likely to promise in the Middle East. (Bevin still wanted South Africa to 'look after the east coast of Africa'.) The CRO paper was endorsed. At a subsequent discussion in the Defence Committee, Strachey (now a War Office minister) reluctantly accepted that they must look on South Africa as an ally, but Emanuel Shinwell (now Minister of Defence) remained profoundly unhappy about seeming to give tacit approval to apartheid by any military co-operation. Attlee (who had not yet really turned his mind to southern Africa) summed up correctly if inconclusively: 'it was a matter of great importance'. However, it clearly had been decided that co-operation with South Africa was to remain a prime object of British policy.[51]

But not the only object. Six months later, Gordon Walker produced his own prodigiously thorough and perceptive analysis of the situation, seeking more definitely to balance necessary co-operation by a policy of containing South African expansion. 'This would mean that we do not regard as our sole objective the emancipation and political advancement of the African in all our African colonies.' Of course this would remain a major objective, but 'we must not subordinate all else to it'. A shift towards closer association with Rhodesian settlers had to be faced. There was a real danger that, to avoid domination by Africans (as a supposed consequence of 'political advancement'), white settler communities would throw in their lot with the Union. This was at least as grave a danger as the eruption of African discontent. Containing South African expansion should thus be 'a policy of *equal* weight and importance in our eyes with the political advancement of the Africans in our Central and East African colonies'. If British communities revolted and linked themselves to the Union, the apartheid policies they detested would be established in the heart of Britain's African empire: 'Millions of Africans would be subjected to oppression. Terrible wars might even be fought between a white-ruled Eastern Africa and a black-ruled Western Africa'. They would in the end fatally have 'betrayed our trust to the Africans', who would be 'calamitously worse off'.[52]

This apocalyptic scenario provided the rationale for the Central African Federation. Enthusiastically advised by G.H. Baxter of the CRO and the ubiquitous and utterly pragmatic Cohen, Gordon Walker was the principal ministerial advocate of creating in central Africa a British bloc to contain Afrikanerdom, provided Africans could be persuaded to accept it.[53] He won Griffiths to his side, but Creech Jones and others remained unconverted to this solution, believing other means could be found for achieving its political and economic purposes without upsetting Africans. Attlee fully understood the case for such a federation in principle, but to him, as always, what mattered was 'tide rather than froth'. Drawing on his Indian experience, he believed the vital thing was the long-term trend of growing African nationalism, which, if given insufficient outlet, might go sour from frustration. The fatal flaw he discerned in the scheme of federation as it ultimately emerged was that it froze the progress of African political advancement by stabilizing the whole framework on the Southern Rhodesian model. The Federation thus ran counter to the basic premise of Labour's African policy, and he rejected it.[54]

Retiring as High Commissioner in 1951 after seven years, Baring summarized the three guidelines which had emerged for Britain's South African policy. One, counteract the magnetic new South African nationalist expansion in the north. Two, preserve and develop the High Commission Territories. Three, regularize relations by co-operating as often as possible and always being very careful to avoid sweeping condemnations, which would only 'unite and inflame' all white South Africans behind Malan. There was thus no simple policy for dealing with Afrikanerdom, but a subtle symbiosis of two parallel strategies, co-operation and containment.[55]

In fact there was no simple policy for dealing with any of the problems of Africa. Throughout the continent the Labour government found that the successful adoption of clear new policies was limited by the tension between Cold War strategic imperatives and their ideally required rational disengagements or moral stands. Neither politically nor economically were centralized blueprints possible. Inadequate British resources, and the stubborn facts of the African environment stopped dead in its tracks any striking advance towards an 'economic new deal'. Politically, in principle Attlee was convinced by Indonesia and Vietnam that 'failure to meet reasonable nationalist aspirations led to an ever-worsening position'. But he did not think Africans were as civilized as Asians, and he foresaw a danger in too rapid a transition.[56] The resultant policy was thus not one of wholesale 'decolonization' or 'dismantling the empire'. Labour ministers themselves invariably called their policy merely one of 'political advancement'. And this political advancement was not thought practicable as yet in much of Africa. Progress was uneven. The Gold Coast and Nigeria were seen as exceptions. Attlee lectured the Northern Rhodesian African National Congress about there being 'a long way to go' and 'no short cuts to political maturity'. Political advancement in East and Central Africa was held up by the supposedly immature and irresponsible nature of its nationalism, but also by the presence of white settlers.[57] Fear of driving them into the arms of an expansionist South Africa was a major reason why the Labour government did not take up earlier recurrent proposals (most notably those of Harold Macmillan in 1942) for an assault on the privileges of the Kenya settlers.[58] East and Central Africans themselves were not thought ready to be of use as collaborators in the task of containing Afrikanerdom. Every region indeed had leaders who were seen as mere demagogues, bent only on capturing the colonial state and driving the British out as quickly as possible. This was not at all the kind of future the government intended. In the short term, local government would be used 'to call in the masses to keep the balance', and close control would remain meanwhile. The long-term aim was gradual political advancement towards self-governing states which were broadly-based, stable, viable, friendly, non-Communist, and firmly within the Commonwealth.[59] Labour ministers may well have been involved in a 'controlled colonial revolution' (the phrase is Gladwyn Jebb's),[60] but their emphasis was distinctly on the *control* of the process. This gradualism was essential because they were determined to maintain as far as possible the structure of British global interests in the fight against Communism. Paradoxically, however, as Attlee saw so clearly, 'an attempt to maintain the old colonialism would . . . have immensely aided Communism'. Decolonization was a gigantic footnote to the Cold War.

NOTES

1. Dalton Papers (L.S.E.), I/35/17, Diary, 24 Feb. 1947; CAB 128/10, CM.75(47)5, 9 Sept. 1947.
2. CAB 129/37(3), CP(49)245, Annex A, 18 Oct. 1949.
3. Bevin Papers (P.R.O.). FO 800/435/116, conversation with Portuguese ambassador, 23

Oct. 1948, & 118, minute to Prime Minister, 6 Nov. 1948; FO 800/444/29, minute to Prime Minister, 16 Sept. 1947; CAB 21/2278, minute by Attlee, 16 Sept. 1947; Dalton Diary, I/34/13.
4. CAB 21/2277, minute 29 Oct. 1946, & 2280, minute, 23 Dec. 1949; CAB 134/786, CCM(54)1; C.R. Attlee, *As It Happened* (London, 1954), 189.
5. CO 537/5361, D.R. Rees-Williams (Parliamentary Under-Secretary, C.O.), report on West African tour, 27 Sept. 1948.
6. CAB 129/16, CP(47)10, memo. 4 Jan. 1947; CO 847/36/2/24, speech by Cripps to African Governors' Conference, 12 Nov. 1947 (AGC.22).
7. CO 537/5699/89 A, 16 June 1950.
8. DO 35/4023/62, speech at opening of the African Conference, 23 Sept. 1948. Attlee regarded this occasion as important enough for him to address, but he was prevented by illness (CAB 21/2279, Attlee to Creech Jones, 12 Oct. 1948).
9. Attlee and Gordon Walker Papers (Churchill Archives Centre, Cambridge), ATLE 1/24/1; GNWR 1/7.
10. CO 847/25/7; CO 847/35/6/1 (Cartland memo.) & 7; CO 847/37/1/21.
11. CO 537/4589 (esp. note by Colonial Secretary, Oct. 1949), & 5708, & 5698; CO 936/56/6; CAB 129/24, CP(48)36; FO 371/107032 (UP.134/1), & 107076 (UP.247/10).
12. CO 847/36/1, minute by I. Thomas, 18 Jan. 1947; PREM 8/922, A(49)1.
13. CO 847/35/6, esp. No. 2, memo. by Cohen, 3 April 1946, and minute, 24 Jan. 1947.
14. CO 847/35/9/3, minute by Cartland, 29 Dec. 1947; CO 847/38/3, memos by R.E. Robinson on some recent trends in native administration policy (March 1947). Robinson described the 'pyramid of councils' as 'essentially an organisation for the political education of the rural Africans, and a scaffolding round which territorial political unity can be built' (CO 847/44/3, memo. on the development of British principles of native administration, 1927–47).
15. CO 847/35/6; CO 847/36/1/9, minutes by Creech Jones, 5 May 1947, and report of the committee on the conference of African governors, 22 May 1947 (? by Cartland), esp. Appendix II (AGC.1, 'The general political development of colonial territories', by Caine), and Appendix III (AGC.2, 'Constitutional development in Africa', ? by Cohen). Ivor Thomas wrote that local government would give Africans 'self-government in the matters that really touch them' (minute, 30 May 1947). The most prominent misinterpretation is by D. Williams in *Cambridge History of Africa, vol. 8, From c. 1940 to c. 1975* (Cambridge, 1984), 341, writing about the Gold Coast in 1946: 'independence – perhaps in 15 years' time. This was a sort of date . . . Creech-Jones [sic], or . . . Cohen had in mind'.
16. CO 847/37/5/9, minute 5 of African Governors' Conference, and Cohen to Sir John Hall, 29 Oct. 1947; CO 537/4625, minute by Creech Jones, 1 March 1949.
17. CAB 134/55, CA(48)8, 29 Oct. 1948; CAB 134/56, CA(49)1, 19 Jan. 1949; CO 1015/770/43.
18. CAB 134/55, CA(48)19; CAB 128/15, CM.21(49)5, 21 March 1949; FO 371/73038, speech by Thomas to international study conference on overseas territories of Western Europe, Amsterdam, June 1948.
19. CO 537/7098; FO 371/80130.
20. CO 537/5698/69, & 5699/102.
21. CO 936/217, F.O. study paper, prepared by Permanent Under-Secretary's Committee, 21 Nov. 1952, and Sir Thomas Lloyd to Sir William Strang, 9 Sept. 1952.
22. CO 537/5921/5, & 5929/2, & 5698/66, & 5699/102.
23. CO 537/5698/69, International Relations department secret paper on 'The Colonial Empire today', May 1950, section III, drafted by S.H. Evans.
24. CO 537/3558/122, Creech Jones to Sir G. Creasy, 18 March 1948; CO 96/795, & 796/24 C.
25. PREM 8/924; CAB 128/16, CM.58(49)3, 13 Oct. 1949; CAB 129/36(2), CP(49)199.
26. CO 537/7181/5, Arden-Clarke to Cohen, 12 May 1951, and minute by Cohen, 11 June 1951.
27. CO 537/5787/52, & 7166; CAB 128/17, CM.30(50)6, 11 May 1950; CAB 129/43, CP(50)94; PREM 8/1310.

28. CO 554/298/13, Macpherson to Lloyd, 18 Jan. 1952.
29. CO 936/198/7, memo. 20 Nov. 1951.
30. CO 967/62, Creech Jones to Sir Philip Mitchell, 17 Oct. 1948; CO 537/5698/69; CO 822/114/2, minute, 20 Sept. 1946; CAB 134/1, A(49)2, 5 July 1949. Creech Jones also told Mitchell he had many doubts about the 'essential rightness of some aspects of our past policy, the basic rightness of our being in Kenya, the conditions and distribution of land in Africa'. British past folly and occasional perversity had brought intractable problems, but equally in Kenya difficulties were 'in no small part due to African suspicion and ignorance, and their own failures in social and political development' (and not only to European settlement), and they ought to be more appreciative of the contribution of Western civilisation, 'which they have almost unwittingly enjoyed'.
31. CO 537/5923; PREM 8/1113, CA(50)2; CAB 128/18, CM.76(50)1; CAB 129/24, CP(48)43; CAB 129/43, CP(50)270. See D.W. Throup, *The Economic and Social Origins of Mau Mau* (London, 1987).
32. CO 537/1468, & 1474, minute by J.S. Bennett, 30 May 1946; CO 537/2081, minute by Cohen, 1 Feb. 1947, & 2087, esp. No. 18, Bennett to Brig. Benoy, 31 March 1947; CAB 129/9, CP(46)165, memo. 18 April 1946.
33. CO 537/2088; PREM 8/1231, DO(48)9, 30 April 1948; PREM 8/1478, COS(49)381.
34. PREM 8/946, & 1388/I (1946), Bevin to Lord Stansgate, 31 Aug. 1946; CAB 128/5, CM.58(46), 7 June 1946; CAB 128/19, CM.23(51)6, 2 April 1951; FO 800/435/153, & 457/176, minute by Bevin to Prime Minister, 15 Dec. 1947.
35. CAB 128/20, CM.51(51)2, 12 July 1951, & CM.60(51)6, 27 Sept. 1951; CO 936/217, minute by Trafford Smith, 22 July 1952. See W.R. Louis, *The British Empire in the Middle East, 1945–51* (Oxford, 1984).
36. CAB 129/1, CP(45)144, memo. on future of Italian colonies, 1 Sept. 1945; CAB 131/1; CAB 131/2; PREM 8/515, memo. 19 Feb. 1946; FO 800/475, & 476. Attlee predicted: 'It may be that we shall have to consider the British Isles as an easterly extension of a strategic area, the centre of which is in the American continent, rather than as a power looking eastwards towards the Mediterranean to India and the East' (memo. 19 Feb. 1946).
37. CAB 131/2–5, passim, esp. DO(46)99 (COS, 5 Aug. 1946), & DO(46)40, memo. by Bevin, 13 March 1946; CO 537/1883, & 2515; FO 800/451/144, Montgomery to Bevin, 25 Sept. 1947.
38. CAB 131/2, DO(46)40, memo. by Bevin, 13 March 1946; Dalton Diary, I/34/12–13, 22 March 1946; CO 537/1231/102, COS(46)271; CO 537/1233.
39. CAB 131/2, DO(46)48, COS report, 2 April 1946; CAB 131/4, DO(47)27, memo. by A.V. Alexander, 17 March 1947, & DO(47)9/4, 26 March 1947; CO 537/1230, & 1231/102, COS(46)271; DO 35/2373, JP(48)122, & COS(49)6; FO 371/73042, & 73043; CO 967/58. A tentative alternative was a train-ferry crossing the northern part of Lake Nyasa to an outlet at Mikindani, which would get Northern Rhodesian minerals to the coast by the quickest route, but not achieve the Cape-Kenya link (PREM 8/923, Marquand Report).
40. DO 35/2380, memo. 19 Dec. 1947; FO 800/435.
41. PREM 8/923. P.C. Gordon Walker in the CRO welcomed Creech Jones's paper as 'very sensible' (DO 35/2380, minute, 8 Jan. 1948).
42. CAB 130/31, GEN. 210/1; PREM 8/733, & 923, EPC(48)35/4, 9 Nov. 1948.
43. CO 537/3030; PREM 8/923, report by H.A. Marquand on visit to Africa, 2 April 1948, and address to press conference, 18 March 1948.
44. FO 800/435/3, & 444/29; FO 371/73037, & 73038, & 73039; CO 537/3032.
45. CO 537/5896 (Griffiths); DO 35/3140/55; FO 371/76351, & 91171.
46. CO 537/5929; CAB 134/1, A(49)2, CO memo. 5 July 1949; CAB 131/10, DO(51) 17/3, 18 June 1951 (Gordon Walker); DO 35/3140; PREM 8/1284, minute by C. Syers, 22 Aug. 1950. See R. Hyam, 'The political consequences of Seretse Khama: Britain, the Bangwato and South Africa, 1948–52', *Historical Journal*, 29 (1986), 921–47.
47. CO 537/4596; DO 35/3811. Noel-Baker told a deputation led by Tom Driberg, MP, 3 March 1949: 'Our policy is not in the slightest degree influenced by economic, financial, or strategic considerations, not at all. It is influenced by this: 40 years ago

Campbell-Bannerman made a self-governing unit of the Union, to which our Liberal Parliament then agreed. Since then we have worked with them in the Commonwealth on many matters and many South African statesmen have, in our view, rendered great services to the world: we want to go on doing that, we want to keep that co-operation, we don't want to have an all-out quarrel with another member of the Commonwealth in the creation of whose self-government we still take a considerable national pride'.

48. CO 537/5710, minute by W.I.J. Wallace, 19 Sept. 1950; CO 936/123, minute by W.G. Wilson, 12 March 1952: CO 936/125/162; CO 936/217, Lloyd to Strang, 9 Sept. 1952.
49. CO 537/5708, & 5709; FO 371/88560, & 88561, & 88566; CAB 128/17, CM.28(50)3, 4 May 1950; CAB 129/39, CP(50)88. The paper was drafted by Sir E. Beckett, W.G. Wilson and A.N. Galsworthy, together with suggestions from N. Pritchard, and vetting by Cohen, Lloyd, J. Martin, and Sir K.O. Roberts-Wray (the legal adviser); it was then discussed with ministers H. Shawcross and J. Dugdale.
50. CAB 129/42, CP(50)214, 25 Sept. 1950; DO 35/3839; CO 537/5710/142; FO 371/88566. The paper was drafted by G.E. Crombie of the CRO, but a great deal of consultation went into it (e.g. with R.R. Sedgwick, G.H. Baxter, C. Syers, and J.S. Garner), and it was 'much travelled' between departments too, so that in its final form responsibility for it was spread widely. Griffiths for the C.O. and Younger for the F.O. signified their general agreement with it.
51. CAB 128/18, CM.62(50)4, 28 Sept. 1950; FO 800/435/153; CAB 131/10, DO(51)17, 18 June 1951; PREM 8/1284.
52. CAB 129/45, CP(51)109, memo. by Gordon Walker, 16 April 1951, after visit to South Africa, Southern Rhodesia and High Commission Territories.
53. See R. Hyam, 'The geopolitical origins of the Central African Federation: Britain, Rhodesia and South Africa, 1948–53', *Historical Journal*, 30 (1987), 145–72.
54. CO 1015/89/13, BBC talk by Creech Jones, 15 April 1952; CO 1015/144/15, and CO 1015/770, visit of Attlee to Central Africa, August 1952. In this matter Attlee was more far-sighted than Cohen, who had become too personally involved with the federal scheme. Cohen's determination to bring Federation into being was not, however, somehow out of line with his West African policy: there is only a paradox if his commitment to 'decolonisation' is exaggerated. His African policy was consistent: in all parts of Africa he wanted to retain the initiative against extremists, and *control* nationalist movements. He opposed withdrawal of the federal proposals on the ground that it would abandon the field to irresponsible 'outright nationalists', which would only give impetus to European extremists. Africans should therefore, as he put it, be brought round to 'a true realisation of their own interests', confronted as they were by the 'Afrikaner menace' (DO 35/3601/104; CO 1015/59, minute, 31 Oct. 1951; CO 1015/64/36 B, to Sir G. Rennie, 16 Nov. 1951).
55. DO 35/3140/55, & FO 371/91171, Baring's 'final review' dispatch to Commonwealth Relations Secretary, 30 June 1951; see also Gordon Walker Papers, GNWR 1/9, Diary, 2 April 1950.
56. *As it happened*, 191.
57. CO 1015/770/43. Cohen expressly described Northern Rhodesian African opinion as 'immature and unorganised politically' (CO 537/7203/7, memo. 18 April 1951).
58. CO 967/57, Sir A. Dawe's memo. on East Africa, July 1942, and 'Mr Macmillan's counter-proposals', 15 Aug. 1942.
59. CO 847/35/6, minute by Sir F. Pedler, 1 Nov. 1946; CO 537/3561, report on West African tour by Rees-Williams, 27 Sept. 1948.
60. FO 371/107032 (UP.134/1), Sir G. Jebb to Foreign Secretary, 12 Jan. 1953.

Ronald Robinson and the Cambridge Development Conferences, 1963–70*

by
D.K. Fieldhouse

Many have speculated about what Ronald Robinson was doing academically during the ten years after 1961, that pivotal date in the literature of modern imperialism when he and Jack Gallagher published *Africa and the Victorians*. Before then there were his articles in the *Journal of African Administration*, the famous article on 'The Imperialism of Free Trade' in 1953, written with Jack, and his own chapter in the *Cambridge History of the British Empire*, Vol. III, which came out eventually in 1959. But after 1961 there was only the previously written chapter (again with Jack) on 'The Partition of Africa' in the *New Cambridge Modern History*, Vol. XI, published in 1962, and a short introduction to the English edition of Henri Brunschwig's *French Colonialism*. Thereafter the next generally known (and extremely influential) publication was his 'Non-European Foundations of European Imperialism: Sketch for a Theory of Collaboration', originally given at a seminar in Oxford in 1969 but published in R. Owen and B. Sutcliffe's *Studies in the Theory of Imperialism* in 1972. So why were there no more seminal publications in this decade?

One possible answer is that RER was organizing, chairing and then editing the published proceedings of a series of summer conferences on the theme of Third World economic development – the Cambridge Development Conferences; and one aim of this essay is to draw attention to RER's role in these now little-remembered conferences. But the aim must extend beyond this: to use the conference proceedings and reports as a mirror of changing attitudes during the 1960s to the problems of Third World development, as RER himself was to do in his chapter on 'Practical Politics of Economic Development' in the collection of selected papers and reports of the proceedings of the Conferences from 1964 to 1968 which was published, with him as editor, in 1971 as *Developing the Third World: The Experience of the Nineteen-Sixties* (Cambridge, 1971). Or, to pose a definite question, what light do the records of these conferences throw on the evolution of ideas on development during what the United Nations called 'The Development Decade'?

I

To understand the character of the Development Conferences of the 1960s it is necessary to go back to their origins. Their genesis can be traced indirectly to the 'Memorandum on Post-war Training for the Colonial Service', submitted in February 1943 by Major Sir Ralph Furse, Director of Recruitment at the Colonial Office.[1] Its starting point was that members of the Service had, since 1924, been given courses of varying lengths at Oxford, Cambridge or elsewhere before their first overseas posting, but that thereafter had no further training or opportunity to consider their territorial problems in a larger context. Furse therefore proposed 'a second course' after their first 'period of apprenticeship' whose aims would be

> in general to check, criticize and clarify the experience the cadet has gained, to counteract the 'bolshevist' tendencies which are said to be most common about the fifth to seventh year of service . . .; to deflate his conceit if he thinks he knows too much; and to fortify his morale after any shocks which his idealism had received during his apprentice tour.

He should also be given a broader view of what was going on in other parts of the empire and the larger issues of colonial policy.[2] This second course should be held at Oxford, Cambridge and London, though Furse was concerned that only appropriate academics should be involved:

> We should want our officers, at all stages of their careers, to believe in the value of what they are doing and to believe that the British Empire is, and has been, on the whole a beneficent institution. A professor of Colonial History who insisted on teaching that the Empire had been acquired by piracy and was only retained to satisfy the greed of a few capitalists might be a serious inconvenience.[3]

Furse's proposals were in most respects adopted by the Devonshire Committee whose report was made in July 1945, though not published until 1946. There was to be a 'second course' at the three universities lasting two academic terms from October; but it should be preceded by a Summer School at Oxford or Cambridge lasting two to three weeks, which would be attended by all members of these courses. The School would be housed in one college. It would aim to be 'generally refreshing and stimulating'; to 'give officers from various territories and branches a chance to exchange experience and ideas'; to 'provide a good and easy meeting ground for the locally recruited officer, the man from the Dominions, and the native of this country'; to 'give a man the opportunity to meet those who are authorities upon his special subject'; and to provide 'a time for the discussion of certain subjects which are important to the colonial servants but which lie a little outside the regular lines of colonial history'.[4]

In the event Cambridge was chosen and the first Summer School was held at Queens' College in August 1947. As an institution it lasted (with a gap in 1950) until 1962, though, after the first School it was called the 'Colonial Office Summer Conference on African Administration', with a sub-title indicating the central theme of the year. A pattern soon became established. In addition to hearing a number of speeches by experts or dignitaries, the 180 or so members were divided into half a dozen study-groups, each of which was provided in advance with a preparatory paper in which a particular aspect of the general topic for the year was set out for discussion. At the end of the fortnight each group prepared a report and these papers and reports were subsequently printed as Colonial Office confidential prints. The list of speakers at the first conference reads like a roll-call of all the great and good in contemporary colonial affairs, and there were always a number of distinguished speakers – 32 of them in 1951, for example – backed up by a solid phalanx from the Office. Among these officials from 1947 to 1949 was RER, but his name does not appear again until 1954, by then as one of the 'other members'; nor thereafter until 1961, when the nature of the institution was changing.

That year, in fact, was the start of a new era and is the main focus of this essay. The conference now became the responsibility of the Cambridge University Overseas Studies Committee, which had existed since the early 1920s to run the colonial service course; but the bureaucratic back-up and financial support came from the Department of Technical Co-operation, of which Sir Andrew Cohen had recently become Director General. This was critical for RER's future role in the Conferences. In 1947 he had joined the new Colonial Office African Studies Branch as research officer (known, he recalls, as 'Thinker').[5] Cohen was then chief of the Africa Division of the Office and the two were evidently close. Cohen was presumably the guiding spirit behind the new-model conferences. He gave the opening address at the 1961 meeting (though it was not printed in the proceedings, which were now published for public sale by the Overseas Studies Committee at Cambridge) and was listed as attending all the conferences until 1965. It is clear that the new form of the conference was his creation and was closely related to the functions and objectives of the new DTC, renamed and transformed into the Ministry of Overseas Development (ODM to distinguish it from the Ministry of Defence) in 1965. These changes reflected and symbolized the fact of decolonization. The time for servants of the imperial power to discuss the minutiae of African administration had passed. The need was now to enlighten their indigenous successors as politicians and administrators; and their primary concern was with economic development, not good government. The 1961 Conference was the last on administration: thereafter all were on aspects of development and from 1965 they were generically described as the 'Cambridge Conferences on Development', with retrospective effect to 1962, since that of 1965 was numbered 'the Fourth'.

It is evidence of the attractiveness of these conferences – no doubt helped by the congenial atmosphere of a Cambridge college in late summer – that they lasted, with gaps in 1967, 1969, and 1971, until 1972. RER chaired all the conferences from 1961 to 1970, edited their published proceedings, provided an Introduction to each of them and much longer summaries of the papers and discussions under the name of 'Argument of the Conference' from 1963 to 1966. Finally, he edited and contributed to the collection of select papers published as *Developing the Third World. The Experience of the 1960s* (Cambridge, 1971). It may have been no accident that his translation to Oxford in 1971 came only a year before the last of the conferences, though Dr Paul Howell, who organized the later conferences, says that 'they were discontinued after [1972] largely because the Overseas Study Committee thought that they were not cost-effective, particularly in view of the diminishing number of representatives from the developing countries themselves'. The rest of this essay will examine the proceedings of these Conferences, year by year, to 1970, with particular emphasis on RER's recorded contribution.

II

Although 1961 marked a new departure, the first three conferences of the new dispensation form a bridge between the old didactic meetings, attended mostly by British colonial officials, and the later conferences, which were essentially opportunities for experts on economic development to discuss problems among themselves and with laymen from overseas countries. In 1961 and 1962 the previous pattern continued, with short conference briefing papers for each discussion group, though now their authors were, for the first time, named in a footnote; and the subject matter and approach were still dominated by Colonial Office preoccupations during this period of transferring power. In 1961 it was still with 'Local Government in Africa', mainly a review of changes and problems since the 1948 Local Government Despatch had pointed the way from indirect rule towards local democracy. In 1962 it was 'Training for Development', which concentrated on meeting African needs for efficient administrators, businessmen and educationalists.

The 1963 Conference, however, marked the start of a new era. Although still nominally restricted to 'African Development Planning' and while most members came from Africa, its focus was on Third World development as a whole. Technically the main innovation was that there were now considered and quite substantial papers by a variety of experts in the then burgeoning science of development economics. In the following years this new pattern was maintained, with an increasing proportion of the papers written by specialists of international standing in their fields from a much more theoretical standpoint. Simultaneously the membership consisted more and more of British and American specialists in development and fewer lay members from overseas until, by the later 1960s, the conference represented mainly the huge international network of those who theorized or attempted to practise economic development in the Third World.

III

The 1963 Conference is of particular interest because, unlike most of its successors and despite its nominal restriction to Africa, it dealt with virtually the whole range of major problems of Third World economic development and thus set up, as it were, topics which were considered separately and in more detail later. This conference therefore provides a snapshot view of contemporary attitudes at a time when faith in the prescriptions of the economists and planners was still strong and when there was general optimism about future prospects for the Third World. Four main subjects were discussed: 'The Techniques and Strategy of Planning'; 'The Role of Agriculture in Development'; 'Education'; and 'Aid'.

It seems clear that everyone took it as axiomatic that planning was essential to successful development. This was not surprising, since the colonial powers had adopted indicative planning for colonies from the middle 1940s and the conventional wisdom of almost all economists in the 1950s had been that such an approach was essential to make the best use of scarce resources.[6] The conference was therefore concerned with the use of planning and the problems it faced rather than with its rationale. Five main aspects were discussed. First it was agreed that lack of data and of efficient administrative agencies made precise and sophisticated planning in Third World countries impracticable: 'to be realistic, the methods cannot be more specific than the existing data allow'.[7] Second, the great need was to reconcile overall with sectional plans and to keep both flexible. The main disagreement was over the relative size of public and private sectors and how to finance the former. Deficit financing was regarded as potentially dangerous: in particular 'contractor credit should be used extremely cautiously',[8] perhaps a reference to Ghana's heavy use of such credits since 1961. On the other hand, the force of Keynesian theory was reflected in the belief that a developing country 'should normally be working on the brink of inflation. Hence the financial art of planning is one of brinkmanship – to keep the economy on the edge without allowing it to fall right over'.[9] Domestic financing of investment should be based mainly on government monopoly of export commodities through marketing boards – 'the most successful and least painful method in African experience. . .'.[10]

Probably the most contentious issue discussed was the relative priority to be given to agriculture and industry. The 1963 Conference seems to have been divided between representatives of African states, who were generally in favour of an 'industry first' strategy, and others, including some economists, who held that agriculture must come first. The compromise conclusion was that agriculture must be made competent to provide a surplus with which to pay for industrialization. This meant expanding exports to earn foreign exchange by helping peasants to produce more by traditional methods on the assumption that they would respond to the right stimuli; though there was no attempt to square this with exploitation of producers through low marketing board prices. What they needed was better communications, marketing facilities, information on prices, and credit facilities, all backed up by better research and extension services. Conversely, capital-intensive farms and estates and provision of sophisticated equipment were a waste of money. Farming must pull itself up largely by its own bootstrings.

The third main theme was education and manpower; and here there was concern at the huge proportion of public revenues and development expenditure then being laid out by many African states on this and other social services. Primary education must take priority, but even so it should aim at sustainable literacy and dissemination of useful skills rather than providing the basis for further education. Secondary and tertiary education should be restricted to defined social purposes and must avoid creating a large surplus of people with locally unusable skills, as had already happened in India.

Finally, the conference took a broad view of aid. It accepted the conventional target of 1 per cent of the GNP of donor countries, but made no serious attempt to define the purpose of aid or to justify it: Conference concentrated mainly on problems relating to different types of aid. It must not be related to the political or ideological purposes of donors. Multilateral was preferred to bilateral aid; but since most aid would necessarily be bilateral and much of it tied to purchases from donor countries, the debate turned mainly on how the restrictive effects of this might best be mitigated.

The 1963 Conference was the last which attempted to tackle the whole range of development issues and necessarily did so rather superficially. It was a layman's conference. It was clearly felt that in future a narrower focus was needed and it was decided that the next conference should concentrate on problems of industrialization. The stage was thus set for what proved perhaps the most exciting of these conferences in 1964.

IV

The 1964 Conference provided the opportunity for a full-scale debate over two major issues in development policy: the relative priority to be given to agriculture and industry and the use of 'intermediate' rather than 'high' technology in developing countries.

RER described the first of these as 'a dramatic confrontation between the champions of "Agriculture first", drawn up on Arnold Rivkin's paper, and those of "Industry first", defending Khalid Ikram's thesis'. In the wings of what he called 'good theatre' was N.F. de Figueirido, who contributed a paper on 'Latin American Industrial Development', written as a comment on these other papers and the discussion they evoked.[11]

Rivkin's case for the primacy of agriculture set out the traditional argument that all economic development, and particularly industrial growth, had historically derived from improvement in the performance of agriculture. Much of his paper consisted of quotations from or references to then popular writers, in particular W.W. Rostow's *The Stages of Economic Growth* and P.T. Bauer and B.S. Yamey's *The Economics of Underdeveloped Countries*.[12] Rivkin's case (as RER pointed out in his Argument) had been most clearly stated by W.A. Lewis in his Report on *Industrialisation in the Gold Coast* (Accra, 1953), which had been commissioned by Nkrumah in his first year as prime minister but was subsequently almost totally ignored by his government. Industry must grow on the back of agriculture because agriculture alone could provide the necessary conditions: a food supply, saving the cost of importing it; demand for all industrial products; commodities for processing and exports to earn foreign exchange. Agriculture would also create employment for an increasing population far better than industry. Finally, it could generate a surplus which could be used by the state to finance development of the modern sector. Thus steady growth of productivity in the agricultural sector was a necessary foundation for an industrial expansion which could be sustained indefinitely.

Khalid Ikram's paper, though in fact only an explanatory analysis of why Pakistan had decided to concentrate the bulk of its development resources during the next two decades on industry rather than agriculture, accurately reflects the influences which were persuading most Third World countries to follow this model in the 1960s. Pakistan had three main aims for the the next two decades: to treble the GNP; to provide full employment for a rapidly growing labour force; and to achieve independence from foreign assistance. Industry alone could make these realizable. Historically its growth rate in Pakistan was far higher than that of agriculture. It was less prone to uncertainties caused by weather and market fluctuations. Large-scale industry had a far higher marginal savings rate than any other activity. Increasing the share of foreign currency available for capital goods imports would make it institutionally feasible to reduce imports of consumer goods.

It is important, and at first sight paradoxical, that Ikram's second reason for making large-scale industry Pakistan's leading sector was the need to absorb an expanding population. Agriculture, already sustaining much underemployment, could not provide any more full-time employment; so the modern sector would have to do so. Yet the type of industry envisaged by the planners was both large-scale and capital intensive; so most of the additional labour would have to be absorbed by other types of employment generated by these new industries, particularly in construction and services. Why, then, go for capital- rather than labour-intensive technology? First, since much industrial production had to be exported, nothing less than the best equipment would make these goods internationally competitive. Second, although wages were low, labour costs per unit of production might well be high because of low productivity. Finally, it would be dangerous to have many different types of imported second-hand machinery because spares would be difficult to obtain.

The third main reason for an 'industry first' policy lay in the calculation that, for Pakistan to become independent of foreign aid, exports had to grow at an annual rate of 7 per cent, whereas the evidence since c. 1952 was that agricultural exports could grow at a mere 2–3 per cent. Industrialization would help the balance of payments in two other ways: import-substitution would reduce imports of consumer goods; and by restricting imports of capital goods (by tariffs, licensing, etc.) the capital goods industry would, for the first time, be given adequate protection and incentive, so ultimately saving substantial quantities of foreign exchange.

Ikram, moreover, strongly rejected the concept of 'balanced growth' between agriculture and industry. Agriculture must indeed grow, since it would still be the largest employer of labour in 1985; but industry must be the uniquely favoured 'leading' or 'strategic' sector, for the reasons already outlined, but also because it had 'shown itself to be a major source for the inflow of modern skills and progressive attitudes which are the *sine qua non* of economic development'.[13]

Such arguments, of course, merely reflected the preference of most development economists of the 1950s and early 1960s for industry as the leading sector of less developed countries (LDCs).[14] But the conference, judging by RER's survey of reports of the discussions, seems to have had doubts. De Figueiredo, in his retrospective paper, while favouring industry as the leading sector in most Latin American countries, held that agricultural exports must be relied on to earn foreign exchange in the early period of industrialization; and if agriculture could not do this in its present condition, it should also receive state help. Thus 'balanced' growth policies might be necessary as a second best.

This was certainly the dominant view of the conference. Most members, especially the Africans, thought that agriculture had been given priority for too long under colonialism and would concede only that it should now be given whatever help was available after the needs of industry had been met. It was recognized, however, that industrialization would be successful only if it generated the right sort of industries, and this resulted in much debate. Import-substituting enterprises for the home market were thought the most viable because such infant industries could seldom be competitive. They should be as simple as possible in the first stage and use local raw materials in the hope that they might eventually be able to export. Preferential regional marketing arrangements were important to provide economies of scale. Export subsidies could be used to offset artificially high domestic costs. Even so there were dangers. Imported capital goods would be a strain on the balance of payments. More serious, as RER summarized the possible effects in a conceptual Third World Ruritania,

> under the strain of subsidising too many [inefficient manufactures], the entire economy slides into a depression from which it will not soon recover. But before this Ruritania has slithered very far it would have hit the inevitable balance of payments crisis, showing that indiscriminate industrialisation cannot pay.[15]

The other main and closely related debate of 1964 turned on the nature of industrial technology best suited to the Third World. E.F. Schumacher, then relatively unknown as Chief Economic Adviser to the British National Coal Board, but subsequently famous as the author of *Small is Beautiful*,[16] put forward the then barely ventilated case for the use of labour-intensive rather than capital-intensive modes of industrial production. His case against the latter had three main foundations. It led to high unemployment. Most of the population of Third World countries did not benefit from the wealth created by capital-intensive urban industries. The capital needed to create such industries was beyond the savings capacity of these poor societies and therefore necessitated dangerous levels of borrowing abroad. The solution to all three problems, wrote Schumacher in a near tautology, was intermediate technology, which 'must be appropriate to the country in question'.[17] His prescription was for central planners to prescribe for 'districts' which had some 'inner cohesion', rather than for a state as a whole. Manufacturing equipment could then be designed to meet the needs and factor endowment of particular districts. Typically a start would be made with equipment to make simple consumer goods, including building and building equipment, agricultural implements and also capital equipment for these and other 'intermediate technology industries'.

> It is only when, so to say, the circle is closed, so that, on the whole, the people are able to make their own tools and other equipment that genuine economic development can take place. In a healthy society which employs an appropriate technology the argument that unemployment cannot be conquered for want of capital could never be true because there would always be the possibility of turning unused labour to the production of capital goods.[18]

Here, then, we are near the source of a debate which has continued to rage into the mid-1980s. At this early stage the essentials of the counter-argument, later to be elaborated by A. Emmanuel,[19] were outlined by Nicholas Kaldor. As reported by RER, he pointed to two main weaknesses in the Schumacher case. First, the more modern and efficient the equipment, the higher the output per unit of capital: hence 'methods of production with the best capital/output ratio give the most economical use of capital when you are short of it'. Second, the limit to the amount of paid employment is set by the quantity of wage goods available to pay for their work. 'The latest technology will produce more manufactured wage goods than labour-intensive techniques, so you will be able to pay more wages to more people.' Yet, in the last resort, it was agricultural surplus which decided the amount of wages a poor country could afford, since food was the primary need.

> If we can employ only a limited number of people in wage labour, then let us employ them in the most productive way, so that they make the biggest possible contribution to the national output, because that will also give the quickest rate of economic growth.[20]

The debate which followed was predictably a drawn battle. RER reported that the dominant view was that 'there must be a middle way for both economic and cultural reasons'.[21] But if so, this *via media* was clearly not discovered, though, according to him, at least one important point was made which experience during the next two decades proved correct. The major reason for the adoption of capital-intensive industry in poor countries was to be found in institutional factors rather than economic analysis. At almost every stage there was a built-in bias towards capital intensity. Foreign donors preferred to pay for single, large, prestigious projects, using their own technology rather than provide funds for a multiplicity of small indigenous ventures which they did not and could not control. Development agencies would lend at perhaps half the current commercial rate of interest for such prestige projects. For their part, Third World governments normally allowed capital goods in free of duty and lowered the real cost of capital by tax incentives and artificially high rates of exchange. Finally the strength of labour unions and statutory minimum wages raised industrial wage levels to the point at which labour-intensive methods of production were uneconomic. Until and unless such practices were altered there was no scope for labour-intensive industrial development.

Of the rest of the 1964 Conference little can be said, though it dealt with a number of major long-running issues: the relative advantages of state and private enterprise; the role of foreign aid; the position of trade unions; and the need to make modern technology compatible with traditional cultures. Seen from the standpoint of the mid-1980s, perhaps two main features of contemporary thought stand out.

First, the fundamental issues have changed very little: agriculture versus industry, high versus low technology, the state versus private enterprise, domestic versus foreign capital, the role of foreign aid, and the impact of foreign technology on traditional cultures. The debate has become more sophisticated but few if any of these issues have been resolved.

Second, however, there has been a major change in the amount of optimism with which such matters are considered. In 1964, while obstacles to growth were obvious, the general assumption was that these could and would be eliminated, given sufficient intelligence and good will on the part of all concerned. Twenty years later much if not all of that optimism has evaporated: the obstacles seem greater than ever. Industry has almost everywhere failed to act as a dynamic leading sector and state-run industry has usually remained a net consumer of resources, almost nowhere making a net contribution to capital accumulation. There has been no satisfactory resolution of the dichotomy between high and low technology. In most parts of Africa, if not elsewhere, agriculture has been bled near to death, but the surplus extracted has mostly been squandered. Food supplies, particularly in Africa, have failed to keep up with population and the volume of export crops has in many places actually declined. Faith in the ability of governments to plan constructively or to carry out their plans, high in 1965, has almost disappeared. Conversely it is significant that what has become a major issue in the modern debate – the probity and competence of successor governments – could not then be discussed at all because, in that first decade of African independence, it had simply to be taken on trust.

V

Unqualified optimism was not, however, as characteristic of the 1965 Conference, which may perhaps mark a watershed. Whether or not there was any connection, this was also what RER described as a 'star-studded gathering' which included far more British members and especially economists than any previous meeting, among them those he called 'the dread engines of scientific theology commanded by Drs Balogh and Kaldor, Mrs Joan Robinson, Drs Street, Pazos, Meier, Berrill, Farley, Schumacher, Hanson. Little, White, Mates, Soper, Selwyn, Mrs Kumar and many more'. This conference also produced some well-remembered aphorisms: ' "Loop before you leap" – the only solution to the population obstacle'; 'statesmen never steal. They always appropriate', answered by 'developing the economy is like persuading a centipede to move quickly. The state can only expect to move ten of its legs. Who is going to move the other thousand (*sic*)' and so on.[22] In short, the Cambridge Conference was becoming an exciting forum for a broad discussion of the evolving theory and practice of development.

But the reason why the 1965 Conference now looks like a watershed is that for the first time the emphasis was on failure or partial failure of Third World development, a moment when the nostrums of the development economists of the previous decade were looked at critically in the light of increasingly disturbing evidence that they were not working as planned. Much that emerged might well have been written or said 20 years later, though by then with more certainty and less residual hope.

The key paper of the conference was 'The Development Decade in

Perspective' by G.M. Meier, a Stanford economist.[23] Meier's basic argument, based on the limited statistics then available, which related mostly to Asia and Latin America rather than to Africa (for which very little statistical information before about 1960 was or is available), was that, far from accelerating, development seemed to be slowing up. He pointed at the start to seven main areas of disappointment. The rate of growth per capita (though not aggregate) was slower in the early 1960s than in the 1950s. Investment relied very heavily on foreign aid. Little progress had been made in equalizing incomes in Third World countries. Industrial expansion was failing to absorb population growth. Agriculture was growing slowly, and often not as fast as population. The volume of Third World exports was not growing as fast as exports from more developed countries (MDCs), and their export/import ratio was deteriorating with serious balance of payments implications. Public and mostly non-productive sectors were growing at the expense of productive private sectors. Finally, modernization was resulting in enclaves and huge urban conglomerations.

Meier went on to consider why these problems had developed and, in particular, how far plans and planners were responsible. Adopting what is now a common view, but was then regarded as reactionary, he argued that the very existence of plans expressed important biases: ideological hostility to capitalism; desire to equalize incomes; dislike of foreign control; prejudice against the 'inferior' activity of primary production; above all the belief that modern Third World conditions were so different from those in the West in its earlier period of development that the old formulae would no longer work. However justified these prejudices might be, it was clear that planning had so far failed to come to terms with reality. Most economists saw development as a theoretical problem and could not convert their equations into concrete plans of action in a Third World setting: the more sophisticated their theories, the less useful when applied. The result was a plethora of 'empty phrases such as "a big push"; or "balanced growth"'.[24] The real social, political and administrative problems involved had been largely ignored, plans had seldom been implemented in a reasonable order and most administrative systems had been quite unable to carry them out.

Meier's conclusion – 'In lieu of prognosis' – points to what was to become the 'conservative' formula of the early 1980s. Since planning had proved so generally ineffective and state control so widely incompetent, the need was now for 'lighter' planning and less central control, except possibly in countries such as India or China where there was intense pressure of population on land and other resources and where there were large domestic markets. Elsewhere governments should stimulate the private sector by providing help of all kinds – for example credit and infrastructure – and by simplifying legal and administrative controls. They should adopt more realistic price structures, exchange rates and trade controls. Agricultural productivity must be improved by better prices, lighter taxes and more help of all kinds to small farmers. Exports must be increased to relieve foreign exchange bottlenecks. The external debt-servicing problem – already becoming serious for some states – must be tackled by the West through more aid, by liberalization of the international gold standard and by relaxation of GATT restriction on preferential trade. Finally, LDCs must seriously tackle their own social problems: 'an improvement in the quality of human life cannot be simply awaited as an object of development, but is necessarily an instrument of development'.[25]

Meier's paper clearly provoked intense controversy. On one side there were those who clung to the faith of the 1950s. The statistics might be misleading. The apparent slowing down of exports was due to less favourable terms of trade, not lagging production. The social investment of the past had not yet provided dividends: 'once you have achieved a certain advance in social improvement, these social inputs combine with the economic inputs and make something like an economic breakthrough'. Aid was essential, not a measure of Third World failure. The Conference seems to have been satisfied with these emollient responses: things were not as black as the statistics suggested; and in fact aggregate growth rates for the Third World did not slow down until the later 1970s. Nevertheless there was clearly some support for Meier's argument, leading to a debate between what RER called the 'social' and the 'aid and private enterprise' approach to development: that is between those who believed that intellectual and psychological changes were necessary before modernization could work and others who thought that economic inputs alone could do the job. A compromise conclusion was that external stimuli were effective only with complementary internal changes.[26]

Meier had mounted one attack on the conventional wisdom on planning; Stanley Please of the World Bank mounted another.[27] His target was the belief that in LDCs the state must be the main mobilizer of domestic financial resources and that it should do so through taxation (in whatever form) rather than by domestic borrowing. This assumption, he said, had two roots. First, in poor societies voluntary savings were likely to be small, so saving had to be compulsory. Second, the state had a lower propensity to consume and a higher propensity to invest than private individuals. The state moreover could take a long rather than a short-term view of social needs. The result, as Please indicated in a table, was that the proportion of GNP taken by Third World governments in the previous decade had risen substantially and looked like rising further.

This fact gratified supporters of state economic dominance; but Please pointed to another side of the coin. The proportion of public revenue used for investment had not risen as fast as its other receipts: that is, many states were spending a larger share of the surplus they extracted on current outgoings. This raised the question whether those who, like Kaldor, pressed for ever higher levels of taxation in LDCs, were right in holding that it would be well and constructively spent. Please pointed to two main reasons for doubt. First, much and probably an increasing share of the public revenues of LDCs was being spent on specifically non-developmental objects, such as defence, public buildings and an enlarged civil service. Second, even that part spent on things such as education and social services, which might help development in the long run, included substantial elements of mere consumption. Thus the danger of a high-taxation, state-oriented system was that once taxes were 'in the kitty', a poor government would be unable to resist the temptation to use them to cover current expenditure, and would then be forced to borrow abroad to pay for investment. Hence there was no certainty that rates of public investment were directly related to levels of taxation. In short, it was unwise to assume that all LDC governments were rational decision-takers, acting in the best interests of future generations. They were more often concerned primarily with their own immediate political and group interests, which were best served by high state expenditure and current consumption.

Please suggested two possible policy implications. Governments must impose more self-discipline: earmarking revenues for particular purposes might be one way of doing so. Second, there might be a case for relying more on private savings and domestic borrowing, which in turn would require higher interest rates and possibly the issue of inflation-proofed bonds.

Such radicalism was clearly too much for the Conference to swallow. RER obviously accepted this propensity of governments to spend in 'the crisis of great expectations'. Patronage was clearly important: 'nothing binds the ties of national unity or oils the wheels of cooperation so much as patronage in the form of current expenditure'.[28] But others clearly found the topic embarrassing because it impugned the wisdom and probity of new states: as one speaker put it, 'the fact is that developing countries are just short of money',[29] as if this exonerated them from all need for economy. Nor was there any support for earmarking particular funds for investment. Proponents of heavy taxation and state control of investment counter-attacked strongly. One speaker, described by RER as '[the] most eminent advocate' of heavy taxation, argued that, while governments might be good or bad, the need was to transfer spending power from the rich minority to the state:

> it is still true generally speaking that however bad the government, the social utility of every unit of money spent by public authorities is greater than when it is left in private hands. There is very little private saving in the vast under-developed areas.[30]

This then orthodox view seems to have been generally accepted, which was not surprising since most members were either economists committed to such ideas or representatives of LDC governments which had a vested interest in high government incomes and expenditure. Discussion therefore focused on the best ways to raise more taxes: import duties, excises and levies on peasant production were deemed most practicable, and there seemed to be no realization that extraction of the peasant's surplus by marketing boards might adversely affect his productive effort.[31]

Seen in the round, the 1965 Conference is important because, while it was the first to focus on the limited achievements of development and the first at which there was serious dissent from the conventional strategies of state-planned and state-based growth, such doubts and criticisms were largely buried under the conventional wisdom of the previous decade. Hope clearly triumphed over accumulating evidence that things were not, in most countries, going as well as they should have been.

VI

In format the 1966 Conference closely followed that of 1965, with 15 papers and over 180 members, some of them very distinguished. The subject also should have proved stimulating. Yet one senses that this was not a very exciting event. In his Introduction RER for once did not enthuse; and it is probably significant that in his later compilation of select papers he included only two from this gathering. Conversely he printed three sections of his own Argument, the first, uniquely, under his own name as '"The Case for Economic Aid" by Ronald Robinson', as contrasted with the normal 'Cambridge Conference Report'.

This is probably significant. Read after 20 years most of the papers and the greater part of the discussion as recorded seem to avoid the fundamental question of 'why' and to concentrate on practical questions of 'how'. Only one paper, written by Chief S.O. Adebo, of the Permanent Nigerian Mission to the UNO, formally posed the question 'Why Aid?'; and he did little more in five pages than distinguish between the virtues of 'military aid', 'emergency economic aid' and 'economic aid aimed at strengthening of [sic] the recipient country's economy', without attempting to rationalize any of these motives.[32] Some of the other writers included short rationalizations of the current functions of aid; but no one dealt with its historical origins or seriously challenged its utility. The two papers which came nearest to providing a considered critique of aid were those given by Hollis B. Chenery of the Harvard Centre for International Affairs and Thomas Balogh of Oxford, then Economic Adviser to Harold Wilson's Labour Cabinet, both of which will be considered below. Hence it was left to RER to put aid in an historical context; and since this probably represents his own most individual and idiosyncratic contribution to the published records of these conferences, its argument must be considered with some care.

RER's case for aid stemmed directly from the central assumptions of the Gallagher-Robinson article, 'The Imperialism of Free Trade' as later developed in *Africa and the Victorians* and 'The Partition of Africa'.[33] Aid in the 1960s must be seen in the context of the long-wave relationship between the West and the Third World. Before c. 1960 most economic relations between MDCs and LDCs were determined by private rather than public interests and objectives. In the nineteenth century European investment in trade and production in LDCs was in the hands of private capitalists and was entirely unplanned: 'Thus haphazardly the underdeveloped regions were first harnessed to the industrial chariot'.[34] Only in the Americas and British settler colonies were the results constructive: in most parts of Asia and Africa 'the uncontrolled activity of private European traders and investors sooner or later involved chaos'.[35] For this there were three main reasons. Much of the capital transferred was for military or consumption purposes and had no economic value. There were no development plans and no ability to plan. Above all, indigenous regimes crumbled as they found it impossible to carry the burden of so much unproductive debt. Thus 'Imperialism [at the end of the nineteenth century] was to be the price of the chaotic egocentricities of free trade during the previous three quarters of a century'[36]

Imperialism evolved into colonialism, which, true to the doctrine of 'The Imperialism of Free Trade', was described as second-best for the West. Nor was it satisfactory for the colonies: colonial rule was 'not the best possible solution to relations between developed and underdeveloped societies' because colonial regimes were expensive and because 'Alien administrators, like traditional rulers, rarely embarked upon revolutionary innovations'.[37] Yet colonialism did at least generate Western-style administrative agencies and 'the popular will to modernize'; so that by the time of decolonization the new states were, for the first time, ready and able to absorb Western technology and investment and to make proper use of them.

But here there was a paradox. Just when these apparently attractive conditions existed and when the new states most needed foreign investment, private capital in the West became relatively unenthusiastic about investment in the Third World. Why was this? RER rehearsed four then standard explanations. The West was increasingly using substitutes for Third World commodities; profits in the West were higher than in LDCs; social policies in the West limited private accumulation for investment; and confidence in the stability of the new states was low. As a result private capital concentrated on the West: 'And so the rich countries are getting comparatively richer and the poorer countries poorer'.[38]

Development aid, government to government, had thus become essential to fill the gap left by private capital. Answering the further question 'Why is aid vital?' RER provided three answers. Domestic savings in LDCs were inadequate in size and in any case could not provide foreign exchange for essential imports. Western private capitalists would not invest in agriculture or infrastructure, concentrating on the import-export sector as in colonial times; whereas these countries now needed to integrate their economies. Trade alone would not pay for essential imports, even if the West removed obstacles to its expansion.[39] Aid, and aid alone, could thus fulfil seven vital functions: solve balance of payments problems; pay for the infrastructure to grow to the point at which private foreign capital would be attracted; help to provide the basis for political and social stability by giving governments the means to buy and reward support; prevent great power rivalries over Third World countries; provide outlets for the West's otherwise unsaleable products, and so have a multiplier effect on the world economy; and finally fulfil a humanitarian role, relieving famine and other morally unacceptable forms of suffering in poor countries.[40] But ultimately, as he had put it earlier in this analysis. aid was a moral obligation:

> Originally it was the advanced countries that imposed the international economy on under-developed societies. It would be almost indecent therefore for the advanced countries to reject their historic responsibility for making the enforced relationship work constructively today.[41]

There are many elements in this critique that might be debated; but perhaps the most surprising thing is that it did not outline the historical origins of aid in the earlier colonial policies of Britain and France, which largely explained its peculiarities in the 1960s: in particular that it had originated in a desire to enable colonies to pay for capital goods which would otherwise have had no market; that it broadened during the post-1945 era into a device for persuading colonial nationalists that the imperial relationship could provide substantial material advantages so long as they remained colonies; and that in the era of decolonization aid became primarily a political weapon in the cold war. Such facts are not necessarily incompatible with RER's argument, but they are essential if one is to understand some of those features of aid in the 1960s which the conference thought worth discussion.

These, in essence, were two: the economic functions of aid and therefore the criteria on which aid should be dispensed; and the alternatives of bilateral and multilateral aid. The first of these was the subject of Chenery's key-note paper, 'The Effectiveness of Foreign Assistance'.[42] In his Argument RER described Chenery and his supporters as 'the hard-nosed school' because they believed that aid resources should be concentrated 'to the places where they have the maximum catalytic and multiplier effects specifically on economic productivity rather than be scattered indiscriminately'.[43] Chenery in fact argued that the only case for aid was to enable LDCs to remove bottlenecks and achieve greater co-ordination in development planning. All aid should be investible: it should not be used to subsidize current consumption. As investment 'the productivity of aid . . . is equal to the marginal productivity of additional capital'; and one unit of aid should generate 3.3 units of growth in GNP.[44] Ultimately the aim must be self-sustaining growth without continued reliance on aid, which depended both on the marginal domestic savings rate exceeding the required investment rate and on exports expanding to close the balance of payments gap.

Such results depended on efficiency in allocating and using aid. This involved more care in the choice between different types of aid (project or programme, tied or untied) by the donors but above all careful selection of those recipients who could make the best use of resources and rigorous controls and checks on how the aid was used. His conclusion was that the size of aid allocated to particular recipients must depend on performance, which in turn would involve better programming and reporting; but as recipients became more efficient they might be freed of supervision. A successful country would be rewarded by more aid, not penalized as in less need, until it eventually achieved self-sufficiency. He concluded, however, with the less rigorous proposition that

> the aim should be a rapid growth rather than . . . maximum efficiency in the use of aid. . . . In countries where additional aid can be used to get growth started, it is likely to turn out to have been very productive in the long run even if the short-run productivity of investment seems low.[45]

The conference's reaction to Chenery's hard message resembled that of the previous conference to Meier. His proposals for selective aid were attacked on humanitarian and emotional grounds and also because most felt that it would not be possible to measure performance comparatively.[46] In fact, according to RER, there seems to have been general optimism about the use and effects of aid: it was admitted that 'a little aid has been wasted in muddle and corruption', most believed not more than one per cent; but the broad picture was regarded as 'very promising indeed'.[47] The common reaction seems to have been that more aid, rather than more control, was needed; and also that there should be less tied or project aid and more programme and multilateral aid (that is, distributed by international agencies such as the World Bank, not by individual donor countries).

On the second main issue of the conference, multilateral versus bilateral aid, Balogh, in his paper 'Bilateral Aid' provided an iconoclastic note of dissent from the standard preference for multilateral aid.[48] His paper began with a realistic list of ten reasons why Third World development had been so disappointing after the optimism of the 1950s, which included most obvious domestic and external influences and ended with 'tribal, feudal or religious attitudes, incompatible with collective and individual social responsibility, cohesion and economic incentives or orderly planning and administration'.[49] His deduction was that a mere increase in the volume of aid would not overcome these social and political obstacles to growth; but equally that the present volume of aid could not safely be reduced and must be made more effective. This could be achieved as well if not better by bilateral, country to country, aid as by multilateral aid. Balogh, indeed, seemed more concerned to point to defects in multilateral aid and its distributors than to the benefits of bilateral aid. He devoted some eight pages to these defects, which he summarized under three main heads. International agencies, particularly those influenced by the USA, were likely to demonstrate the same ideological and political bias and favouritism to particular recipients as individual donors. The World Bank and other agencies depended on funds provided by private financial institutions, merely acting as redistributing agents who charged a commission, and were therefore liable to favour conservative policies; though agencies such as IDA, which received outright contributions from governments for distribution, were less prone to conservatism. Finally, those who made policy in these agencies, the international civil servants, were really unaccountable to anyone, and their bias, together with the limited knowledge held by many of the 'experts' they employed, might result in a serious imbalance in the pattern of aid.[50]

As to the merits of bilateral aid Balogh was less specific. The main case for it seemed to be political. As Economic Adviser to the Labour Cabinet he was acutely aware of the difficulty of generating more aid in an economy plagued by balance of payments problems. In such a situation British aid must be largely tied to save foreign exchange. Moreover, it was only possible to sustain the existing level of aid if it was linked to Britain's continuing sense of responsibility for its one-time colonies in the Commonwealth.

> This Commonwealth responsibility also creates a political will, because of the moral obligation felt, to make sacrifices which otherwise would not be made. *Thus bilateral aid in many circumstances represents an addition to what otherwise would be forthcoming* [sic] on a multilateral basis where much vaguer and looser moral considerations apply, however important and admirable such general aims or feelings are.[51]

Moreover, since 1964 the Labour government had improved Britain's ability to give aid wisely by establishing the Ministry of Overseas Development, which had a Cabinet-level minister to remove aid from the political influence of the Foreign or Commonwealth Offices, and the Institute of Development Studies (IDS) in Sussex. It also offered interest-free loans to the poorest recipients of aid. British bilateral aid could thus be expected to become at least as effective and disinterested as that from other agencies; moreover, given a Labour government, Britain might be less conservative in its assessment of Third World needs and monetary policies than international agencies.[52] Indeed, the debate was largely spurious: 'The real difference is between sensible and foolish allocation of aid'. Plans were 'mostly nonsense' because of inadequate data and oversimplification of complex human and physical realities to make planning feasible. He concluded that

> What we need is hard-headed, socially conscious and morally animated professional planning and skilful education. What we need is a strict co-ordination of bilateral and multilateral aid on the basis of sub-regional plans in which the political and moral impulse in both contributing and receiving countries are fully mobilised.[53]

Balogh seems not to have converted his audience: according to RER the general view remained that 'Multilateral aid has big advantages from every point of view, except that it is hard to get'.[54] Facing realities, however, the conference devoted most of its time to considering how best to improve bilateral aid; among many other needs aid donors should not exclude provision for local costs in recipient countries. This particularly affected peasant agriculture, which was not susceptible to project planning and depended for development on a more general improvement of the infrastructure, on small loans and extension services. Thus at the end the conference had moved on to agriculture; and in the last section of his Argument RER expressed his own estimate of its importance. 'Ultimately, I believe, we have to alter the whole structure of peasant agriculture in much the same way as we have to alter the structure of the economy as a whole.'[55] And, at the end, 'Plainly it is time to put more stress on aid as a means of bringing about a more equitable distribution of the profits of development. For this reason the subject of the next Cambridge Conference is to be "Rural Development" '.[56]

VII

This next conference, however, did not take place for two years, the first break in the annual routine since 1950. There were other innovations. For the first time since 1966 RER did not provide an Argument: his recorded contribution was to be chairman and joint editor (with Peter Johnston of the ODM) of the published proceedings and to write a short Introduction which summarized the main thrust of the proceedings. In place of his Argument there were brief 'Personal Impressions', by other members, of the papers and discussions under each of the five main 'Heads' into which the subject was divided. Finally, the ratio between overseas and British members of the conference, in rough balance in 1966, now tilted sharply on the domestic side: it had become primarily a British debate with a minority of overseas contributors.

For the purposes of this essay this conference has less interest than its predecessors. None of the papers nor, so far as one can judge from the reports, the discussions, really dealt with fundamentals. On the other hand, it was significant that there was now almost universal agreement with the proposition, quite unacceptable in 1964 and 1965, that agriculture, particularly food production, was of primary importance. No one now seems to have argued that an 'industry first' strategy would pull up agriculture behind it. Indeed, virtually all the development models discussed emphasized that agriculture must be the basis for industrial growth; and Dr K.A. Busia, then Chairman of the Political Committee and from 1969 to 1972 Prime Minister of Ghana, pointed out sadly that 'This . . . was the advice given in 1953 to Ghana by Professor Arthur Lewis. But it was not heeded, and the consequences of following a different course have been disastrous'.[57]

With this fundamental principle so generally accepted, the conference could concentrate on alternative strategies for agricultural development; and here too one can see a reaction against earlier belief in the need to replace traditional peasant modes of production by modern large-scale mechanized techniques. The general view was now that summarized by Dr E.M. Godfrey of Manchester University:

> the need to undermine, reform or abolish traditional social institutions in order to modernise agriculture has been grossly over-rated. Most experience shows that, provided the economic incentive is big enough and certain enough, the peasant will adopt improved methods and adjust the social order accordingly.[58]

This view was supported, among others, by Professor Edmundo Flores, who held that in Mexican experience the scale and degree of mechanization were less critical factors in improving production than location, provision of water, adequate prices and other incentives offered to farmers.[59] There was general agreement that land reform (that is, the break-up of big estates) was desirable mainly, as E.H. Jacoby of Stockholm put it, because of 'the additional efforts by the cultivator provided by changes in the tenure system'; that is, peasants would work harder if they owned their land, a simple point made nearly two centuries earlier of the peasantry of France by Arthur Young.[60] There also seems to have been a swing against earlier acceptance of the need to squeeze the peasant to extract a surplus for public revenue. It was still generally accepted that he must be 'exploited' in the sense of taking part of his product; but it was now also realized that if he was squeezed too hard he would stop producing. It was therefore essential to establish precisely what level of prices would keep him working hard, even though this implied some danger of higher costs in the economy as a whole; and he must be given as much state help as possible to compensate him for his efforts.[61]

Thus the only substantive issue in debate was the best way to distribute resources: whether to spread them thinly over the mass of the peasantry or concentrate them where they would have the greatest effect – among the more enterprising and successful minority. Discussion turned on the concept of a 'two-tier' system of agriculture, which implied concentrating fertilizer, improved seeds, irrigation, etc., on a selected minority of farmers and areas, treating the rest of the rural sector as more or less a static holding operation to sustain the bulk of the population and prevent them from drifting to the towns. It is unclear from the reports on which side of the line the balance of opinion lay.

Yet there is no doubt that the general tone of the papers and reported discussions seems, on the printed page, to have been pessimistic: agriculture remained a major problem late in that Development Decade and was holding back general economic growth. It is therefore somewhat surprising that, in his Introduction, RER took a very optimistic line. The reappraisal of doctrine was 'full of hope. It may be after all that the developing countries have begun their long-awaited agricultural revolution in the nineteen-sixties'. 'Happily it looks as if the agricultural problem will have become so much easier by the nineteen seventies that much of the old doctrine can be thrown into discard.' This improvement was due partly to states putting more resources behind the farmer, partly to 'a dramatic break-through in farming techniques which, even in over-populated South Asia, promises to convert agricultural shortages into increasingly substantive surpluses in spite of the increase of population within the next decade.'

Indeed,

> This Cambridge conference was the first at which we were not so much concerned with the problem of how to overcome agricultural shortages as with the question of what might be done with surpluses. That would be an historic turning point indeed. . . . If this normally pessimistic conference has read the signs right, agriculture will after all prove to have been the great success story of the Development Decade.[62]

It is difficult, at least in the printed conference proceedings, to find any basis for such optimism. W. Allan, of the Cambridge School of Agriculture, for one, talked of 'the sluggish growth of agriculture and the explosive expansion of population' as possible major causes of the fact that, in that ninth year of the 'Decade of Development' its objectives were 'further from achievement than they were at the beginning'.[63] Unfortunately the 1970s were not, for most parts of the Third World, to justify RER's optimism about the performance of agriculture.

VIII

In his Foreword to the 1970 Conference[64] RER stated confidently that these 'mixed or generalist conferences' had proved 'remarkably useful as a forum for challenging established orthodoxies and reflecting new trends of policy and thought in development studies' and concluded that there was 'every expectation that [the conference] will hold up as candid a mirror to the experience and ideas of the development endeavour in the seventies as it did in the sixties'.[65] But it was not to be: for whatever reasons this was to be the last but one. At least in terms of the number and distinction of those attending and providing papers 1970 suggested no decline: most of the stalwarts of previous years were there. But there were perhaps signs that the formula of a 'mixed or generalist' conference was losing its utility. As had been seen, during the 1960s the conference had changed entirely from an instrument for enlightening colonial administrators into a forum for relatively high level discussion among mainly European and American theorists, while retaining some elements of its didactic function for practical politicians and civil servants. The report of this conference suggests that these two functions no longer combined as they had done in the past. The science of development economics had moved on and become more specialized and specific. The very broad policy options discussed in so cavalier a manner in earlier years now seemed too crude and elementary. Conversely, so the report of this conference suggests, the sharper and more specific issues raised by the experts in 1970 were blunted and lost their point when bandied around in a large conference by non-experts.

The papers and proceedings of 1970, however, provide a useful check on the progress of some of the major themes that had surfaced on and off since 1963, indeed on the general evolution of development economics in that Development Decade. In a sense its very subject – unemployment in LDCs – suggests at least the partial failure of the grand development strategies of the previous two decades. As D.H. Morse, recently retired after 22 years as Director-General of the International Labour Office, put the matter in his key-note paper 'The Employment Problem in Developing Countries', the 1960s had shown conclusively that substantial aggregate growth had not automatically generated employment. Indeed it had resulted in increased unemployment and widening social disparities. His conclusion, supported by Hans Singer and Dudley Seers, was that GNP must be 'dethroned' as the sole or main aim and measure of LDC development. The pursuit of growth must now be accompanied, and if necessary modified by, strategies to maximize employment and generate greater equality in incomes. Planning should aim first at employment and only then estimate the resultant growth of GNP. Means to achieve this should be land reform, more public works, more labour-intensive industrial methods (backed by correction of fiscal and other policies which tended towards capital-intensive investment), better education in relevant subjects, reduction of international obstacles to LDC exports and the liberalization of aid to promote these objectives.[66]

It is clear that this 'dethroning of GNP' set the cat among the pigeons: as RER commented,

> These issues made this the most perplexed of all Cambridge conferences. Usually they are in two minds – a consensus with a minority dissenting. This one was in five or six minds, which shows how hard planners find it to wrench development theory and practice away from growth rates so as to take the employment problem fully into account.[67]

John White of the Institute of Development Studies, which was to become a main home of this new approach, recorded the cut-and-thrust of the debate in plenary session, as did all others who commented on group discussions. The strongest opposition to Morse came from those who, like Kaldor, had all along distrusted concepts such as 'intermediate technology' (still being pressed here in a paper by Schumacher) and who pointed out that there was no simple dichotomy between growth and employment or between high and intermediate technology. Frances Stewart and Paul Streeten's paper 'Conflicts between Output and Employment Objectives' pointed to this same weakness of the Morse approach. There was no simple trade-off between GNP and employment, for a choice of either objective now must affect the other later. Thus, to go for high employment and labour-intensive production now might well result in lower growth, smaller savings and so less employment in the future.[68]

According to RER and White, no consensus emerged on these opposed issues of principle; but some general argument developed over the practical measures that needed to be taken. It would be wrong to give up the general aim of increasing the aggregate national product; but it was desirable to plan to change the composition of the output, putting more weight on rural production by deploying resources from urban areas. To make this possible LDCs should end the distortion of factor prices – the result of overvalued exchange rates, high import tariffs and trade controls, low interest rates and high wages. This case was pressed by many, including E.J. Berg, later author of the World Bank's *Accelerated Development in Sub-Saharan Africa* (1981), which was to recommend precisely these objectives. But how this was to be achieved in the face of very strong historical, institutional and political vested interests in LDCs does not seem to have been discussed in 1970. A decade and a half later the same problems remain.

The 1970 Conference may be taken to symbolize the end of an era in perhaps two main ways. First, the papers as a whole and the discussions as reported reflect a growing pessimism which contrasts very strongly with the guarded optimism of the early years. In most LDCs aggregate growth, contrary to the pessimism of Meier in 1965, had been sustained: the 1960s were the best recorded decade for the Third World. Yet the results were almost uniformly regarded as unsatisfactory. Development, in short, had taken place, but it had not had the beneficial results predicted. Few if any LDCs had become self-sustaining in terms of savings and capital accumulation. Some were already – long before the oil crisis of 1973/4 and the intensified indebtedness of the later 1970s and beyond – in a serious economic mess. The benefits of growth had rarely permeated below the level of the urban elite and the employed urban work-force. Rural producers (though few statistics were produced at the conference to demonstrate the fact), were mostly worse off than they had been a decade earlier and were migrating in vast numbers to already overcrowded towns. This in turn was generating for the first time unacceptably large numbers of evident and enumerated unemployed. Such facts made nonsense of development as it had been conceived in the 1950s and threw very real doubt on the prescriptions of the first generation of development economists. One result was that radicals were extrapolating from Latin American experience and attempting to apply dependency theory to other continents. Another was the rise of a conservative consensus which put much of the blame on the policies adopted by LDCs and the incompetence with which they were applied.

The other interesting feature of the 1970 Conference was that it demonstrated that the virtual unanimity of earlier development theory, with its emphasis on aggregate growth through high investment, state dominance and industrialization, had largely dissipated. Where once the few dissenters, ranging from P.T. Bauer with his distrust of state action and therefore indicative planning, to Schumacher and his dislike of capital-intensive industry, were regarded as eccentric or reactionary, now they had powerful allies. The god of growth had proved to have feet of clay; the rising gods were full employment, fair play for the peasants, and meeting what were to be called 'basic needs' before contemplating affluence for any. This represents a revolution in thinking which has gone much further by the mid-1980s. How much the Cambridge Conferences contributed to these intellectual shifts is impossible to say: probably not much, since their primary purpose was to disseminate the ideas of intellectuals to the men of decision and action. But at least their reports form a valuable mirror to intellectual change; and it is not the least of RER's achievements that he should have contributed so much to ensuring that these meetings are as stimulating to those who now read their proceedings as they evidently were to those who took part in them.

NOTES

* The subject of this essay was suggested to me by Dr Andrew Porter, one of the editors of this volume. I had considerable difficulty finding out about certain features of these conferences because some of those most directly concerned are dead and I can trace no records of the Overseas Studies Committee. I could, of course, have got all the information I needed from Ronald Robinson; but the fact that the *Festschrift* was to be a surprise made this impossible. I have therefore had to work largely within the four corners of the published records and may well have missed important aspects of the conferences.

1. Reprinted on 22–46 of *Post-War Training for the Colonial Service*, Report of a Committee Appointed by the Secretary of State for the Colonies, London, 1946 [the Devonshire Committee].
2. Ibid., 30–31.
3. Ibid., 34. There was, in fact, no danger of this happening in the 1940s, with Reginald Coupland at Oxford, V.T. Harlow in London and E.A. Walker at Cambridge, all firm believers in the 'beneficent' character of the British Empire.
4. Ibid., 14.
5. 'The Journal and the Transfer of Power, 1947–51', *Journal of Administration Overseas*, xiii, 1, (1974), 255. The *Journal* began in 1947 as a typescript *Digest of African Administration* in the Colonial Office and later became printed as the *Journal of African Administration*.
6. For convenient surveys of the evolution of planning theory and its rationale, see I.M.D. Little, *Economic Development. Theory, Policy and International Relations* (New York, 1982); T. Killick, *Development Economics in Action* (London, 1978). Killick attended the 1964 Conference as a lecturer in the University of Ghana.
7. R.E. Robinson (ed.), *African Development Planning* [the Cambridge Conference of 1963: hereafter 1963 Conference] (Cambridge, 1964), 8.
8. Ibid., 11.

9. Ibid., 10.
10. Ibid., 10.
11. R.E. Robinson (ed.), *Industrialisation in Developing Countries* [the Cambridge Conference of 1964] (Cambridge, 1965), 5. Rivkin was then an Economic Adviser in the World Bank; Ikram was on the Planning Commission of Pakistan; de Figueirido was Director of the Joint United Nations Economic Commission for Latin America and related institutions of the UN.
12. Cambridge, 1960; Cambridge, 1957.
13. Cambridge Conference, 1964, 75.
14. Perhaps the best known proponent of the case for industry as the leading sector was A.O. Hirschman: see in particular his *The Strategy of Economic Development* (New Haven, 1958). For surveys of the vast literature see also Little, *Economic Development* and Killick, *Development Economics*.
15. Cambridge Conference, 1964, 15.
16. E.F. Schumacher, *Small is Beautiful* (London, 1973).
17. Cambridge Conference, 1964, 94.
18. Ibid., 96.
19. A. Emmanuel, *Appropriate or Underdeveloped Technology* (1981: English edn. Chichester, 1982).
20. Cambridge Conference, 1964, 28.
21. Ibid., 31.
22. R.E. Robinson (ed.). *Overcoming Obstacles to Development* [The Cambridge Conference of 1965] (Cambridge, n.d.), 1.
23. Ibid., 44–61.
24. Ibid., 50.
25. Ibid., 57.
26. Ibid., 5–6, quoted by RER as 'the words of [the] chief protagonist [of the case for optimism]'; ibid., 6–8.
27. 'Mobilizing Internal Resources through Fiscal Measures', ibid., 101–112.
28. Cambridge Conference, 1965, 13.
29. Ibid., 14.
30. Ibid., 16. This was probably Nicholas Kaldor who, the previous year, had published an article, 'Taxation for Economic Development', *Journal of Modern African Studies*, I (1963).
31. G.K. Helleiner's, 'The Fiscal Role of the Marketing Boards in Nigerian Economic Development', *Economic Journal*, 74 (1964), expressed the then standard view that marketing boards were the best way of extracting value from peasants without serious adverse effects on them or the economy. Later evidence suggests that he was wrong in most cases.; see also his *Peasant Agriculture, Government and Economic Growth in Nigeria* (Homewood, IL, 1966).
32. R.E. Robinson (ed.), *International Co-operation in Aid* [the Cambridge Conference of 1966] (Cambridge, 1968), 57.
33. This paper and the rest of RER's 'Argument' is dated 1968 in *Developing the Third World*, whereas the other reprinted papers from this conference are dated 1966. This is presumably because the proceedings of the 1966 Conference were not published until 1968 due, as RER stated in his Introduction, entirely to his own failure to act earlier. So presumably the views he expressed here represented his later thoughts superimposed on the records of the conference.
34. Cambridge Conference, 1966, 9.
35. Ibid.
36. Ibid., 10.
37. Ibid., 11.
38. Ibid., 12.
39. Ibid., 13.
40. Ibid., 14–16.
41. Ibid., 9.
42. Ibid., 61–77.

43. Ibid., 21.
44. Ibid., 63.
45. Ibid., 76.
46. Ibid., 22–6.
47. Ibid., 51.
48. Ibid., 104–20.
49. Ibid., 109.
50. Ibid., 110–18.
51. Ibid., 111.
52. Ibid., 118–19.
53. Ibid., 119–20.
54. Ibid., 30.
55. Ibid., 54.
56. Ibid., 55.
57. R.E. Robinson and P. Johnston (eds.), *The Rural Base for National Development* [the Cambridge Conference of 1968], (Cambridge, 1968), 13.
58. Ibid., 47.
59. Ibid., 73–5.
60. Ibid., 17; Arthur Young, *Travels in France* (1794: reprinted London, 1900).
61. Cambridge Conference, 1968, 120–21.
62. Ibid., 1–2.
63. Ibid., 39–40.
64. R.E. Robinson and P. Johnston, (eds.), *Prospects for Employment Opportunities in the Nineteen Seventies* [the Cambridge Conference of 1970] (London, HMSO, 1971).
65. Ibid., 1.
66. Ibid., 5–13.
67. Ibid., 3.
68. Ibid., 77–94.

Published Writings by R.E. Robinson

'The Relationship of Major and Minor Local Government Authorities', *Journal of African Administration* I, 1 (Jan. 1949), 30–33.

'The Member System in British African Territories. A Note by the Colonial Office African Studies Branch', ibid., 2 (April 1949), 51–9.

'The Progress of Provincial Councils in the British African Territories', ibid., 2 (April 1949), 59–68.

'The Administration of African Customary Law', ibid., 4 (Oct. 1949), 158–76.

'Why "Indirect Rule" has been replaced by "Local Government" in the Nomenclature of British Native Administration', ibid. II, 3 (July 1950), 12–15.

John Gallagher and Ronald Robinson, 'The Imperialism of Free Trade', *Economic History Review*, 2nd ser., VI, 1 (1953), 1–15 [reprinted in A.G.L. Shaw (ed.), *Great Britain and the Colonies 1815–1865* (London, 1970), 142–63; W.R. Louis (ed.), *Imperialism. The Robinson and Gallagher Controversy* (New York and London, 1976), 54–72; and J.A. Gallagher, *The Decline, Revival and Fall of the British Empire* (ed. Anil Seal: Cambridge, 1982), 1–19].

'Something of Brebner', *Cambridge Review* LXXIX, 23 Nov. 1957, 190. [Obituary Note for J.B. Brebner]

'Imperial Problems in British Politics, 1880–1895', in E.A. Benians, Sir James Butler, and C.E. Carrington (eds.), *The Cambridge History of the British Empire, Volume III, The Empire-Commonwealth, 1870–1919* (Cambridge, 1959), 127–180.

Ronald Robinson and John Gallagher with Alice Denny, *Africa and the Victorians. The Official Mind of Imperialism* (London and New York, 1961) pp. xii + 491.

'The Official Mind of Imperialism', in *Historians in Tropical Africa: proceedings of the Leverhulme Inter-Collegiate History Conference, held at the University College of Rhodesia and Nyasaland, September 1960* (Salisbury, Southern Rhodesia, 1962), 197–208.

Ronald Robinson (ed.), *Cambridge University Overseas Studies Committee. Summer Conference on Local Government in Africa. 28 August–9 September 1961 at King's College, Cambridge* (Overseas Studies Committee, Cambridge, 1962) pp. 79. [RER was author of 'I. 'Introduction', 5–7.]

Ronald Robinson and John Gallagher, 'The Partition of Africa', in F.H. Hinsley (ed.), *The New Cambridge Modern History, Volume XI, Material Progress and World-Wide Problems, 1870–1898* (Cambridge, 1962), 593–640.

Ronald Robinson (ed.), *Cambridge University Overseas Studies Committee. Summer Conference on Training for Development, 26 August – 8 September 1962 at King's College, Cambridge* (Overseas Studies Committee, Cambridge, 1963), pp. 80. [RER was author of the 'Introduction', 5.]

Ronald Robinson (ed.), *African Development Planning: Impressions and Papers of the Cambridge Conference on Development Planning, 22 September – 5 Oct. 1963, at Queens' College, Cambridge* (Cambridge University Overseas Studies Committee: Cambridge, 1964), pp. 148. [RER was author of Pt. I, 'Introduction', 5–6, and Pt. II, 'The Argument of the Conference', 7–41.]

Ronald Robinson (ed.), *Industrialisation in Developing Countries: Impressions and Papers of the Cambridge Conference on the role of Industrialisation in Development, 6–19 September 1964, at King's College, Cambridge* (CUOSC: Cambridge, 1965), pp. iv + 203. [RER was author of Pt. I, 'Introduction', and Pt. II, 'The Argument of the Conference', 1–53.]

Ronald Robinson (ed.), *Overcoming Obstacles to Development: Impressions and Papers of the Fourth Cambridge Conference on Development Problems, 12–25 September 1965 at Jesus College, Cambridge* (CUOSC: Cambridge, 1966), pp. iv + 179. [RER was author of Pt. I, Introduction, and Pt. II, 'The Argument of the Conference', 1–43.]

Introduction to Henri Brunschwig, *French Colonialism 1871–1914: Myths and Realities* (London, 1966), pp. vii–x.

Ronald Robinson (ed.), *International Co-operation in Aid: Impressions and Papers of the Fifth Cambridge Conference on Development Problems, 4–17 September 1966 at Jesus College, Cambridge* (CUOSC: Cambridge University Press, 1968), pp. iv + 238. [RER was author of Pt. I, 'Introduction', and Pt. II, 'The Argument of the Conference', 1–55.]

'Hare and Tortoise', *The Economist*, 28 Sept. 1968, 49. [Review of Ronald Hyam, *Elgin and Churchill at the Colonial Office, 1905–1908.*]

Ronald Robinson and Peter Johnston (eds.), *The Rural Base for National Development: Papers and Impressions of the Sixth Cambridge Conference on Development Problems, 24th March to 4th April 1968 at Jesus College, Cambridge* (CUOSC: Cambridge University Press, 1970), pp. v + 178. [RER was author of the Introduction, 1–3.]

R.E. Robinson (ed.), *Developing the Third World: The Experience of the*

Nineteen-Sixties (Cambridge Commonwealth Series: Cambridge University Press, 1971), pp. viii + 289. [RER was author of Ch. I, 'Practical Politics of Economic Development'; Chs. VI, VIII, XVI, XVIII, XX, XXII and XXIII reproduced sections from his contributions to the reports of the Conferences on Development of 1964, 1965, and 1966.]

Ronald Robinson and Peter Johnston (eds.), *Prospects for Employment Opportunities in the Nineteen Seventies: Papers and Impressions of the Seventh Cambridge Conference on Development Problems 13th to 24th September 1970 at Jesus College, Cambridge* (Foreign and Commonwealth Office, Overseas Development Administration; CUOSC; HMSO, London, 1971), pp. v + 246 [with Foreword, and Introduction, by RER, 1–4].

'Non-European foundations of European Imperialism: sketch for a theory of collaboration', in Roger Owen and Bob Sutcliffe (eds.), *Studies in the Theory of Imperialism* (London, 1972), 117–42.

'The Journal and the Transfer of Power 1947–51', *Journal of Administration Overseas*, XIII, 1 (Jan. 1974), 255–8.

'Sir Andrew Cohen Pro-Consul of African Nationalism (1909–1968)', in L.H. Gann and P. Duignan (eds.), *African Proconsuls. European Governors in Africa* (Stanford, 1978), 353–64.

'European imperialism and indigenous reactions in British West Africa, 1880–1914', in H.L. Wesseling (ed.), *Expansion and Reaction* (Leiden, 1978), 141–63.

'Conclusion I.', in A.H.M. Kirk-Greene (ed.), *Africa in the Colonial Period. The Transfer of Power: The Colonial Administrator in the Age of Decolonization. Proceedings of a Symposium held at St. Antony's College, Oxford, 15–16 March 1978* (Oxford, 1979), 178–81.

'The Moral Disarmament of African Empire 1919–1947', in Norman Hillmer and Philip Wigley (eds.), *The First British Commonwealth. Essays in Honour of Nicholas Mansergh* (London, 1979), 86–104. [Originally published as a Special Issue of *The Journal of Imperial and Commonwealth History*, VIII, 1 (Oct. 1979).]

'Andrew Cohen and the Transfer of Power in Tropical Africa, 1940–1951', in W.H. Morris-Jones and G. Fischer (eds.), *Decolonisation and After. The British and French Experience* (London, 1980), 50–72.

Africa and the Victorians. The Official Mind of Imperialism (2nd. edition, 1981), pp. xxiii + 518 [being a reprinting of the first edition, together with RER's Explanation, pp. ix–xxiii, and Afterthoughts, 473–99].

'Oxford in Imperial Historiography', in Frederick Madden and D.K.

Fieldhouse (eds.), *Oxford and the Idea of Commonwealth. Essays presented to Sir Edgar Williams* (London, 1982), 30–48.

W.R. Louis and R. Robinson, 'The United States and the end of the British Empire in tropical Africa, 1941–1951', in P. Gifford and W.R. Louis (eds.), *The Transfer of Power in Africa: Decolonization 1940–1960* (New Haven, CT, and London, 1982), 31–55.

Review of D.J. Morgan, *The Official History of Colonial Development*, 5 vols. (1980) in *The Journal of Imperial and Commonwealth History* XII, 1 (Oct. 1983), 132–5.

'Imperial Theory and the Question of Imperialism after Empire', in R.F. Holland and G. Rizvi (eds.), *Perspectives on Imperialism and Decolonization. Essays in Honour of A.F. Madden* (London, 1984), 42–54. [Originally published as a Special Issue of *The Journal of Imperial and Commonwealth History*, XII, 3 (May 1984).]

'New structures, new mentalities', *Times Literary Supplement*, 16 Aug. 1985, 895. [Review of Michael Crowder (ed.), *The Cambridge History of Africa, Vol. 8, From c. 1940 to c. 1975*; and William Tordoff, *Government and Politics in Africa*].

'The Excentric Idea of Imperialism, with or without Empire', in Wolfgang J. Mommsen and Jürgen Osterhammel (eds.), *Imperialism and After: Continuities and Discontinuities* (London, 1986), 267–89.

Review of Norman Etherington, *Theories of Imperialism. War, Conquest and Capital* (1984), *English Historical Review* CII (1987), 260–1.

S. Forster, Wolfgang J. Mommsen, and R.E. Robinson (eds.), *Bismarck, Europe and Africa: the Berlin Africa Conference 1884–85 and the Onset of Partition* (Oxford, 1988).

'The Conference in Berlin and the Future in Africa, 1884–85', in ibid., 1–32.

'British Imperialism: The Colonial Office and the Settler in East-Central Africa, 1919–63', in Enrico Serra (ed.), *Imperialism: the British and the Italian Experiences Compared. Proceedings of the Second British–Italian Historians' Conference held at Catania, 2–4 October 1987* (forthcoming, Rome, 1989).

Notes on Contributors

Christopher Andrew has been Fellow of Corpus Christi College, Cambridge, and University Lecturer in History since 1967. He has published extensively on French foreign and imperial policy frequently in collaboration with A.S. Kanya-Forstner, with whom he wrote *France Overseas: The Great War and the Climax of French Imperial Expansion* (1981). His other main area of research is the history of intelligence services; he is a founding joint editor of *Intelligence and National Security*, and the author of *Secret Service: The Making of the British Intelligence Community* (1985).

David Fieldhouse has been Vere Harmsworth Professor of Imperial and Naval History in Cambridge University since 1981, and Fellow of Jesus College in that University. He taught at Haileybury between 1950 and 1952, after which he became Lecturer in Modern History at the University of Canterbury, New Zealand. Between 1958 and 1981 he was Beit Lecturer in Commonwealth History at Oxford University, and (after 1966) a Fellow of Nuffield College. His many publications include *The Colonial Empires* (1966), *The Theory of Capitalist Imperialism* (1967), *Economics and Empire, 1830–1914* (1973), *Unilever Overseas* (1978) and, most recently, *Black Africa 1945–1980* (1986). He is at present writing a history of the United Africa Company.

Robert Holland is Lecturer in History at the Institute of Commonwealth Studies in London University. He studied at Jesus College, Oxford, and carried out his doctoral research at St. Antony's College. In 1976–77 he was Beit Junior Lecturer in Commonwealth History at Oxford University. He is the author of *Britain and the Commonwealth Alliance, 1918–39* (1981), *European Decolonization, 1918–81: An Introductory Survey* (1985) and co-editor (with Andrew Porter) of *Money, Finance and Empire, 1790–1960* (1985). He is currently completing a contribution (on the twentieth century) to the *Fontana History of England*.

Ronald Hyam has been for more than 25 years both Fellow and Librarian of Magdalene College, Cambridge, having previously studied under Ronald Robinson at St John's College in that University. He is the author of *Elgin and Churchill at the Colonial Office, 1905–1908: The Watershed of the Empire-Commonwealth* (1968), *The Failure of South African Expansion, 1908–1948* (1972), *Britain's Imperial Century, 1815–1914: A Study of Empire and Expansion* (1976), and (in collaboration with Ged Martin) of an essay collection entitled *Reappraisals in British Imperial History* (1975). His current research and writing span documentary editing and a general interpretation of decolonization after 1945, and a more light-hearted study of the sexual dimensions of British empire and imperialism.

A.S. Kanya-Forstner is Professor of History and Associate Dean of the Faculty of Graduate Studies at York University, Toronto. A graduate of the Universities of Toronto and Cambridge, he was a fellow of Gonville and Caius College, Cambridge, from 1965 to 1972. He is the author of *The Conquest of the Western Sudan: A Study in French Military Imperialism* (1969) and (with Christopher Andrew) *France Overseas: The Great War and the Climax of French Imperial Expansion* (1981).

Wm. Roger Louis is Kerr Professor of English History and Culture in the University of Texas at Austin, and a Supernumerary Fellow of St. Antony's College, Oxford. His publications include *Imperialism at Bay: the United States and the Decolonization of the British Empire, 1941–1945* (1977) and *The British Empire in the Middle East, 1945–1951: Arab Nationalism, the United States, and Postwar Imperialism* (1984). He is currently completing two books, respectively entitled *The Last Three Viceroys* and *The End of the British Empire in the Middle East, 1952–1958*.

Colin Newbury is Senior Lecturer in Commonwealth History and Fellow of Linacre College, Oxford. A New Zealander by birth, he has taught at the University of Ibadan and has been Visiting Professor at Duke University, the University of Hawaii and Stanford University. He is the author of a two-volume collection of select documents entitled *British Policy Towards West Africa* (1965, 1971) and of *The West African Commonwealth* (1964). More recently he has written extensively on the Pacific and published articles on imperial economic history, chiefly concerned with labour issues. He is currently engaged on a study of the diamond trade and South Africa.

Andrew Porter is Reader in History at King's College, London. Having studied at St. John's College, Cambridge, he took up his first lecturing appointment in 1970 at Manchester University, before moving to London in 1971. He is the author of *The Origins of the South African War: Joseph Chamberlain and the Diplomacy of Imperialism, 1895–1899* (1980), *Victorian Shipping, Business, and Imperial Policy: Donald Currie, the Castle Line and Southern Africa* (1986) and co-editor (with Robert Holland) of *Money, Finance and Empire, 1790–1985* (1985). Most recently he has written and edited (with A.J. Stockwell) *British Imperial Policy and Decolonization. Volume I: 1938–51* (1987). He has now completed the second volume of the latter work (which runs to 1964), and is continuing his research in the field of missionary history and British expansion.

Michael Twaddle is Lecturer in Commonwealth Studies in the University of London. His initial interest in overseas history was aroused by Ronald Robinson while an undergraduate at St. John's College, Cambridge. Subsequent experience in Uganda and RER's encouragement to collect 'oral stuff' on recent African history led to postgraduate and linguistic studies at the School of Oriental and African Studies ('the Mecca for this sort of thing', in RER's view) under Roland Oliver and Ronald Snoxall and a further period at Makerere. He is shortly to publish a major biography of Semei Kakungulu – initially African ally but ultimately embarrassing critic of British imperialism in East Africa.

George Shepperson was William Robertson Professor of Commonwealth and American History at Edinburgh University between 1963 and 1986, and is now Emeritus Professor in that University. After studying at St. John's College, Cambridge, he served in the King's African Rifles between 1943 and 1946. He arrived in Edinburgh to lecture in Imperial and American history in 1948. Subsequently he was a Visiting Professor at Chicago University, Makerere College, Dalhousie University and Rhode Island College. He is the author (with Thomas Price) of *Independent African: John Chilembwe and the Origins, Setting and Significance of the Nyasaland Native Rising of 1915* (1958; first paperback edition, 1987) and *David Livingstone and the Rovuma* (1964).

H.L. Wesseling is Professor of Contemporary History and Director of the Centre for the History of European Expansion at Leiden University. He is the author of *Soldaat en Krijger. Franse opvattingen over leger en oorlog, 1905–1914* (1969) and editor of *Expansion and Reaction: Essays on European Expansion and Reactions in Asia and Africa* (Leiden, 1978). His most recent major publication is *Vele Ideeën over Frankrijk. Opstellen over geschiedenis en cultuur* (1987). Professor Wesseling's current research and writing is concerned with the history of the partition of Africa.

For Product Safety Concerns and Information please contact our EU representative GPSR@taylorandfrancis.com
Taylor & Francis Verlag GmbH, Kaufingerstraße 24, 80331 München, Germany

www.ingramcontent.com/pod-product-compliance
Lightning Source LLC
Chambersburg PA
CBHW051643230426
43669CB00013B/2422